Demographics and Innovation in the Asia-Pacific

DEMOGRAPHICS AND INNOVATION IN THE ASIA-PACIFIC

Edited by Karen Eggleston,
Joon-Shik Park, and Gi-Wook Shin

Stanford | Walter H. Shorenstein
Asia-Pacific Research Center
Freeman Spogli Institute

THE WALTER H. SHORENSTEIN ASIA-PACIFIC RESEARCH CENTER (Shorenstein APARC) addresses critical issues affecting the countries of Asia, their regional and global affairs, and U.S.-Asia relations. As Stanford University's hub for the interdisciplinary study of contemporary Asia, we produce policy-relevant research, provide education and training to students, scholars, and practitioners, and strengthen dialogue and cooperation between counterparts in the Asia-Pacific and the United States.

The Walter H. Shorenstein Asia-Pacific Research Center
Freeman Spogli Institute for International Studies
Stanford University
Encina Hall
Stanford, CA 94305-6055
http://aparc.fsi.stanford.edu

Demographics and Innovation in the Asia-Pacific
may be ordered from:
Brookings Institution Press
https://www.brookings.edu/bipress/
books@brookings.edu

Walter H. Shorenstein Asia-Pacific Research Center, 2021.
Library of Congress Control Number: 2021936293

First printing, 2021
ISBN 978-1-931368-63-6

Contents

Tables and Figures

Tables

Figures

Abbreviations

AI	artificial intelligence
CES-D	Center for Epidemiologic Studies Depression Scale
CHARLS	China Health and Retirement Longitudinal Study
CRADA	Cooperative Research and Development Agreement
EAP	Economically Active Population survey
ELSA	English Longitudinal Study of Ageing
ESR	economic support ratio
GDP	gross domestic product
GIS	geographic information system
GM	genetically modified
GNP	gross national product
HILDA	Household, Income and Labour Dynamics in Australia
HRS	Health and Retirement Study
IA	intelligence augmentation
ICT	information and communication technologies
ILO	International Labor Organization
IADL	instrumental activity of daily living
IT	information technology
JMA	Japan Medical Association
JSTAR	Japanese Study of Aging and Retirement
KPI	key performance indicator
LASI	Longitudinal Aging Study in India

LFPR	labor force participation rate
MNES	Medical Network Systems
NBER	National Bureau of Economic Research
NSFIE	National Survey of Family Income and Expenditure
NTA	National Transfer Accounts
OECD	Organisation for Economic Co-operation and Development
R&D	research and development
SAGE	Study of Global Aging and Adult Health
SARS	Severe acute respiratory syndrome
SHARE	Survey of Health, Ageing and Retirement in Europe
SOEP	Socio-Economic Panel
TFR	total fertility rates
WHO	World Health Organization
WPS	Workplace Panel Survey

Contributors

KAREN EGGLESTON is senior fellow at the Freeman Spogli Institute for International Studies (FSI) at Stanford University, director of the Stanford Asia Health Policy Program, and deputy director of the Walter H. Shorenstein Asia-Pacific Research Center at FSI. She is also a fellow with the Stanford Center for Innovation in Global Health and a faculty research fellow of the National Bureau of Economic Research. Eggleston earned her PhD in public policy from Harvard University, studied in China for two years, and was a Fulbright scholar in Korea. Her research focuses on comparative health systems and health reform in Asia, especially China; government and market roles in the health sector; supply-side incentives; healthcare productivity; and economic aspects of demographic change.

JAMES FEYRER is a professor of economics at Dartmouth College. He received his PhD from Brown University and his BS from Stanford University. His work is primarily in applied macroeconomics. His work on the impacts of demographics and trade on growth has been influential in policy circles. In particular, his work on the impact of globalization on output has informed the Brexit debate. He has published articles in the *Quarterly Journal of Economics*, the *American Economic Review*, the *Review of Economics and Statistics*, the *Journal of the European Economic Association*, among other journals.

TAIYO FUKAI is a project researcher in the Department of Economics at the University of Tokyo.

APARAJITA GOYAL is a senior economist at the World Bank in Washington, D.C. Her work focuses on microeconomic issues of development, with a particular emphasis on agriculture productivity, poverty, technological innovations, and digital economy. She has worked on operations, policy advice, and analytical activities in Latin America, Africa, and South Asia. Her research has been published in leading academic journals such as the *American Economic Review, Journal of Human Resources, Journal of Development Economics,* and has also been featured in popular press such as *Frontline, The Economist,* and the *Wall Street Journal,* among others. She holds a PhD in economics from the University of Maryland, an MSc from the London School of Economics, and a BA in economics from St. Stephen's College, University of Delhi, India.

HIDEHIKO ICHIMURA is a professor in the Graduate School of Public Policy and Graduate School of Economics at the University of Tokyo. He received his PhD in economics from MIT and BA in economics from Osaka University. Prior to the University of Tokyo, Ichimura taught at University College London and the University of Pittsburgh.

SUN HO JEONG is a lecturer and research fellow at the Communication and Media Research Center, Ewha Womans University, South Korea. She received a PhD in journalism from the University of Texas at Austin, a Master of International Affairs from Columbia University, and a BA in journalism from Ewha University. Jeong's primary research interests include journalism in the context of digitization and globalization, and the role of digital media in fostering social change. She has published in academic journals including *Information, Communication and Society, International Communication Gazette, International Journal of Communication, Journalism,* and *Journalism Practice,* among others.

DONG-IL JUNG is a professor of human resource management and organization in the Division of Business Administration at Sookmyung Women's University in Korea. He graduated from Seoul National University with bachelor's and master's degrees in sociology and received his PhD in sociology from Cornell University. His work is in the areas of interorganizational network, social construction of organizational identities, and organizational learning in complex systems. His current projects include the diffusion of innovation and emergence of collective norms in platform-based organizational communities, the formation and evolution of network in music- and film-production industries, and the coevolution of knowledge networks and supply networks in the global automobile production market.

KYUNG-HEE KIM is a professor in the Media School at Hallym University and the director of the Institute for Communication Arts and Technology (iCat). She received her PhD from Ewha Womans University. Her research focuses on the interplay of digital culture, news organization, and gender. She has written and edited several books on social media, media literacy, and gender. She has also published in numerous journals including the *Journal of Computer-Mediated Communication*, *Media, Culture and Society*, and *Asian Journal of Communication*.

YOUNG BUM KIM is an associate professor at Hallym University Institute of Aging. His primary research interests include social gerontology and comparative welfare state study. He received his master's and PhD degrees from Yonsei University in Korea. He received the Outstanding Article Award as a co-author from the American Sociological Association's Section on Inequality, Poverty, and Mobility in 2012. He has served as the editor-in-chief for *Regional Sociology,* a Korean journal. Recently he has been studying the relationship between social relationships and the mental health of Korean elderly.

KENJI E. KUSHIDA is a research scholar at the Japan Program at the Shorenstein Asia-Pacific Research Center at Stanford University. He holds a PhD in political science from the University of California, Berkeley, an MA in East Asian studies and BAs in economics and East Asian studies, all from Stanford University.

His research streams include 1) information technology innovation, 2) Silicon Valley's economic ecosystem, 3) Japan's political economic transformation since the 1990s, and 4) the Fukushima nuclear disaster. He has published several books and numerous articles in each of these streams, including "The Politics of Commoditization in Global ICT Industries," "Japan's Startup Ecosystem," "Cloud Computing: From Scarcity to Abundance," and others. His latest business book in Japanese is *The Algorithmic Revolution's Disruption: A Silicon Valley Vantage on IoT, Fintech, Cloud, and AI* (Asahi Shimbun Shuppan 2016).

CHULHEE LEE is a professor of economics at Seoul National University. After receiving his doctoral degree from the University of Chicago in

1996, he taught at SUNY Binghamton before returning to Seoul in 1998. His major research topics are the economic status and labor-market behaviors of older persons, and the interactions of ecological environment, socioeconomic status, and health over the life course. Since 2001, Lee has been involved, as project leader and senior investigator, with the management of the NIH-funded Early Indicators project, which constructed and analyzed longitudinal data on Union Army soldiers. He has also participated in various projects creating and studying new data in Korea, such as the Korea Longitudinal Study of Aging, the panel data on Korean Health Insurance, and the sample of military records in Korea.

Lee's research on the health and retirement of U.S. Civil War soldiers has been published in *American Economic Review*, *Journal of Economic History*, *Explorations in Economic History*, and *Social Science History*. He has also published papers on the retirement of Koreans in *Economic Development and Cultural Change* and *Journal of Population Ageing*. His recent work on the long-term effects of in utero exposure to violent events such as the Korean War and the 1980 Kwangju uprising and on the changing relationship between unemployment and health has appeared in the *Journal of Health Economics*, *Social Science and Medicine*, *Asian Population Studies*, and *Health Economics*. He is currently working on various demographic issues in Korea, including the effects of parental gender norms on intra-family time allocation, the causes and consequences of changing sex ratios at birth, long-term factors of health and standards of living, and explanations for decline in marriage and fertility.

RIKIYA MATSUKURA is an associate professor at Nihon University and a researcher at the Nihon University Population Research Institute. Since 2002 he has also been a guest researcher and lecturer of demographic analysis at the Statistical Research and Training Institute of the Japanese Ministry of Internal Affairs and Communications. As a UN consultant, Matsukura has contributed to the formulation of the most recent five-year economic plan for the Lao People's Democratic Republic. He has more than 20 years of experience in demographic research, focusing on the development of statistical methods for complicated models and the application of these methodologies to socioeconomics and population. In recent years he has contributed to the development of the National Transfer Accounts economic indices.

NAOHIRO OGAWA is a population economist who specializes in studying the effects of demographic changes on economic growth and social security systems. Aside from economic impacts of low fertility and rapid population aging, his research has included a variety of other population-related issues, such as family organization and values shifts, and assessment of policies regarding employment, marriage, retirement, and care for the elderly. Japan is the world forerunner in population aging, and in the past decade Ogawa has led efforts to introduce new methodology for measuring intergenerational transfers in Asia and convey the lessons learned in Japan to other Asian and world countries.

Ogawa has published numerous academic papers in internationally recognized journals. His jointly written or edited journals and books include *Fertility Change in Contemporary Japan, Human Resources and Development along the Asia-Pacific Rim, Population Aging, Intergenerational Transfers and the Macroeconomy, Ageing in Advanced Industrial States: Riding the Age Waves, Volume 3* and *Low Fertility and Reproductive Health in East Asia.*

Ogawa has served on councils, committees and advisory boards set up by the Japanese government and international organizations such as the World Health Organization and the Asian Population Association. Currently he is a visiting fellow at the Asian Development Bank Institute, and serves as the distinguished visiting research fellow at the Social Wellbeing Research Center and the University of Malaya.

JOON-SHIK PARK is a professor in the Department of Sociology at Hallym University, in Chuncheon, Korea. He received his PhD from Yonsei University in Korea. His research focuses on employment and regional studies. Park began his academic career as a researcher on labor and employment issues in Korean society. Recently, he has been interested in comparing social economy and local regeneration in the context of global social and economic crisis. His most recent books, articles, and project reports cover such issues as the impact of globalization on employment regimes and local societies; social dialogue and integration; and creative innovation for sustainable local development. Park has served as president of the Korean Regional Sociological Association and dean of the Social Science School at Hallym University. He is now a member of the Korean government's Presidential Commission on Policy Planning and leads the commission's Inclusive Society Division as its chairperson. He is also serving as Hallym University's vice president of vision and cooperation.

GI-WOOK SHIN is a professor of sociology at Stanford University and senior fellow at the Freeman Spogli Institute for International Studies, where he is director of the Walter H. Shorenstein Asia-Pacific Research Center. As a comparative and political sociologist, his research has concentrated on nationalism, development, and international relations.

Shin is the author/editor of 20 books and over 50 articles, most recently *Strategic, Policy and Social Innovation for a Post-Industrial Korea: Beyond the Miracle* (2018); *Superficial Korea* (2017); *Divergent Memories: Opinion Leaders and the Asia-Pacific War* (2016); and more.

Shin is not only the recipient of numerous grants and fellowships, but also continues to actively raise funds for Korean/Asian studies at Stanford. He gives frequent lectures and seminars on topics ranging from Korean politics to North Korea and historical reconciliation in Northeast Asia. He serves on councils and advisory boards in the United States and South Korea and promotes policy dialogue between the two allies.

Before coming to Stanford, Shin taught at the University of Iowa and the University of California, Los Angeles. After receiving his BA from Yonsei University in Korea, he was awarded his MA and PhD from the University of Washington.

Preface

This volume is based on the papers presented at the Stanford-Hallym Asia-Pacific Innovation Conference in Chuncheon, Korea, in June 2019. The conference was part of our ongoing Asia-Pacific Innovation Project at the Walter H. Shorenstein Asia-Pacific Research Center, which aims to produce academic and policy research that will help promote innovation and entrepreneurship in Asia. In the project, we have examined the industrial organization of businesses and innovation clusters and how such environments affect entrepreneurship. We also studied the impact of public education and financial policies pursued by East Asian countries to promote innovation and entrepreneurship.

At the June 2019 conference and in this book, we focus on examining innovation, technology, and demographic change. As the population of many Asian countries is aging rapidly, it is now more important and relevant than ever to better understand the relationship between aging and innovation. In this book, we seek to answer the most pressing questions on this issue—what policies can promote innovation and entrepreneurship by both the young and old in an aging population? We also explore the impact of aging on the social and economic landscape and how such demographic changes affect the labor force and productivity, and we discuss the ways in which population aging and technology can influence each other.

My colleague Karen Eggleston led this part of the project in close collaboration with Joon-Shik Park of Hallym University. It was our pleasure to work with the Institute for Communication Arts and Technology, the Institute of Life and Death Studies, and Leaders in

Industry-University Cooperation at Hallym. I am very grateful to Choongsoo Kim, president of Hallym University, for his support of the conference and to the Hallym University Development Foundation and the National Research Foundation of Korea for their financial contribution. At our center, Kristen Lee has provided administrative support, working closely with the Hallym team. George Krompacky assisted in editing and publishing this volume.

Gi-Wook Shin
Director
Shorenstein APARC

Demographics and Innovation in the Asia-Pacific

1 Demographics and Innovation in the Asia-Pacific

An Introduction

Karen Eggleston and Joon-Shik Park

Few concepts are as critical for sustained improvement in living standards as innovation. New ideas and ways of doing things, technologies and inventions, and greater productivity in transforming inputs into outputs—these aspects of innovation define how societies and economies progress and develop. However, little is known about how innovation interacts with two of the largest forces shaping the twenty-first century: the demographic transition and the economic and geopolitical re-emergence of Asia.

This book delves into how demographic change shapes the supply of innovation and the demand for specific kinds of innovation in aging Asia. Social scientists from several Asia-Pacific countries offer multidisciplinary perspectives from economics, demography, political science, sociology, and public policy. Each of the eight chapters focuses on questions of political economy and policy surrounding demographic change and innovation. Topics range from the macroeconomic productivity effects of population age structure, to the microeconomic labor force effects of changing demographics and technology, to the broader implications for human well-being.

This introductory chapter first provides an overview of demographic change in the region and several leitmotifs in the research. We then provide a tour of the book, previewing the central argument of each chapter, before offering a few concluding thoughts about a future research agenda.

Acknowledgement: This book was supported by the Ministry of Education of the Republic of Korea and the National Research Foundation of Korea (NRF-2015 S1A5B4A01037022).

Asia's Demography

Throughout this volume, the authors illustrate the multiple aspects of demographic change in the Asia-Pacific, from the historical process of declining fertility to urbanization and gender imbalance. Most prominent among the demographic trends, however, is the extent of population aging, and how aging interacts with innovation.

While we all know that populations around the globe are aging, the extent to which East Asia leads the world in the magnitude and scope of the demographic transition bears underscoring. Figure 1.1 illustrates population aging trends for the Asian economies covered in this volume and some comparators with the standard metric of proportion of older adults. Figure 1A shows the increase in share of population in the traditional retirement ages (65 and older) between 2017 and 2050, and figure 1B shows the increase of the "oldest of older people" (age 80 and older) over the same period. Note that the countries of East Asia—especially Asia's Organisation for Economic Co-operation and Development (OECD) countries of Japan and South Korea—have some of the oldest age structures on the planet, with Korea's pace of change strikingly rapid. Between now and 2050, the population that is age 65 and older will increase to more than one in four Chinese, and to more than one in three Japanese and Koreans. China's median age already exceeds that of the United States, at a much larger absolute scale and at a lower per-capita income. India is much younger, although it is still aging. India's share of age 80+ will almost triple, albeit while remaining less than 3 percent, whereas in Japan and Korea, more than 15 percent of the total population will be age 80 or older according to projections for 2050.

As figure 1.1 illustrates, this pace of aging in East Asia far surpasses that of the United States or the OECD average, while India and other parts of South and Southeast Asia are considerably younger. Thus, the demographic challenges facing Asia range from how the oldest age structures can continue innovation for improved well-being, to how some of the younger age structures can reap the demographic dividend from productively engaging large working-age cohorts for social progress.

How will these large demographic changes shape the future of the world's most dynamic economies? The constituent chapters delve into the multiple close links between innovation and populations, as well as

FIGURE 1.1 Asia's population aging in comparative perspective, 2017–50

A. Increase in percentage of population age 65 and older between 2017 and 2050

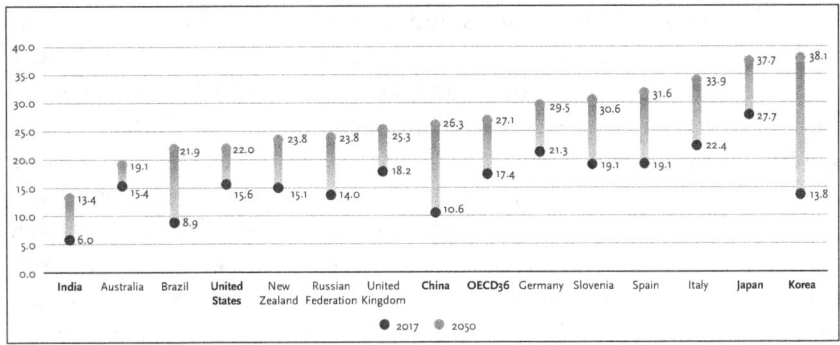

B. Increase in percentage of population age 80 and older between 2017 and 2050

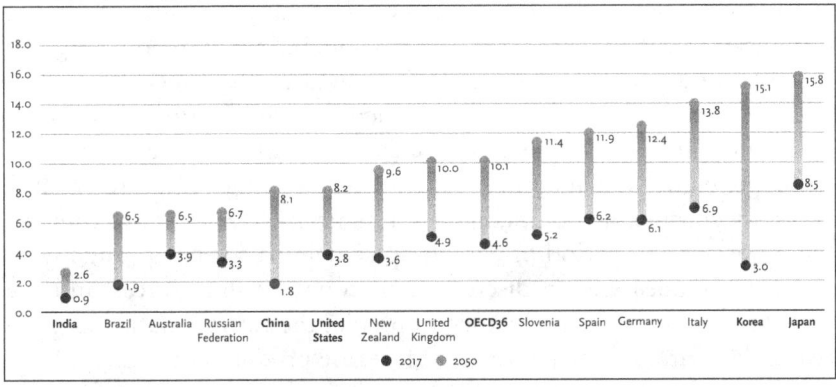

SOURCE: Health at a Glance 2019: OECD Indicators. *OECD Library*. Data extracted from OECD Health Statistics 2019, OECD Historical Population Data and Projections Database, 2019. Data link: https://doi.org/10.1787/888934018260.

whether those links represent causal relationships, and which way the causal arrow points.

A Tour of the Rest of the Volume

The first half of the book focuses on how demography shapes productivity and the labor supply of older workers. Contributions shine a spotlight on topics ranging from the macroeconomic productivity effects of demographic change analyzed by Feyrer, to the microeconomic labor force effects of changing demographics and their interaction with new technologies, as analyzed by Ogawa et al. and Chulhee Lee. This introduction discusses the primary contours of each chapter in turn.

In chapter 2, "Demographics and Productivity in Asia," James Feyrer of Dartmouth examines the macroeconomic relationship between workforce demographics and aggregate productivity in Asia. First, he describes the patterns of demographic change across the region, including the timing of fertility decline to below-replacement levels and changes in the working-age population. Then, in careful empirical analyses that build upon and extend his earlier work, Feyrer shows that changes in aggregate productivity among over 100 countries between 1960 and 2010 are significantly correlated with the age structure of the countries' workforces. In addition to multiple variants of these cross-country regressions, Feyrer discusses possible mechanisms for how demographics might impact productivity, including the implications of demography for management quality and innovation. Applying the regression results to the demographic structure of specific Asian countries, Feyrer confirms that the high-income Asian nations like Japan and Korea, and even some middle-income countries of the region, will no longer enjoy a "demographic dividend" boosting aggregate productivity. By contrast, lower-income Asian nations like India are entering the more positive period of demography, helping to spur productivity. Feyrer concludes with a discussion of countervailing forces and the need for caution in using history to predict the future relationship between demographic structure and aggregate productivity.

In the third chapter, Karen Eggleston examines the case of China in "Demographics and Innovation in China: Correlation or Causation?" She starts by reviewing the literature regarding demography and innovation, and some evidence of the causal arrow running from innovation to demographics in China's case (e.g., public health interventions have spurred China's demographic transition since the Mao era). The remainder of the chapter probes the correlation of demographic change in the post-Mao era with innovation in China's economy, and whether the causal arrow may also run from demographics (in terms of scale and age structure) to innovation. Focusing on the most recent decade, she provides statistics on research and development investment and patents in China in comparative international perspective, and discusses several key industries in more depth, including healthcare technologies and the impacts of the COVID-19 pandemic on China's economy and innovation.

Whether future predictions about productivity and age structure hold true depends to a significant degree on whether future cohorts of older adults will be healthier than earlier generations, with ill health "compressed" into older ages and capacity to function independently preserved well into conventional retirement years. This is the question addressed in the fourth chapter, by Naohiro Ogawa, Hidehiko Ichimura, Taiyo Fukai, and Rikiya Matsukura, providing new empirical evidence on the changing cognitive performance and untapped work capacity among older persons in Japan. The first part of their chapter provides a broad overview of rapid changes in the demographic and economic landscape in postwar Japan, including fertility and mortality patterns, economic growth and the "two demographic dividends," the age structure of the workforce, and the recent modifications to traditional employment practices. The authors stress that, in light of fiscal pressures, Japan needs effective policies to boost national productivity. They evaluate the cognitive performance and work capacity of Japan's aging labor force by using detailed individual-level data from the Japanese Study of Aging and Retirement (JSTAR). Ogawa, Ichimura, Fukai, and Matsukura find that the cognitive performance of Japanese aged 60 to 75 is similar to that of their counterparts in many European countries. Moreover, higher educational levels, better childhood nutrition, and other improvements in health suggest that the future older adults in Japan may be even more mentally fit than the current generations. Thus, they suggest that putting these older workers into productive employment could boost Japan's gross domestic product by 3.2 to 6.0 percent. Their analyses suggest that, despite the declining overall and working-age population, Japan's labor force could harness older workers to bolster the workforce in productive ways going forward.

But will the jobs to harness this work capacity exist? And will the older citizens be willing to take those jobs? These were open-ended questions even before COVID-19. They are all the more pressing, given the economic devastation in the wake of a pandemic that may reignite the debate about older workers "stealing" younger workers' jobs, and give reluctant employers an excuse to dismiss or avoid older workers in the name of protecting their health. Thus, a pressing question is whether older workers will be able to adjust to the changing job requirements and technologies, and whether the productivity of older adults will be sufficient for employers to hire them in those positions. Some historical perspective from the United States and Korea in the next chapter provides a less sanguine perspective.

Chulhee Lee, a prominent Korean economist, contributes the fifth chapter, "Sectoral Shift, Technological Change, and Older Labor: Evidence from the United States and Korea." As he writes, the labor force participation of middle-aged and older citizens and its interaction with technological change remains critical for understanding how aging impacts innovation. His chapter provides evidence for how economic and technological changes affected older workers during the industrialization periods of 1880 to 1940 in the United States and 1960 to 2015 in South Korea (hereafter Korea). His research contributes to the limited literature empirically examining how technological changes affect young and older workers differently. These contributions cover technological changes that impact both the appropriateness or quality of matching individuals' skills to specific jobs, as well as sectoral shifts in employment between industries with different flexibility in work schedules. Examining the early twentieth century United States and how industry-specific technological, organizational, and managerial characteristics affected older male manufacturing workers, he analyzes rich data from Union Army veterans as well as the Integrated Public Use Microdata Series. Comparative empirical analysis focuses on South Korea's economic development era when it moved from a largely agrarian to an industrial economy, when urbanization and agricultural decline were offset by the increased labor force participation of older men in rural areas. In addition, analyzing a 2 percent random sample of Korea's population and housing censuses between 1980 and 2000, Chulhee Lee finds that pressure to leave the labor market at middle or older ages differed across sectors, with employment for older adults somewhat stable in agriculture and other sectors like insurance and real estate, compared to manufacturing. The most important factor explaining the labor force participation rate of older males in Korea has been the relative decline in the agricultural workforce, with additional impetus from industrial structure shifting away from the sectors most conducive to older workers.

Finally, Professor Lee discusses the important lens of technological change and its disproportionate impact on older workers, who face obsolescence of skills, less efficiency in learning, and limits on mobility across locations and jobs. Using Workplace Panel Survey data from 2005 to 2015, he confirms the negative effect that automation and information technology investments have on the employment of older workers in Korea. Thus, Lee's research reinforces and expands upon the cross-country productivity impacts of age structure highlighted by

Feyrer. Based on his analysis of individual- and firm-level data from both the United States and Korea, Lee concludes that "the remarkably parallel findings obtained from the two countries at different times strongly suggest that radical changes in technology may bring unfavorable labor market consequences for older people, at least compared with the young" and present an additional challenge for aging societies in search of innovation.

If technological change to date has clearly had a negative impact on older workers, perhaps future technological change could be friendlier to older populations. After all, we know that societies will need to promote longer work lives to support the sustainable financing of social protection while protecting living standards (Eggleston and Fuchs 2012). Thus, endogenous innovation for older-age structures seems critical. In the subsequent sections of the book, we explore whether technology itself is being developed, or will be developed, to assist older workers, focusing on endogenous innovations for an aging population. Such innovations mitigate the labor-replacing effects of new technologies and may enable productive harnessing of the growing populations of older but still cognitively engaged and physically functional workers.

What is the political economy of technological development itself in aging economies, from subsidizing robots for long-term care in Japan (Eggleston ⓡ Lee ⓡ Iizuka 2021) to developing innovations that "upskill" older workers (as discussed in Kushida's chapter)? These are some of the topics covered in the latter half of the volume, with themes of aging, technology, and the political economy of innovation. The focus of these chapters turns toward the aging population as consumers of technologies and drivers of innovations to meet their own needs, as well as the political economy of spatial development, agglomeration economies, urban-rural contrasts, and differential geographies of aging.

In chapter 6, Kenji Kushida addresses how Japan's aging demographics have affected pathways of technological development. After a brief overview of Japan's demographic challenges, Kushida examines a series of specific sectors within which technological innovations address labor shortages and the needs of older workers. The cases range from construction, agriculture, and transportation, to digitalization of administrative records in healthcare, land transactions, and housing. Kushida emphasizes that the demographics of Japan's aging society have galvanized a wide range of corporate efforts, supported both directly and indirectly by the government, to aggressively develop artificial intelligence and related technologies. The examples and case studies provide a vivid picture of how Japan's economy adapts and leverages population aging in search of a new competitive advantage, counterbalancing the narrative of "lost decades" in one of the world's largest economies and the society with the oldest age structure.

To offer a window on the diversity of Asia's demography and how it shapes innovation in various sectors, we next turn to India and its vital agricultural sector. While agriculture may seem far removed from what high-growth entrepreneurship connotes (e.g., visions of Silicon Valley "unicorns"), it is important to remember that farming remains the foundation of hundreds of millions of livelihoods across Asia. Moreover, agricultural productivity shapes global disparities and catch-up growth. Indeed, the difference between rich and poor countries in real labor productivity is more than thirty-five-fold in agriculture, compared to less than fivefold in nonagricultural sectors (Restuccia, Yang, and Zhu 2008).

While India's demography is far younger than that of Japan, many aspects of innovation for India's sustainable development are also closely linked to its demography. In chapter 7, "Technology for Agriculture Productivity in India," Aparajita Goyal and Karen Eggleston describe the demographic challenges facing India, home to the world's largest rural population. The authors assess the need for innovation to raise agricultural productivity in India to reduce poverty and reap the "demographic dividend" that earlier spurred the economic development of its now aging East Asian neighbors.

The book concludes with two chapters on Korea and the political economy of aging and innovation. Technologies for aging societies are not confined to enabling a productive workforce or formally measured economic output. Instead, technologies can also be critical for broader social issues of meaningful lives and continuing social engagement. Healthy aging includes social connectedness—especially highlighted during the COVID-19 pandemic and the need for physical distancing with social connection. But "digital divide" means that those who might benefit the most from connecting through technologies—older persons who are isolated—are least able to engage, even in a very tech-savvy society like Korea, with the filial piety of young people helping the older generation.

Technologies' importance for meeting the demographic challenges of Asian societies extends beyond the work-a-day issues of employment. In the twenty-first century, those in and outside the labor force rely increasingly on technologies of communication to connect with society on multiple levels. The 2020 pandemic has underscored the importance of communication while physically distancing, especially for older persons, who are the most vulnerable to infectious disease, but unfortunately also the most likely cutoff from social integration if unable to access information and communication technologies (ICT). It is this aspect of the social value of ICT technologies that is explored in chapter 8, "Population Aging, ICT Innovation, and Media Literacy in South Korea," by Sun-Ho Jeong and Kyung-Hee Kim. South Korea is an "aged society" (defined as having at least 14 percent of its population aged 65 and older), and it is expected to become a "super-aged society," with more than 20 percent of its population over 65 years old in less than a decade. With one in five of its people becoming 65 or older, this population's ability to use media is becoming more important, because it prevents isolation and further contributes to successful aging and quality of life. In this regard, South Korea offers an ideal environment for active aging, with 96 percent of adults connected to the internet. At the individual level, however, a divide due to socioeconomic factors may exist in their access and use of digital media, which calls for discussions at the societal level. In this chapter, the authors analyze topics reflected in the news coverage about the aging population and ICTs between 2000 and 2019, and look at national survey data examining levels of ICT access among older adults in South Korea. Findings indicate that there have been continuous efforts to extend ICT access to older adults by technology companies and local welfare centers. Although there persists a divide in access and use due to socioeconomic factors, reduced differences in the level of education by generation and gender give us the hope of closing the gap in the not-too-distant future.

The volume concludes with Young Bum Kim, Joon-Shik Park, and Dong-Il Jung's chapter, "Population Cliffs, Crisis of Local Society, and the Politics of Innovation in South Korea." South Korea is a particularly important case for studying the local geography of aging, given its rapid aging and extreme concentration of population in Seoul, which has prompted measures such as moving government agencies to a newly developed separate city, Sejong City, over the past decade. The purpose of the chapter is to examine changes in the population and age structure in South Korean regions and to explore their implications for regional development. First, the study describes the change of demographic structure by age in South Korea over the last 20 years according to administrative area, and investigates how those changes to the population structure are related to human-made amenities in each area. Second, the study explains how the quality and quantity of human-made amenities can contribute to fostering regional innovations and suggests strategies for closing the gap between the capital and noncapital areas, thereby achieving regionally balanced socioeconomic development in Korea.

The results of the empirical analysis on the relationship between changes in population and age structure and human-made amenities can be summarized as follows. First, an increase in the senior population is correlated with expansion of cultural and medical facilities. An increase in the ratio of seniors increases the demand for the services they desire and brings about the expansion of the facilities that meet such needs. Second, a reduction in the number of children reduced the number of elementary schools. Third, the number of cultural facilities and medical facilities such as clinics were found to increase when the population increased, and to decrease when the population decreased. The authors suggest that counties in South Korea where the population has already declined considerably may face a situation where the population may not receive the necessary services. Some counties are even missing specific medical facilities, such as maternity clinics.

However, the potential impact of low fertility and aging on innovation is not totally negative. First, if the quantity of human resources was important in the industrial age, their quality is important in the digital era. The reduction in the school-aged population will provide an opportunity to increase the quality of education. Second, population pressure caused by a reduced labor force and increased support costs can promote a range of technological innovations. The various social problems brought about by aging provides the opportunity to boost innovative activities. For instance, Japan's Society 5.0 is a roadmap for transnational growth, which aims to solve social problems, such as labor shortages due to population aging, by applying the technology of the fourth industrial revolution, such as artificial intelligence, robots, and internet of things, across the society. Much progress can be made in technological, cultural, and social sectors related to the health, culture, leisure, and the livelihood of seniors. Such innovation can also contribute to reducing the social burden resulting from a reduced labor force, as well as enhancing social vitality, by expanding the opportunities for seniors to participate in the labor market and the society.

Thus, the question is how to detect and utilize such opportunities. While various factors may be involved in building innovative capabilities in Korea's local regions, a unipolar system, in which a super-big city absorbs all human, financial, and technological resources, may not be an effective way of augmenting nationwide innovation outcomes. From a national standpoint, for instance, two cities, each with a population of five million, may be more conducive for innovation than one city with a population of 10 million. The authors conclude that "multipolarization" of areas, each supporting regional innovation, should be a goal, so that through the dispersion of the population, various forms of innovation using social, economic, spatial, and cultural resources can thrive in all regions. Such innovation initiatives could in turn lead to balanced development and effective responses to population aging.

Future Research Agenda

The terrain covered in this volume, while expansive and focused on key bumps ahead, also points out the vast horizon of unanswered questions. Each author provides windows onto different vistas of inquiry that could themselves constitute books of further conceptual and empirical research. These contributions lay out a research agenda for further policy-relevant research on demography and innovation. What will be the macroeconomic and productivity effects of changing population age structures, and to what extent can and do economy-specific policies shape that narrative? What are the underlying mechanisms linking demography to innovation? Throughout this chapter, we have raised questions that future research will need to address.

At a microeconomic and behavioral science level, the relationship between demography and innovation depends on the responses of individuals, families, communities, and polities, shaped by policy responses designed to change the incentives and framework for innovative activity. While we have reviewed in this chapter many researchers' advice about policies to stimulate appropriate innovation and entrepreneurship, one must filter these recommendations through a skeptical lens. Much careful empirical evidence does point toward responsible approaches. However, we do not have a plethora of well-established policy results for the determinants of economic growth and improved well-being independent of the details of history, institutions, culture, and their interaction with events such as global pandemics and recovery therefrom. Arguably, any narrow focus on economic growth overlooks the broader social goals of raising human well-being beyond material living standards, although raising the latter for the world's poorest should surely remain a central goal.

Will we be able to innovate to not only raise average well-being, but to close disparities while uplifting all? The answer for the Asia-Pacific will depend primarily on the young people of the region. What innovations will spring from the minds of Asia's youth over the coming decades because they are endowed with longer, healthier lives than their grandparents and parents enjoyed? One thing is certain: the interplay between innovation and demographic change will shape the future of Asia, and with it, the globe. Readers in many disciplines will find these expert social scientists' contributions fruitful food for thought for their research and a rich source of case studies for teaching at both the undergraduate and graduate levels.

References

Eggleston, Karen N., and Victor R. Fuchs. 2012. "The New Demographic Transition: Most Gains in Life Expectancy Now Realized Late in Life." *Journal of Economic Perspectives* 26, no. 3: 137–56.

Eggleston, Karen ⓕ Yong Suk Lee ⓕ Toshiaki Iizuka. 2021. "Robots and Labor in the Service Sector: Evidence from Nursing Homes," Stanford Asia Health Policy Program working paper, https://aparc.fsi.stanford.edu/asiahealthpolicy/publication/robots-and-labor-service-sector-evidence-nursing-homes; and NBER Working Paper 28322, https://www.nber.org/papers/w28322.

OECD Library. Health at a Glance 2019: OECD Indicators. https://doi.org/10.1787/888934018260.

Restuccia, Diego, Dennis Tao Yang, and Xiaodong Zhu. 2008. "Agriculture and Aggregate Productivity: A Quantitative Cross-Country Analysis." *Journal of Monetary Economics* 55, no. 2: 234–50.

World Bank. "DataBank. GDP per Capita (current US$)." Accessed June 6, 2020.

Demographics, Productivity, and the Labor Supply of Older Workers

2 Demographics and Productivity in Asia

James Feyrer

This chapter examines the relationship between workforce demographics and aggregate productivity in Asia. The countries of Asia have been experiencing unprecedented changes in the demographic structure of their populations and workforces. Persistently low total fertility rates (TFRs) after a period of high fertility led to a strong demographic dividend with low dependency ratios and a large cohort of prime-age workers. For many of the rich countries in Asia, this period is coming to an end. Figure 2.1 shows TFRs for the high-income countries in Asia (along with Germany and the United States for reference).

Total fertility rates in Japan and Germany have been significantly below the replacement level of 2.1 for almost 50 years, beginning in 1970. Over the next 20 years, the rapidly growing nations of Asia followed suit, with Singapore falling below replacement in 1975, Hong Kong in 1980, South Korea in 1985, and China and Taiwan in 1990. Malaysia was the last to make the transition in 2015. The United States, Australia, and New Zealand have a notably different pattern. They dropped below replacement in 1970, 1975, and 1980, respectively, but they never dropped as far below replacement as the East Asian nations and Germany did by 2015.

Figure 2.2 shows the corresponding fertility trends for the lower-income Asian nations. Vietnam is the only country within this group that has decisively gone below the replacement level. Bangladesh, Nepal, Sri Lanka, and Myanmar have dropped to below the replacement level only recently. India, Indonesia, and Laos are forecast to drop below replacement by 2030, and Cambodia by 2035. The Philippines and

FIGURE 2.1 TFR in higher-income Asian nations, 1950–2050

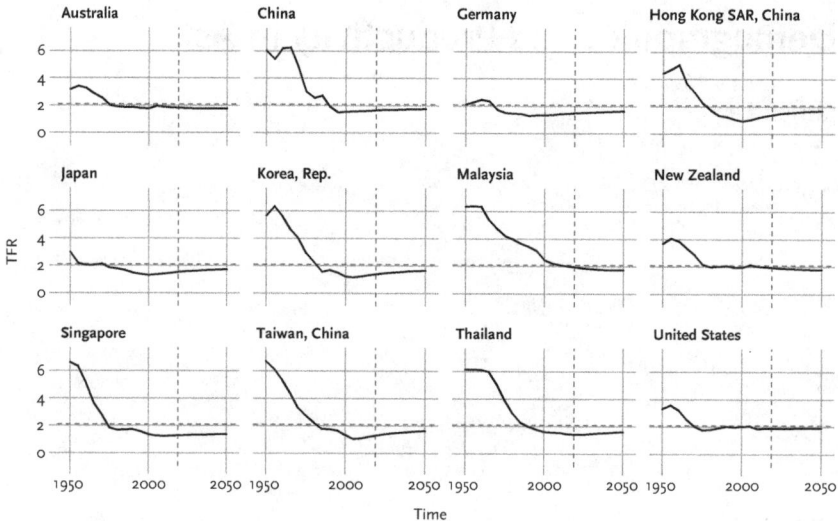

NOTE: TFR is based on medium UN projections; Germany and the United States included for comparison. The replacement level TFR of 2.1 and year 2019 are indicated by the horizontal and vertical dotted lines, respectively.
SOURCE: UN Population Division.

FIGURE 2.2 TFR in lower-income Asian nations, 1950–2050

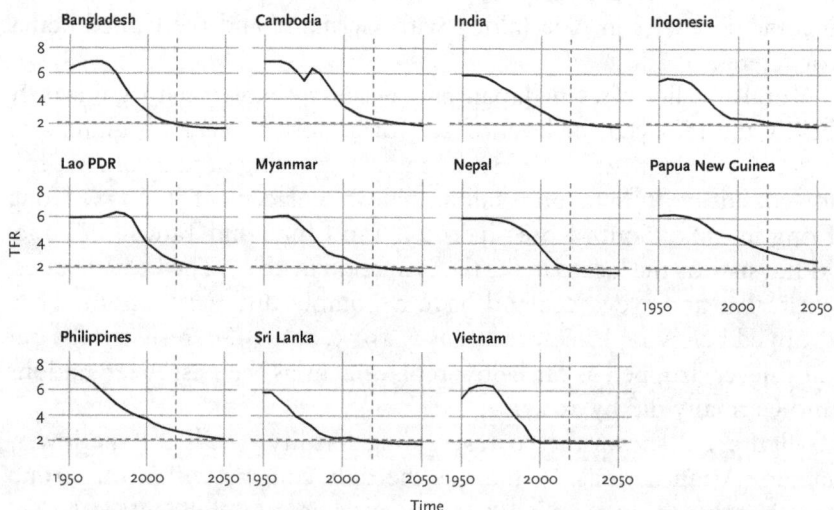

NOTE: TFR is based on medium UN projections. The replacement level TFR of 2.1 and year 2019 are indicated by the horizontal and vertical dotted lines, respectively.
SOURCE: UN Population Division.

TABLE 2.1 The timing of demographic transitions in Asia

Country	2015 TFR	Year below replacement
Japan	1.48	1960
Germany	1.47	1970
United States	1.89	1970
Singapore	1.26	1975
Australia	1.83	1975
Hong Kong	1.33	1980
New Zealand	1.97	1980
Taiwan, China	1.22	1985
South Korea	1.32	1985
Thailand	1.46	1990
China	1.64	1990
Vietnam	1.95	2000
Malaysia	2.01	2015
Sri Lanka	2.03	2015
Bangladesh	2.07	2015
Nepal	2.08	2015
Myanmar	2.18	2020*
India	2.30	2025*
Indonesia	2.32	2030*
Laos	2.62	2030*
Cambodia	2.52	2035*
Philippines	2.88	2055*
Papua New Guinea	3.59	2085*

NOTE: *Forecast; Germany and United States included for comparison.
SOURCE: UN Population Division.

Papua New Guinea are clear outliers, with total fertility rates currently above 2.5.

Table 2.1 summarizes the timing of the transition. There are four clearly defined groups: (1) early transitions with shallow fertility declines (United States, Australia, and New Zealand), (2) early transitions with deep fertility declines (Japan, Singapore, Hong Kong, Taiwan, South Korea, Thailand, China, and Vietnam), (3) just transitioned (Malaysia, Sri Lanka, Bangladesh, Nepal, Myanmar), and (4) pretransition (India, Indonesia, Laos, Cambodia, the Philippines, and Papua New Guinea).

With the exception of the shallow transitioners (all former Great Britain settler colonies), the transitions are all monotonic, from high to low fertility with the differences between them being mostly the start dates. The richest countries in Asia tended to have the earliest transitions. This is almost certainly good news, because the demographic transformations that will happen over the next half century

FIGURE 2.3 Working age population distribution for higher-income Asian nations, 2010

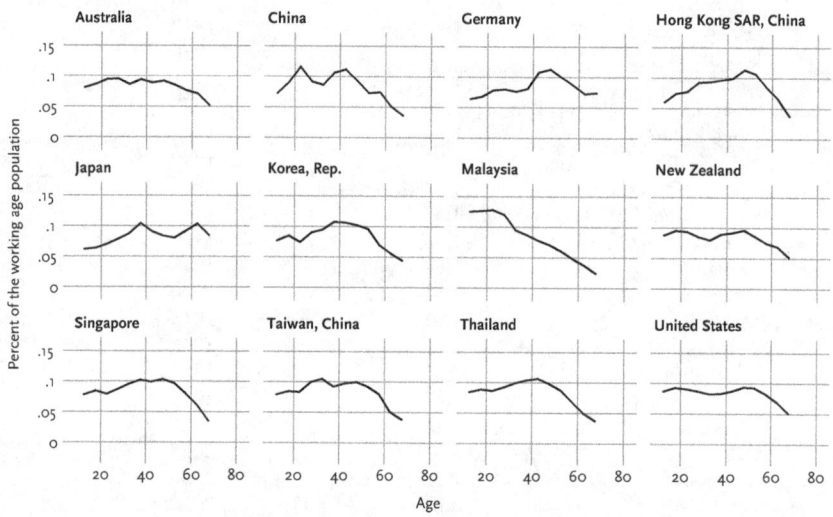

SOURCE: UN Population Division.

are unprecedented. Since there will almost certainly be societal and economic stresses associated with these changes, it is fortunate that the first countries to undergo them are rich and politically stable.

For the earliest demographic transitions, the largest birth cohorts are prime-age workers. Over the next 20 years, these outsized cohorts of prime-age workers are turning into outsized cohorts of retirees. Figure 2.3 shows the distribution of the working age population in 2010 for the higher-income Asian nations. Figure 2.4 does the same for 2030. In 2010 most of the countries have a peak in the age distribution between 30 and 50, the exceptions being Japan and Germany, which are already showing signs of an aging workforce. Malaysia is the other outlier, with a very young workforce. By 2030 all of these economies will have distributions skewed decidedly toward older ages, with the exception of the shallow transition group of the United States, New Zealand, and Australia, and the lone late transitioner, Malaysia.

The forecast distributions for the early and deep transition countries are a new phenomenon in the world. The median age in Japan is forecast to be above 50 by 2025. To put this into perspective, figure 2.5 shows the highest median age in the world in each year for large

FIGURE 2.4 Working age population distributions of higher-income Asian nations, 2030

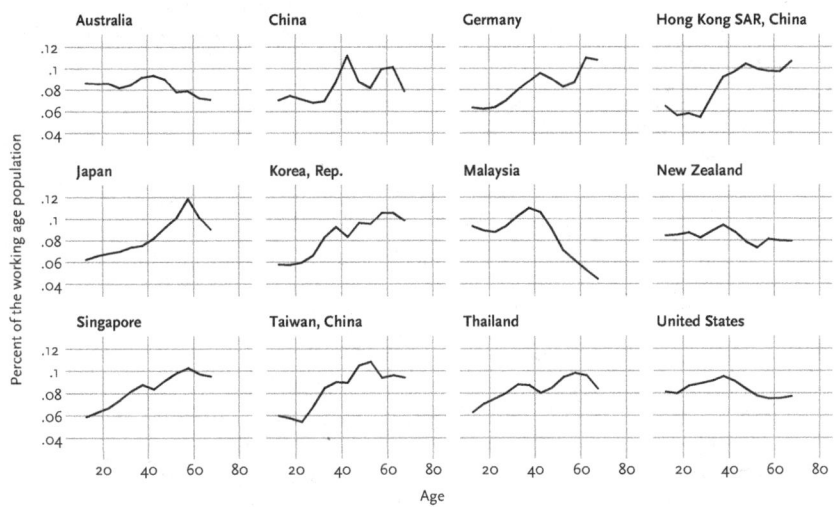

SOURCE: UN Population Division.

FIGURE 2.5 Highest median-age country, 1950–2050

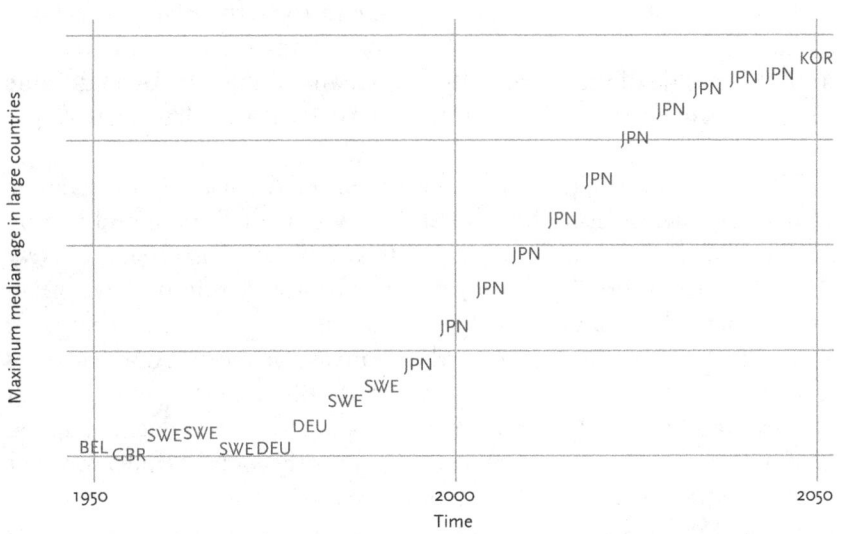

NOTE: Includes only large countries.
SOURCE: UN Population Division.

FIGURE 2.6 Median age by world region, 1950–2100

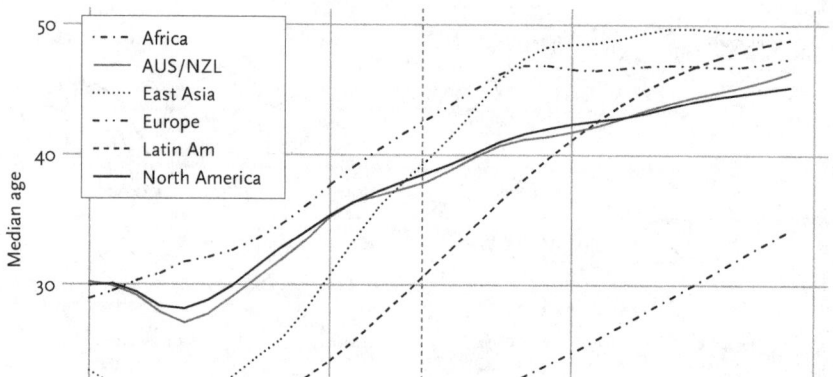

NOTE: Medium UN projections.
SOURCE: UN Population Division.

countries. Until 1995 the highest median ages were in Western Europe and were in the mid-30s until 1980. Japan took the place of Sweden as the oldest nation in the world in 1995 and is forecast to remain so until the middle of the century. By 2050 many of the later demographic transition countries in Asia will join Japan with median ages in the mid-50s.

Figure 2.6 shows the median age by region. As of 2019, the average median age within East Asia is still below that of Europe and is only a bit below the level of the United States, Canada, Australia, and New Zealand. The future (and past) trajectory, however, is remarkable in its steepness. Also of note, and less well known, is that Latin America looks much more like East Asia than Europe or North America in its transition, with a delay of about 20 years. Just as Japan will serve as an early indicator of how the world responds to unprecedented aging, East Asia as a whole may provide lessons for the similar transition that will hit Latin America with a lag of 20 years.

What does this mean for future productivity? From the labor literature, we know that there is a robust relationship between years of experience and income. Assuming that workers are paid their marginal product, this suggests a relationship between worker productivity and age. Aggregating to the national level, this suggests that changes in the age structure of a population will be correlated with changes in productivity. In this way, an aging population may be a more productive one due to experience. However, there may be reason to believe that aging may lower the productivity of workers. For example, there is evidence that cognitive ability declines with age.

Feyrer (2007) investigates the relationship between the age structure of the workforce and productivity. I find that there is a strong and robust correlation between the size of the prime-age workforce, centered on the 40-year-old cohort, and total factor productivity. This impact is significantly larger than expected from standard Mincer evidence on the relationship between wages and experience. This suggests that there are other mechanisms at work beyond simple aggregation of private returns.

The early demographic transition Asian nations have benefited from the aging of their populations over the first 40 years of their transitions by having smaller youth cohorts and commensurately larger cohorts in the prime working years. This is about to reverse as the cohorts above prime age become the largest, as shown in figure 2.4.

In the remainder of this chapter, I will discuss some of the potential mechanisms through which aging populations impact productivity. I will then look at the aggregate evidence and update Feyrer (2007) with new data, considering the implications for future growth of productivity in Asia. Finally, I will consider whether the past is a useful guide for the future for Asia, since the demographic configurations that are forecast are very different from what we have seen in the past.

Channels

Demographics might impact productivity through several different channels or mechanisms. Two seem especially salient.

Idea creation

The first channel is idea creation, or innovation. The creation of new productive ideas and their dispersion through the economy is the main engine of growth in the rich countries of the world. The nonrival nature of ideas generates externalities from the idea creators to the entire workforce. If innovative activity is not spread uniformly across the working life, the demographics of the workforce could have a strong influence on technological change and adoption.

Innovation over the life cycle will be driven by two countervailing forces. First, one must study to get to the research frontier. As technologies become more complicated, this period of training is likely to become longer. This makes it more difficult for the youngest members of the workforce to be the driving force behind innovation. Working in the opposite direction, there is evidence that cognitive function declines over time. A metastudy of the relationship between age and cognition by Verhaeghen and Salthouse (1997) documents the decline in cognitive abilities over the life cycle.

These two factors should generate a life-cycle pattern of innovation. One of the first studies of age and innovation is Lehman (1953). He examines creative output in science and invention and finds that innovative activity varies substantially by age. Across disciplines, peak productivity is found to occur between the ages of 30 and 40.

More recent work by economists have also found a link between age and creative performance. Weinberg and Galenson (2005) find that the peak years for Nobel Prize–winning economists tends to be in their 40s. Jones (2010) studies Nobel Prize winners in the sciences and uses the NBER patent database to study significant new inventions. He finds the age range of 35–45 to be the peak innovative years.

Interestingly, he finds that the likelihood of innovative activity at young ages is falling over time. This is not offset by an increase in innovative activity in later years. Jones conjectures that it takes longer to get to the innovative frontier as technologies become more complex, leaving a shorter window for innovative activity.

Feyrer (2008) adds to this body of evidence by showing kernel density estimates of the ages of patent grantees by year from 1975 until 1995 (figure 2.7). The United States underwent large changes in the age distribution of the workforce between 1975 and 1995. While this is somewhat evident in figure 2.7, the shape of the distribution is quite stable, with a median age of roughly 48 throughout. If it is the case that innovative activity peaks in individuals between the ages of 35 and 45, it is not unreasonable to think that relatively smaller cohorts in these age ranges will lead to lower levels of innovation and lower productivity growth.

In more recent evidence, Azoulay, Jones, Kim and Miranda (2018) study high-growth startups over the past decade. They find the mean

FIGURE 2.7 Age distribution of U.S. inventors granted patents, 1975–95, select years

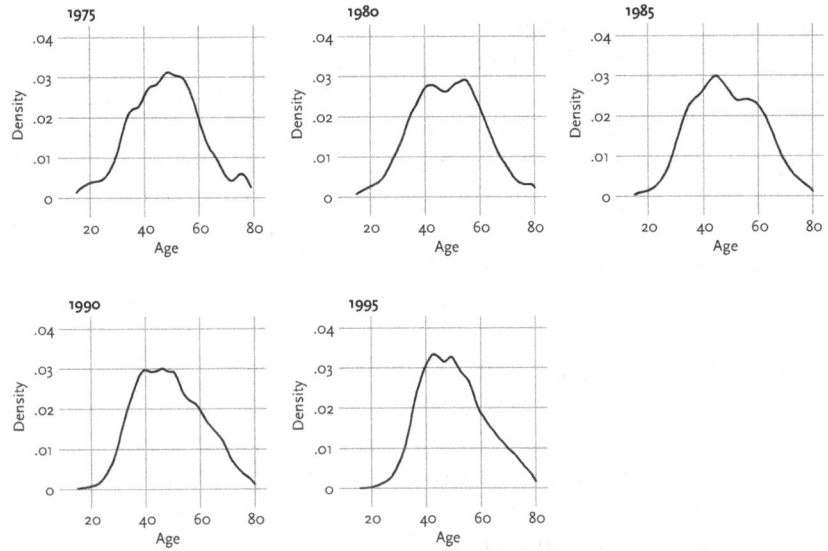

NOTE: Medium UN projections.
SOURCE: IPUMS, author's calculations. For details, see Feyrer (2008).

founder age of the fastest growing companies to be 45. For the top firms, the frequency of founders at ages 30 and 55 is 40 percent lower than at age 45. Once again, there appears to be a comparative advantage in innovation centered around the middle age group in the age distribution.

Idea adoption

While innovation is certainly important, for ideas to be reflected in the output of the economy they must be adopted by firms and contribute to the production process. This is true particularly for those smaller countries where domestic innovation may be overshadowed by the importance of innovation happening in other parts of the globe and then adopted domestically. The innovation described in the previous section is moving the frontier of knowledge outward. In this section we are concerned with how closely countries operate to the frontier by tapping from the stock of world innovation.

Weinberg (2002) finds a tension between age and experience in technology adoption. Because schooling tends to be concentrated early in life, young workers have the advantage of more recent human capital.[1] Younger workers are often better educated in the latest technologies and may also be more willing to take risks. However, younger workers may lack the experience and training to effectively implement new ideas. This leads to a potential point in middle age when a worker's human capital is reasonably fresh and the worker has gained the skills needed to implement the new technologies.

Feyrer (2011) finds that demographic shifts may also matter through the effect on the quality of management. The Lucas (1978) span of control model emphasizes the importance of managers. A firm with a manager of quality x managing n workers and k units of capital will produce the following amount of output:

$$y = xg[f(n,k)] \tag{1}$$

where $f()$ is a standard neoclassical production function, and $g[]$ has decreasing returns. An increase in the quality of the manager raises output and the marginal product of labor and capital for the entire firm, holding inputs constant. Higher marginal products will attract more capital and labor to the firm, but decreasing returns to $g[]$ means that increasing the size of any given firm will reduce per-worker output for any given level of inputs. In equilibrium, all firms have the same marginal products.

Given a distribution of managerial talent, there will be a cutoff level where the highest managerial skill workers manage and the rest work for firms. The higher-quality managers will manage larger firms. There will be a trade-off between adding more managers (allowing for smaller firms) and lowering the overall quality of management.

This suggests that a large influx of young workers will drive down the overall quality of management. Young workers are unsuited for management due to a lack of experience. They therefore need to be managed by the older, smaller cohorts. This will lead to a combination of larger firms for high-quality managers (reducing productivity due to the scale effect) and the employment of a larger number of managers from the older cohorts. These additional managers will be further down the distribution of managerial talent, also lowering productivity.

---

1   Chari and Hoenhayn (1991) find that technologies diffuse slowly due to vintage human capital effects.

FIGURE 2.8 Age distribution of U.S. workforce categorized as managers by decade, 1950–2000

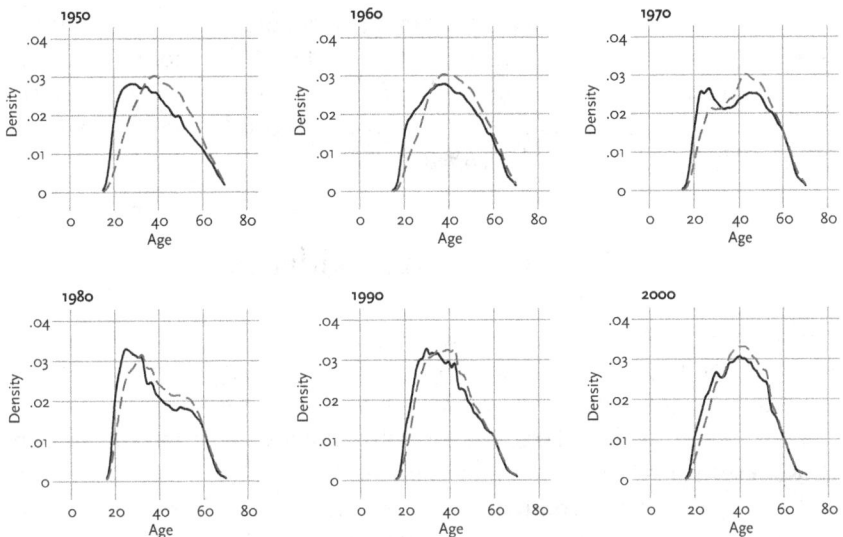

NOTE: Entire workforce represented by solid line, managers by dashed line.
SOURCE: IPUMS, author's calculations.

Figure 2.8 shows the evolution of the age distribution of managers in the United States over time against the evolution of the workforce as a whole. The solid line is a kernel density estimate of the age distribution of the U.S. workforce over time. The dashed line is the age distribution of U.S. workers categorized as managers.

In all the graphs, young workers are underrepresented in management. This is consistent with youth being a barrier to management due to lack of experience. The baby boom first appears in the workforce in the 1970 census, but baby boomers are not much in evidence in the management distribution. Because there is an influx of young workers who need managers, the probability that members of the older cohort are called upon to manage necessarily rises. These additional managers are likely to be less talented. By 1980, the baby boom has fully entered the workforce, but is still quite underrepresented in the managerial workforce.

The beginning of the baby boomers' managerial careers pulls the average age of managers down by four years from 1970 to 1980, from

43 years old to 39 years old. The managerial workforce begins to return to its earlier shape in 1990 as the baby boomers begin to hit normal managerial ages. By 2000 the distribution looks almost identical to the 1960 distribution. The median age of managers in 2000 returns to the level of 1960. Using a calibrated model of the economy, Feyrer (2011) shows that the demographic movements in the United States can explain up to 20 percent of the observed productivity slowdown with the United States in the 1970s.

Cross-Country Evidence

Given these mechanisms at the microeconomic level, it seems sensible to see if age impacts are visible in the aggregate. Feyrer (2007) finds a large impact of the demographic structure of the workforce on productivity and output in a large sample of countries. This section revisits those results, updating them with new data.

For use in a cross-country regression, demographic measures have several useful characteristics that make identification more straightforward than with many variables typically used in this literature. First, demographic measures are strongly predetermined. The current age structure of the workforce was determined roughly 20 years ago and should be predetermined with respect to current output movements. Second, demographics have significant time series variation. This time series variation allows for exploiting the panel nature of the data.

Output in country i at time t, $y_{i,t}$ is assumed to be a function of a time-invariant country fixed effect, f_i, a time trend common to all countries, μ_t, and a vector of explanatory variables $x_{i,t}$,

$$y_{i,t} = f_i + \mu_t + \beta x_{i,t} + u_{i,t}. \qquad (2)$$

The regressors are the proportion of the workforce by age group, with "W10" in tables 2.2 and 2.3 indicating workers between the ages of 10 and 19, "W20" workers between ages 20 and 29, etc. "W60" indicates workers 60 years of age and older. Because these variables are proportions, the sum of all the age groups is one for each country-year pair. The 40-year-old group is excluded and is therefore the reference group. I choose to exclude W40 because the 40-year-old age group generally has the highest coefficient when included. By excluding W40, significant coefficients on the other age groups indicate that they are significantly different from the implied zero coefficient on W40.

Equation 2 will be estimated in first differences. Data for output are from the Penn World Tables versions 6.0 and 9.1 (Feenstra, Inklaar, and Timmer 2015). There have been significant revisions to the Penn World Tables in the last decade that have brought some earlier studies into question, particularly those relying on the time series for identification (Johnson, Larson, Papageorgiou, and Subramanian 2013). The specific series that I am using is *rgdpo*, which is output-side real gross domestic product (GDP) that is adjusted by chained purchasing power parity.

The data on workforce composition are from two sources. The International Labor Organization (ILO) has compiled cross-country data on the number of workers by five-year age groups spanning age 10 to age 65. These are available at 10-year intervals, starting in 1960. Population by five-year age groups is available from the UN. The population data is used to impute the intermediate values for the workforce data.[2]

The Feyrer (2007) sample contained 87 countries from 1960 to 1990. New data will allow us to increase the sample across countries to 106 and across time to 2010. The most expansive sample has 954 observations, compared to the 499 of the original study. Oil exporters are excluded.

The first column of table 2.2 shows results using the same sample and data from Feyrer (2007). The differences between the age groups are extremely large. According to the column 1 estimates, a five-percentage-point shift from the 30-year age group to the 40-year age group is associated with an over 13 percent increase in per-worker output.[3] If this shift occurred over a 10-year period, this would add approximately 1.6 percentage points to output growth in each year.

The remaining columns examine how robust the results from the original paper are to updates to the data that have occurred in the subsequent decade. Column 2 updates the left-hand side from Penn World Tables 6 to Penn World Tables 9.1, with very little change in the results.

---

2 The population demographic data used in the imputation is limited to the working age population in order to avoid contaminating the imputed data with information about dependency ratios.

3 Demographic shifts of this size, while not the norm, are present in the data. Between 1980 and 1990, the proportion of workers in the United States who were between 40 and 49 rose by 4.6 percent.

TABLE 2.2 Output on demographics—updated data

	(1)	(2)	(3) $\Delta ln(y)$	(4)	(5)
$\Delta W10$	−3.181***	−3.685***	−3.392***	−3.347***	−3.569***
	(0.685)	(0.838)	(0.860)	(0.742)	(0.729)
$\Delta W20$	−1.823**	−1.974*	−1.910*	−1.949**	−2.440***
	(0.642)	(0.755)	(0.779)	(0.633)	(0.656)
$\Delta W30$	−2.736***	−2.768**	−2.291**	−2.632***	−2.660***
	(0.734)	(0.821)	(0.760)	(0.670)	(0.630)
$\Delta W50$	−1.894*	−2.443*	−1.254	−0.908	−0.971
	(0.794)	(0.944)	(0.898)	(0.794)	(0.803)
$\Delta W60$	−2.334**	−2.279*	−2.259*	−2.112*	−2.151*
	(0.807)	(1.091)	(0.985)	(1.031)	(1.029)
r2	0.142	0.132	0.127	0.102	0.0959
N	499	435	530	613	742
Countries	87	85	106	85	106
Joint p–value	0.000585	0.000377	0.00406	0.000808	0.000203
PWT version	6	9	9	9	9
Final Year	1990	1990	1990	2000	2000

NOTE: Standard errors clustered at the country level.
All regressions include a full set of time dummies.
*p<0.05, **p<0.01, ***p<0.001.
SOURCE: Author.

The use of the new Penn World Tables allows for more countries to be added. Column 3 uses the same years as columns 1 and 2 but adds more countries. Column 4 keeps the same countries as the original sample but adds years up to 2000. Column 5 uses the extended time period and includes all possible countries. The new results are quite compatible with the old, with the main exception being that the results for the upper age groups become less precise. In addition, the coefficient on the 50-year-old age group falls and is no longer significant as the sample increases.

Table 2.2 starts with the larger country sample and progressively adds years to the sample. Columns 1 and 3 are identical to columns 3 and 5 in table 2.3, and the results are quite similar. Once again, adding years tends to weaken the results a bit at the upper age ranges. This is notable because many countries are seeing unprecedented increases in the relative size of these upper age groups.

TABLE 2.3 Output on demographics—adding years of new data

	(1)	(2)	(3) $\Delta ln(y)$	(4)	(5)
$\Delta W10$	−3.392***	−4.281***	−3.569***	−3.238***	−2.577***
	(0.860)	(0.922)	(0.729)	(0.701)	(0.608)
$\Delta W20$	−1.910*	−2.602**	−2.440***	−2.600***	−2.139***
	(0.779)	(0.912)	(0.656)	(0.691)	(0.629)
$\Delta W30$	−2.291**	−3.146***	−2.660***	−2.640***	−1.813**
	(0.760)	(0.808)	(0.630)	(0.694)	(0.629)
$\Delta W50$	−1.254	−1.825†	−0.971	−0.766	−0.670
	(0.898)	(0.938)	(0.803)	(0.763)	(0.723)
$\Delta W60$	−2.259*	−2.637*	−2.151*	−2.159**	−1.307*
	(0.985)	(1.072)	(1.029)	(0.726)	(0.622)
r2	0.127	0.116	0.0959	0.0942	0.0877
N	530	636	742	848	954
Countries	106	106	106	106	106
Joint p-value	0.00406	0.000142	0.000203	0.000441	0.00305
Final Year	1990	1995	2000	2005	2010

NOTE: Standard errors clustered at the country level.
All regressions include a full set of time dummies.
†p<0.10, *p<0.05, **p<0.01, ***p<0.001.
SOURCE: Author.

Implications

The results of the previous section can be used to provide insight into cross-country productivity patterns.

Cross-country productivity differences

The demographic characteristics of the workforce differ greatly across countries with different income levels. Figure 2.9 shows the proportion of the working age population aged 40–49 across income groups. The poorest nations have a lower proportion of 40-year-old workers than the richer nations in every year. While the other three higher-income groups all show a rising share of workers aged 40–49, the timing of the rise is different in each. For the high-income group the increase in 40- to 49-year-olds is from 1980 to 2000. The

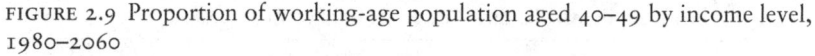

FIGURE 2.9 Proportion of working-age population aged 40–49 by income level, 1980–2060

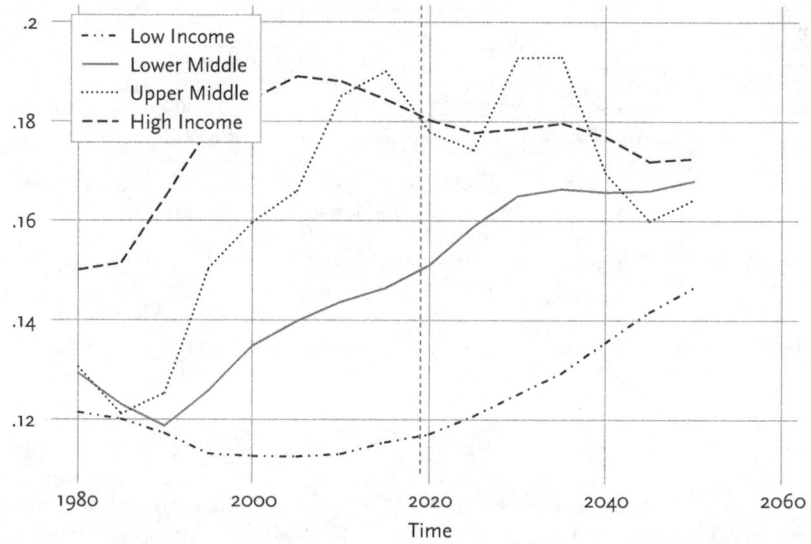

SOURCE: UN Population Division.

upper-middle-income group starts 10 years later with a steeper slope, and the lower-middle group with a shallower slope. The low-income group remains low throughout, with forecasts suggesting movement over the next 30 years.

Given the results of the previous section, we can see that in 1980 the high-income group had much more favorable demographics for productivity than the rest of the countries in the world. Over the last 40 years, the upper-middle group converged with the high-income group in this regard and the lower-middle group is in the process of following suit.

Figure 2.10 shows the proportion of the working age population aged 40–49 across regions. The demographic transition for East Asia looks very similar to that of North America, with a 15-year lag. Figures 2.11 and 2.12 show the proportion of the workforce between the ages of 40 and 49 across a number of Asian countries. For the higher-income countries, the increase in the middle-aged cohort size has provided a significant productivity boost over the last 30 years, but for many, this is about to end and, in some cases, reverse. The

FIGURE 2.10 Proportion of working-age population aged 40–49 by region, 1980–2060

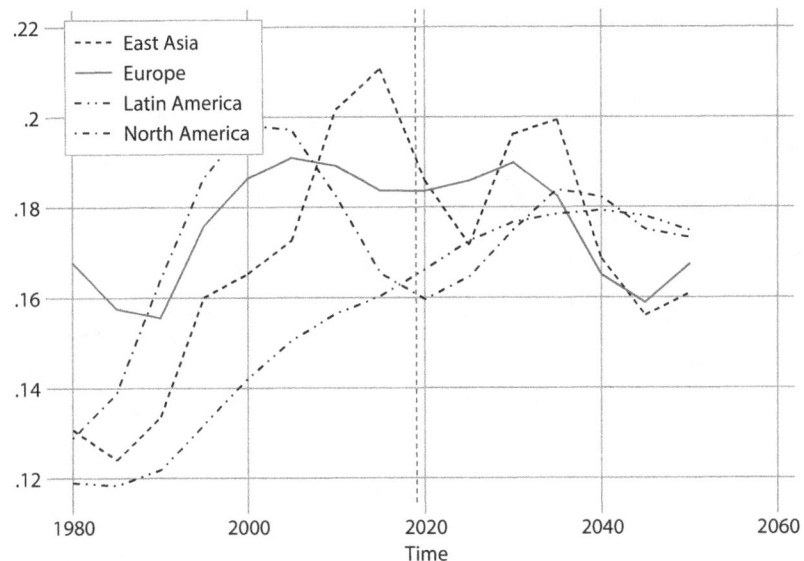

SOURCE: UN Population Division.

FIGURE 2.11 Proportion of working age population aged 40–49 in higher-income Asian countries, 1980–2060

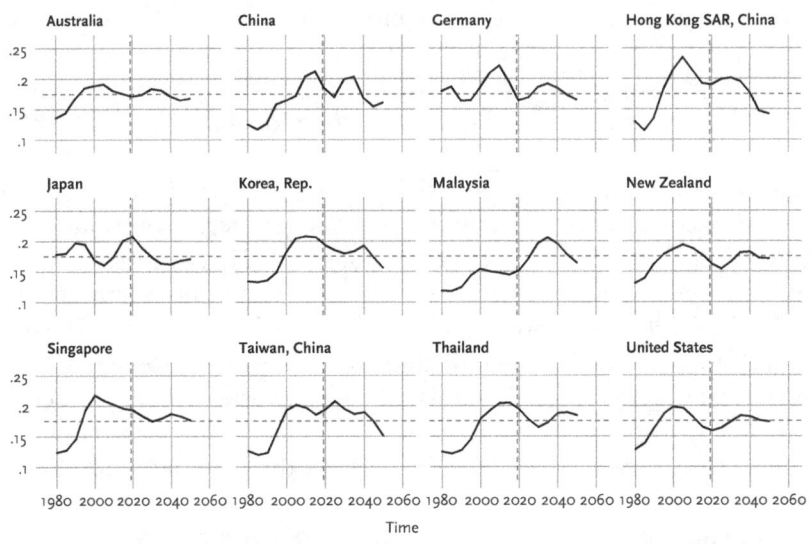

NOTE: The replacement level TFR of 2.1 and year 2019 are indicated by the horizontal and vertical dotted lines, respectively
SOURCE: UN Population Division.

FIGURE 2.12 Proportion of working-age population aged 40–49 in lower-income Asian countries, 1980–2060

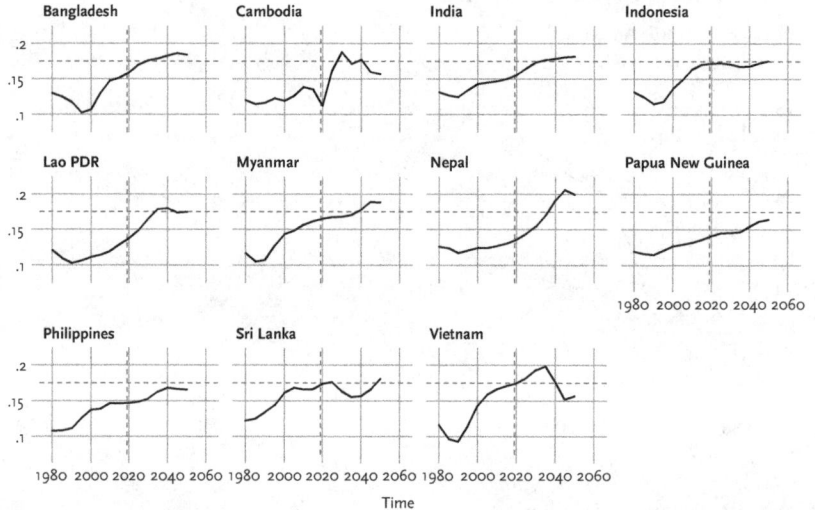

NOTE: The replacement level TFR of 2.1 and year 2019 are indicated by the horizontal and vertical dotted lines, respectively.
SOURCE: UN Population Division.

lower-income Asian nations are all moving into a period where demographics suggest a productivity boost.

The impact of demographics on income

Figures 2.13 and 2.14 use the demographic data, combined with the regression coefficients, to show the past and predicted contribution to the level of TFP over time for the nations of Asia. The levels in these figures are the increase (or decrease) in log points of productivity relative to the world mean attributable to demographic forces, as estimated earlier. For most of the higher-income Asian nations, productivity has been substantially boosted compared to the world average by demographics. Taking South Korea as an example, moving from the world average to 0.4 from 1970 to 2000 suggests that demographic change contributed to over 1 percent per year additional GDP growth over this period. The slope, however, has reversed and South Korea is poised to give back about half these gains over the next 30 years. For the lower-income nations, their demographic structure has been a negative to

FIGURE 2.13 Contribution of demographics to output relative to world mean in higher-income Asian countries, 1950–2050

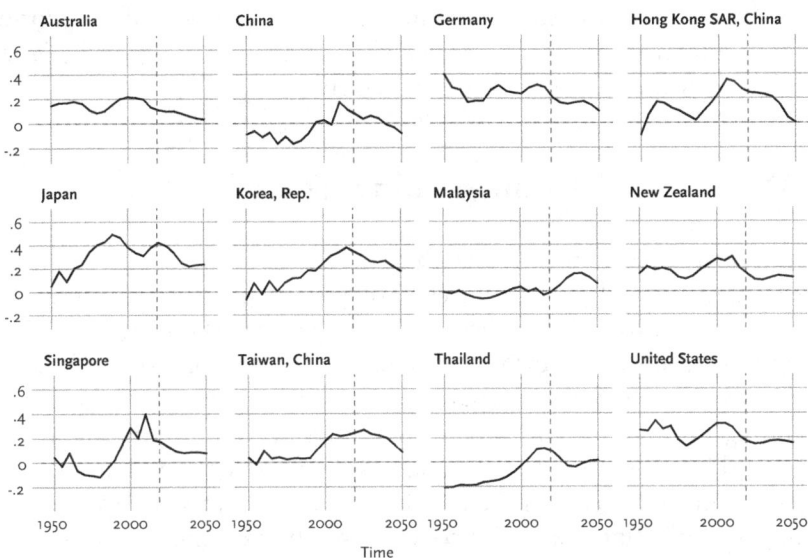

NOTE: The replacement level TFR of 2.1 and year 2019 are indicated by the horizontal and vertical dotted lines, respectively.
SOURCE: UN Population Division.

FIGURE 2.14 Contribution of demographics to output relative to world mean in lower-income Asian countries, 1950–2050

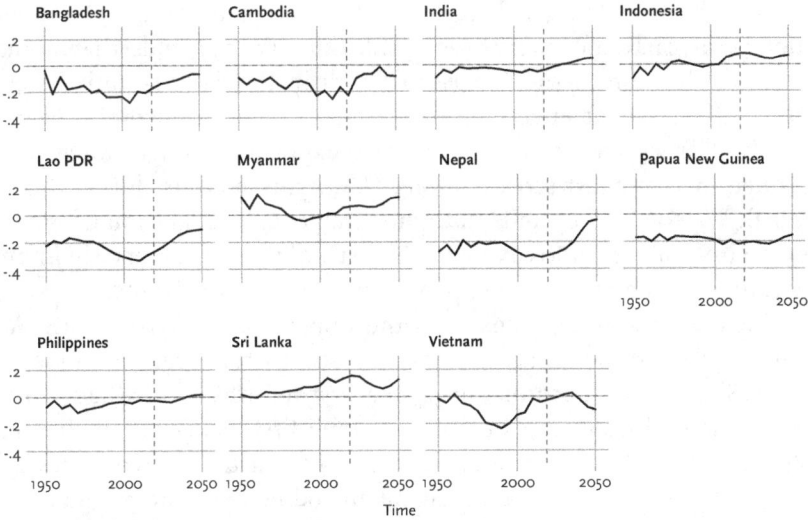

NOTE: The replacement level TFR of 2.1 and year 2019 are indicated by the horizontal and vertical dotted lines, respectively.
SOURCE: UN Population Division.

productivity over the sample period relative to the rest of the world. Most are forecast to move toward the world average, suggesting higher productivity growth rates in the transition.

Countervailing Forces

The previous section suggests that the aging of the higher-income Asian nations will exert a downward pull on productivity over the next 30 years. Recall that these estimates are based on regression coefficients outlined earlier in this chapter. The updating of these coefficients with new data suggests that the downward pull of the oldest working age cohorts may not be as strong in recent years as in the past. Table 2.3 shows that each successive wave of new data moving forward in time weakens the conclusions for the 50- and 60-year-old cohorts, suggesting that older cohorts may be exerting less of a negative pull on productivity over time.

There are several reasons to think that this may be true. First, the cohorts now entering old age had much healthier childhoods than in the past. Vaccinations, sanitation, and food fortification mean that the childhoods of those entering old age in the future will be healthier than those in the past before we even account for modern improvements in medicine.

Over the last decade, there has been a large literature about the impacts of early life interventions. Bleakley (2007) finds that hookworm eradication in the American South in the early twentieth century had significant effects on education and future incomes. Ferrie, Rolf, and Troesken (2012) find that lead exposure through water pipes resulted in lower test scores among U.S. Army recruits during World War II. Watson (2006) finds that improvements in sanitation of Indian reservations in the 1960s explain a big part of the convergence in infant mortality rates between white people and Native Americans.

Much of this work focuses on the impact of in utero health. Almond (2006) shows that cohorts exposed to the Spanish Influenza of 1918, either in utero or during the first months of life, had worse health and socioeconomic outcomes in their lifetime. Feyrer, Politi, and Weil (2017) find that salt iodization in 1924 in the United States led to significant cognitive improvement in iodine-deficient populations. Almond and Currie (2011) do a nice job of surveying this literature.

These studies all point to the idea that the cohorts entering old age now are different from those that came before them. There are some signs that the improvements in conditions at early ages have yielded cognitive benefits at the aggregate level. Flynn (1984) famously pointed out that IQ in the United States was rising about three points per decade. In a metastudy, Trahan, Stuebing, Hiscock, and Fletcher (2014) confirm this finding and suggest that there are no signs that this is diminishing over time.

The idea that current cohorts entering old age differ from their predecessors has significant consequences for population aging. Dickinson and Hiscock (2010) and Salthouse (2015) suggest that some of the evidence for cognitive decline with age is an artifact of longitudinal studies combined with the Flynn effect. Dickinson and Hiscock (2010) suggest that controlling for the Flynn effect can account for 85 percent of the disparity between 25- and 70-year-olds.

Taken together, these studies suggest that the older-aged workforce of the future may look very different from that of the past in ways that impact productivity. This suggests a large degree of caution in using the past as a guide for the future.

Conclusion

This chapter presents evidence that the proportion of prime-age workers has a strong positive influence on productivity through the channels of innovation and idea adoption. This has been a significant contributor to productivity growth for the high-income nations of Asia over the last half century. For the lower-income Asian nations, demographic factors have been a drag on productivity over the same period. This situation is about to reverse. There are indications that as the high-income Asian nations enter a period of significant aging, this demographic change will exert a drag on productivity going forward.

These predictions are very uncertain for several reasons. First, the aggregate evidence is getting weaker over time regarding the negative impact of an older workforce. This may be because the older workers of the past were much different from those of today and of the future, due to better healthcare, nutrition, and conditions during childhood.

The second reason for caution is that the estimates of the impact of demographics on productivity were performed on data that does not include the sorts of demographic configurations that we will see over the next 30 years. In 1975 the highest median age in the world was 35. By 2050 the higher-income nations of Asia will all have median ages above 50. Estimates about the impact of older workers are very much extrapolating from data that does not cover the range of values that we will see in the future.

References

Almond, Douglas. 2006. "Is the 1918 Influenza Pandemic Over? Long-Term Effects of In Utero Influenza Exposure in the Post-1940 U.S. Population." *Journal of Political Economy* 114 (August): 672–712.

Almond, Douglas, and Janet Currie. 2011. "Killing Me Softly: The Fetal Origins Hypothesis." *Journal of Economic Perspectives* 25, no.3: 153–72.

Azoulay, Pierre, Benjamin Jones, J. Daniel Kim, and Javier Miranda. 2018. "Age and High-Growth Entrepreneurship." Working Paper 24489, National Bureau of Economic Research (April).

Bleakley, Hoyt. 2007. "Disease and Development: Evidence from Hookworm Eradication in the American South." *Quarterly Journal of Economics* 122, no.1 (February): 73–117.

Chari, V. V. and Hugo Hopenhayn. 1991. "Vintage Human Capital, Growth, and the Diffusion of New Technology." *Journal of Political Economy* 99, no.6: 1142–65.

Dickinson, Mercedes D. and Merrill Hiscock. 2010. "Age-Related IQ Decline is Reduced Markedly After Adjustment for the Flynn Effect." *Journal of Clinical and Experimental Neuropsychology* 32, no.8 (September): 865–70.

Feenstra, Robert C., Robert Inklaar, and Marcel P. Timmer. 2015. "The Next Generation of the Penn World Table." *American Economic Review* 105, no.10 (October): 3150–82.

Ferrie, Joseph P., Karen Rolf, and Werner Troesken. 2012. "Cognitive Disparities, Lead Plumbing, and Water Chemistry: Prior Exposure to Water-Borne Lead and Intelligence Test Scores Among World War Two U.S. Army Enlistees." *Economics & Human Biology* 10, no. 1: 98–111.

Feyrer, James. 2007. "Demographics and Productivity." *Review of Economics and Statistics* 89, no.1 (February): 100–09.

———. 2008. "Aggregate Evidence on the Link Between Age Structure and Productivity." *Population and Development Review* 34: 78–99.

———. 2011. "The US Productivity Slowdown, the Baby Boom, and Management Quality." *Journal of Population Economics* 24, no.1 (January): 267–84.

Feyrer, James, Dimitra Politi, and David N. Weil. 2017. "The Cognitive Effects of Micronutrient Deficiency: Evidence from Salt Iodization in the United States." *Journal of the European Economic Association* 15, no.2 (April): 355–87.

Flynn, James R. 1984. "The Mean IQ of Americans: Massive Gains 1932 to 1978." *Psychological Bulletin* 95, no.1: 29–51.

Johnson, Simon, William Larson, Chris Papageorgiou, and Arvind Subramanian. 2013. "Is Newer Better? Penn World Table Revisions and Their Impact on Growth Estimates." *Journal of Monetary Economics* 60, no.2 (March): 255–74.

Jones, Benjamin F. 2010. "Age and Great Invention." *Review of Economics and Statistics* 92, no.1: 1–14.

Lehman, Harvey C. 1953. *Age and Achievement*. Princeton University.

Lucas, Robert E. 1978. "On the Size Distribution of Business Firms." *Bell Journal of Economics* 9, no.2: 508–23.

Trahan, Lisa, Karla K. Stuebing, Merril K. Hiscock, and Jack M. Fletcher. 2014. "The Flynn Effect: A Meta-analysis." *Psychological Bulletin* 140, no .5 (September): 1332–60.

Verhaeghen, Paul and Timothy A. Salthouse. 1997. "Meta-analyses of Age-Cognition Relations in Adulthood: Estimates of Linear and Nonlinear Age Effects and Structural Models." *Psychological Bulletin* 122, no.3 (November): 231–49.

Watson, Tara. 2006. "Public Health Investments and the Infant Mortality Gap: Evidence from Federal Sanitation Interventions on U.S. Indian Reservations." *Journal of Public Economics* 90, nos.8 and 9 (September): 1537–60.

Weinberg, Bruce A. 2002. "Experience and Technology Adoption." 2002. Working paper, Ohio State University, May.

Weinberg, Bruce A., and David W. Galenson. 2005. "Creative Careers: The Life Cycles of Nobel Laureates in Economics." *De Economist* (December).

3   Demographics and Innovation in China

Correlation or Causation?

Karen Eggleston

Innovation in many ways defines our age and our aspirations, although no two of us may use exactly the same definition of *innovation*. Economists have long pointed to the centrality of productivity for economic progress; indeed, rising productivity determines long-run improvement in living standards. In that light, the relationship between innovation and demography comes down to how you define innovation—as synonymous with *productivity,* or as a more general social and economic concept, often linked to entrepreneurship and Schumpeterian creative destruction, or a foundational feature of a particular kind of modern economy. For example, the prominent scholar of postsocialist transition, János Kornai, argues that enhanced innovation will be the most important effect of economic system transformation in central and eastern Europe and the former Soviet Union, because "rapid innovation and dynamism are not a random phenomenon. . . but a deeply rooted system-specific property of capitalism" (2014, 3). The People's Republic of China (PRC) also has reformed from a centrally planned to a market-based economy, and increasingly seeks to push the global technological envelope in key industries as a strategy to sustain and deepen its soon-to-be-largest economy in the world.

Economists often equate innovation with productivity change in the long run and analyze the economic impacts of specific forms of technological change like automation and the application of artificial intelligence (AI) to a range of tasks, which may or may not relate directly to population characteristics. Economists tend to agree that specific kinds of innovation, such as automation, profoundly shape economies but need not steal all meaningful jobs from humans. Historically, automation may not have reduced employment, at least according to the Economic Expert Panel of the Initiative on Global Markets at the University of Chicago Booth School of Business, a panel that explores the extent of agreement on public policy issues among a diverse range of distinguished economists.[1] The expert panel expressed much more disagreement and uncertainty about whether information technology and automation stifle wage growth in spite of increased productivity. On innovation and long-term growth, the expert panel also expressed considerable uncertainty, with very few agreeing with the pessimist view that "future innovations worldwide will not be transformational enough to promote sustained per-capita economic growth rates in the U.S. and western Europe over the next century as high as those over the past 150 years."[2] Is the outlook even more optimistic for emerging Asia, or China in particular? Certainly, an increasing share of global innovations are arising from the region, and policymakers seek continued innovation to feed continued increases in per-capita living standards.

Although other social scientists may differ from economists in their approaches, as do the authors of the other chapters of this book, we all explore the close link between innovation and populations. The questions swirl more about whether the link represents a causal relationship or simply a correlation (as the title of this chapter emphasizes), and about which way the causal arrow points, if the relationship is at least partially causal.

To some extent, we know there is a definitive relationship between demographic change and innovation: previous innovations in population

---

1   Sapienza and Zingales (2013) utilize this survey, as do others. According to the official description, the expert panel members "are all senior faculty at the most elite research universities in the United States. The panel includes Nobel Laureates, John Bates Clark Medalists, fellows of the Econometric society, past Presidents of both the American Economics Association and American Finance Association, past Democratic and Republican members of the President's Council of Economics, and past and current editors of the leading journals in the profession. This selection process has the advantage of not only providing a set of panelists whose names will be familiar to other economists and the media, but also delivers a group with impeccable qualifications to speak on public policy matters. . . . The panel data are copyrighted by the Initiative on Global Markets and are being analyzed for an article to appear in a leading peer-reviewed journal." Individual responses are available, including their degree of confidence in each response; see, for example, http://www.igmchicago.org/participants/oliver-hart/ (accessed June 14, 2020).
2   See the summary of the expert panel responses at http://www.igmchicago.org/surveys/innovation-and-growth/ (accessed June 20, 2020).

health science and clinical medicine have enabled lower infant mortality and longer, healthier lives. In China in particular, we know that public health interventions and gains in schooling during the 1950 and 1960s, despite the tragedy of the Great Leap Forward Famine, contributed to the dramatic health improvements during the Mao era that laid the human capital foundation for post-Mao economic growth (Babiarz et al. 2015). Thus, one causal arrow runs from innovation to demography. Health innovations underlie the demographic transition from high and fluctuating birth and death rates to low and stable ones (Lee 2003; Eggleston and Fuchs 2012). With fertility rates dipping below replacement levels decades ago in many of the economies most advanced in this demographic transition, such as in Japan, the aging of earlier cohorts now drives an increasingly inverted population pyramid. Other economies with younger populations, like India, face the challenge of fully harnessing the "demographic dividend" from large cohorts in the working ages (Bloom and Canning 2000; Agarwal et al. 2020). For China, the demographic challenges involve rapid aging and gender imbalance, with the demographic dividend disappearing while urbanization continues to fuel growth.

To what extent does a causal arrow run the other way, from demography to innovation? Broadly, larger populations may generate more ideas, if ideas per capita are relatively uniformly distributed, and if agglomeration effects offset any congestion, environmental damage, or Malthusian negative effects of large populations.[3] And higher educational investments per child—sometimes seen as an inevitable trend with lower fertility rates—enhance the potential for an ever-greater share of the world's population to build on the shoulders of giants to contribute to humanity's store of knowledge and wisdom, from understanding of the human condition to technological inventions and organizational innovations that make our longer lives meaningful.

However, many analysts worry that demographic change slows the engine of innovation, warning that cognitive decline and clogged career paths enfeeble the innovative potential of societies with high proportions of middle-aged and older people, relative to youth. For example, the Chinese economist and entrepreneur James Liang argues that "the most fundamental and irreparable problem of aging is the weakening

---

3   It is on this basis, for example, that Liang asserts that "the three big heavyweights—China, India, and the United States—will be the leading nations of innovation" (2018, 226) well into the future.

of entrepreneurship and innovation, and a sort of degradation in the vitality of the human population taken as a whole" (2018, xv). Others hold up Japan's "lost decades" as evidence of an inevitable erosion of innovation in older economies, sometimes termed "Japanification." Does the empirical evidence support this view? What can China learn from other economies of East Asia or Southeast Asia, like Japan, Korea, and Singapore, about remaining innovative? Will younger South Asia inevitably eclipse East Asia as its younger population surges into the working ages, just as surely as India will soon overtake China as the most populous country in the world? This chapter focuses on China's case, while other chapters of this book probe multiple aspects of these questions for selected other countries of the Asia-Pacific region.

If one is worried about lower innovation in aging societies like China, it might be prudent to consider whether demography is the driver of reduced innovation, or whether population aging is rather a factor correlated with other underlying causes such as declining increases in the quality of human capital (at least as measured by educational attainment), as Gordon (2017) and others have suggested. Bloom, Jones, van Reenen, and Webb (2020) argue that ideas are just getting harder to find overall. Empirically, they show that research productivity is declining sharply, despite increasing research effort as evidenced by data from myriad industries, products, and firms. Since most economic models of long-term increases in living standards posit that research productivity itself is crucial for raising aggregate productivity—in conjunction with sheer numbers of researchers—this lackluster development bodes ill for future innovation. Bloom, Jones, van Reenen, and Webb (2020) provide a telling example: Compared to 50 years ago, over 18 times more researchers are required to achieve Moore's Law doubling of computer chip density. Of course, an older age structure may further compound this relative lack of ideas, even if it is not the direct cause, although "smoking gun" evidence on that point remains hard to find.

An older population may indeed generate fewer "conventional" innovations that have fueled broader economic growth in previous decades, as Gordon (2017) emphasizes.[4] However, countries with older

---

4   Robert Gordon, of course, would not be at all surprised: In his 2017 book *The Rise and Fall of American Growth: The US Standard of Living Since the Civil War,* Gordon argues that the transformative innovations of the previous century, and their boost to long-run economic growth, have mostly come to an end, although the U.S. population age structure is one mitigating factor relative to other high-income countries, such as Japan and most European countries.

populations—including young and middle-aged entrepreneurs in those nations—arguably have a distinct advantage in at least one form of innovation: providing the new ways of thinking and technologies that cater to the needs and capabilities of an older population. Where else to tinker with and rapidly upgrade gadgets catering to 70- and 80-year-olds than in a society in which such consumers are numerous and have many years of healthy life expectancy ahead of them? Several chapters of this book examine this hypothesis of endogenous technological change driven by demography and tailored to the needs of an older population like Japan (e.g., the chapter by Kushida) as well as the political economy of regional responses to aging. China, as the most populous country with a median age higher than that of the United States, represents a huge domestic market for technologies for aging societies that can also be exported to the rest of the globe.

China's demographic change shapes its economy and society in multiple fundamental ways. As Eggleston (2020a) notes, the total fertility rate of the PRC declined to around replacement levels in 1990–95, from approximately 6 at the outset of the PRC in 1950–55, with rapid decline prior to the one-child policy; the rate has been below 2 for about a generation (see Lee and Wang 2001 and sources cited therein). Although the relative importance of socioeconomic change and policy restrictions continues to be debated, clearly China's population is aging at a relatively rapid pace. Economic dependents—both retirees and children—will increase relative to workers, acting as what some call a "demographic headwind" as formidable as the demographic tailwind that accounted for no less than 15 percent of economic growth between 1982 and 2000. The surge in number of workers was amplified by increasing output per worker—from the growth of industry and services, catch-up in technology, China's urbanization and transformation into a market-based economy, and the higher educational attainment of its younger generations (see Eggleston 2020a, b, c, and sources cited therein). Long-run fertility in China remains uncertain, since the relatively recent relaxation of family planning policies will lead to some rebound but perhaps to no more than replacement levels (Jiang, Li, Li, and Feldman 2016). The new births will increase the total dependency ratio in the intermediate term but eventually make filial piety to China's grandparents less of a burden on the young, despite problems from pension policies designed for an earlier era of shorter lives (Eggleston 2020a), as well as the immediate challenges from COVID-19 recession and recovery.

In addition to population aging, China's large gender imbalance shapes labor markets and social tensions (Eggleston 2020a). The sex ratio at birth (SRB)—the number of boys born per 100 girls—has long been abnormal, with the excess of boys to girls much higher in rural areas than in urban areas, despite policies that allowed a second child if the first was a girl. Sex-selective abortion is illegal, but it has contributed to the imbalance. According to the 2010 census, 118 boys were born for every 100 girls. Beijing is aware of potential problems and launched the "Care for Girls" campaign in 2006 to address gender imbalance issues (Jiang, Li, Li, and Feldman 2016). While the fate of poorer rural men (sometimes called "bare branches" because they lack heirs) could exacerbate social tensions, more privileged men may be further driven by the gender imbalance in ways that contribute to economic growth. Indeed, Wei and Zhang (2011) offer empirical evidence in support of their conjecture that increasing marriage market competition due to sex-ratio imbalances has contributed nontrivially to China's recent economic growth.

While some argue that son preference and excess males are a transitional phenomenon, researchers have also drawn links to social tensions arising from this demographic reality, especially for poor rural men who are the most challenged in finding brides. Demography and innovation have a gendered relationship not only in China, but across the region. For example, according to some commentators, it is women's education and career concerns that keep fertility extremely low in some countries, despite pro-natal policies.[5]

Others assert that depopulation may be good for the planet, or that the total cost of raising a child is prohibitive, or that the real culprit behind below-replacement fertility might be the patriarchy that makes women endure the "double shift" of childcare and homemaking along with employment outside the home (especially evident during the pandemic). Perhaps fertility will rebound to a more sustainable level precisely in those societies that fully embrace fathers as equally responsible for child raising. Feyrer, Sacerdote, and Stern (2008) present evidence arguing that

> in the final phase [of three phases] of development, women's labor
> market opportunities begin to equal those of men [and] the increased

---

[5] Liang (2018) writes that "fertility will continue to drop, primarily due to the increase in women's level of education and career, in spite of strong pro-fertility policies" (p. 226).

household bargaining power that comes from more equal wages results in much higher (if not gender-equal) male participation in household production. Female labor force participation is higher than in the intermediate phase. The increased participation of men in the household also reduces the disincentives for women to have additional children, and fertility rates rise compared to the intermediate phase. The intermediate, low-fertility phase might describe Japan, Italy, and Spain in the present day, while the Scandinavian countries, the Netherlands, and the modern-day United States may be entering the final phase. . . . [W]e predict that high-income countries with the lowest fertility rates are likely to see an increase in fertility in the coming decades.

Will low-fertility Asian societies also see a rebound in fertility toward replacement levels? Can and will Asian societies embrace the idea that being a good parent and good employee is possible even for those who lack a Y chromosome?

For obvious reasons, this debate is crucial for China in particular, where gender roles are changing but conventional views of women's place remain contested parts of social dialogue. Of course, China is not alone in facing a gendered dimension to its demographic challenges. They are prominent across the region, from the low labor force participation of women in India, to Japan's "womenomics" policies to promote female labor force participation as a counterbalance to a declining and aging overall population, while eschewing immigration. Will the COVID-19 pandemic set back progress in women's careers in particular, given the (often unspoken) assumption that women take care of the children while they are at home and schools are closed, and that men should be given priority in retaining and regaining jobs during the economic recovery? How these forces play out in China (and other parts of Asia) will shape the demography of the workforce and fairness of the "social contract" for decades to come.

Clearly, demography has already shaped China's economy in multiple ways. Urbanization and gender imbalance will interact with population aging to present policymakers with opportunities and constraints different from those of other countries and China's own past (Eggleston 2020a). The factors that have propelled China's economic growth in the past—including cheap rural labor and catch-up growth toward the technological frontier—almost inevitably will recede in prominence, enhancing the importance of innovation for economic vitality (Wei, Xie, and Zhang 2017). Moreover, the success of China's push for innovation will increasingly depend on how well authorities leverage the private sector not only for job creation and tax revenue, but also as a partner in addressing public goals—what we call "collaborative governance" (Eggleston, Donahue, and Zeckhauser 2021).

Post-Mao China has long showcased the entrepreneurial spirit of the Chinese, but the innovative potential of entrepreneurship has attained particular prominence in recent decades. Entrepreneurship can be difficult to define and measure, although few would dispute that it is a vital element of market-based economies and their prospects for healthy development and contribution to human well-being. Most of the new technologies and creative ideas that engage and enthrall—as well as enrich new firms and established older ones with innovative products and services—can be considered entrepreneurial ventures of one sort or another. Mazzucato (2015) speaks of the entrepreneurial state. And Schumpeter's famous "creative destruction" conjures images of disruptive entrepreneurs launching high-growth start-ups while the economy weeds out lumbering and inefficient older firms, which either never contributed much to value added or have seen brighter days and are now obsolescent (Schumpeter 1950). Decker, Haltiwanger, Jarmin, and Miranda (2014) measure entrepreneurship by the age of firms, rather than their size. Using detailed census data, the authors document declining entrepreneurial activity across virtually all industrial sectors and in all U.S. states, although the causes and consequences remain somewhat obscure. Certainly the 2020 COVID-19 pandemic will fundamentally shape economic outcomes for many years to come, including the scope and scale of entrepreneurial activity in various sectors across countries, perhaps first and foremost in the country where it originated and was among the first to recover.

One factor is certain: recovery and renewed growth to meet China's ambitious goals for eradicating poverty and raising living standards will increasingly depend on success in fostering innovation. China's commitment to that goal is evident in its increasing expenditures on research and development (R&D) in recent years. Figure 3.1 shows R&D spending in 2018 for China in international comparison. Growing R&D investments are evident as China catches up with the United States in devoting between 2 and 3 percent of GDP to R&D despite its much lower GDP per capita. Higher R&D spending is evident for Germany, Japan, and especially South Korea, which invests almost twice the fraction of GDP in R&D that China does (figure 3.1). But the pace of increase in China's investments is especially notable. Over the period

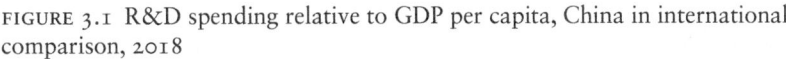

FIGURE 3.1 R&D spending relative to GDP per capita, China in international comparison, 2018

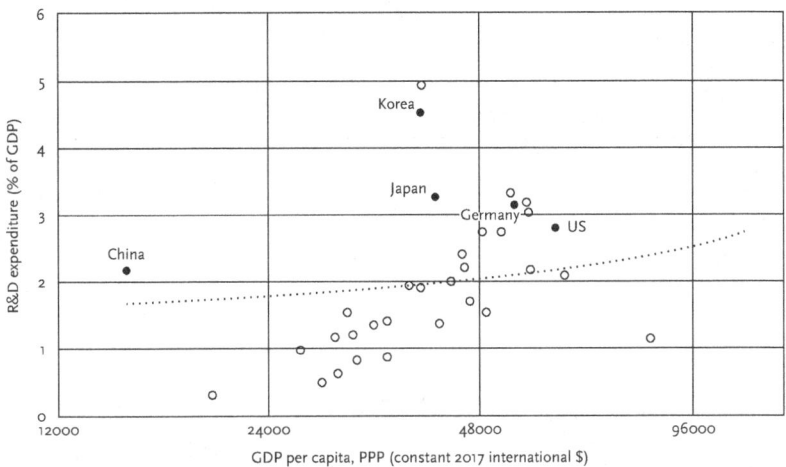

GDP per capita, PPP (constant 2017 international $)

NOTE: Data for all countries are for 2018.
SOURCE: World Bank 2020, OECD 2020a.

from 2000 to 2018, China's spending on R&D as a percentage of GDP has risen rapidly to converge with the average for OECD countries (figure 3.2).

These significant increases in R&D investments have translated into a growing number and quality of patents (figures 3.3, 3.4, and 3.5) and other manifestations of technological competitiveness of China's pre-eminent state-owned and private firms. As emphasized by Wei, Xie, and Zhang (2017), China can further improve the productivity of subsidies and other innovation resources by removing the preference for state-owned enterprises (SOEs) to level the playing field with the private sector.

Despite skepticism about China's industrial policies and favoritism of state firms, research suggests that public policies do indeed play a key role in supporting innovation and entrepreneurship, given that markets underprovide public goods like knowledge. Bloom, Van Reenen, and Williams (2019) synthesize evidence from the United States and other advanced economies to suggest that long-run investment in human capital and short-run R&D tax credits and direct public funding seem the most effective. China has undertaken aspects of both. While educational attainment has increased substantially, including with a

FIGURE 3.2 Gross domestic spending on R&D as a percentage of GDP, China and the OECD average, 2000–18

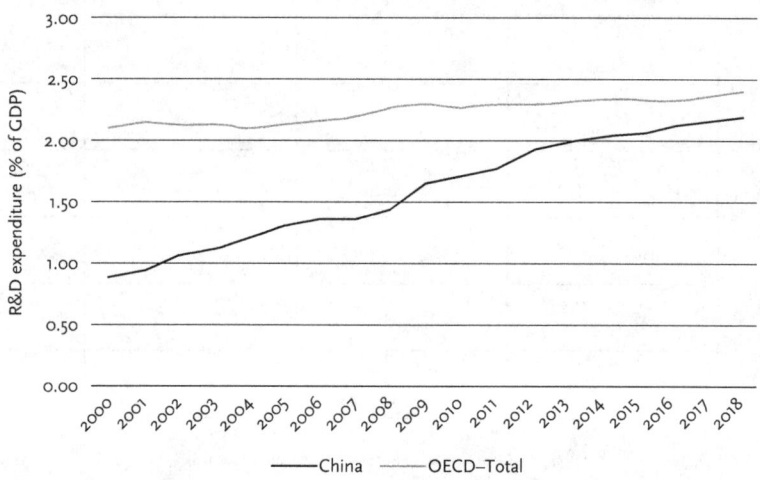

NOTE: "OECD–Total" shows the average percentage of GDP spent on R&D among 35 OECD countries.
SOURCE: OECD 2020c.

FIGURE 3.3 Patent applications from China, World Intellectual Property Organization, 1982–2018

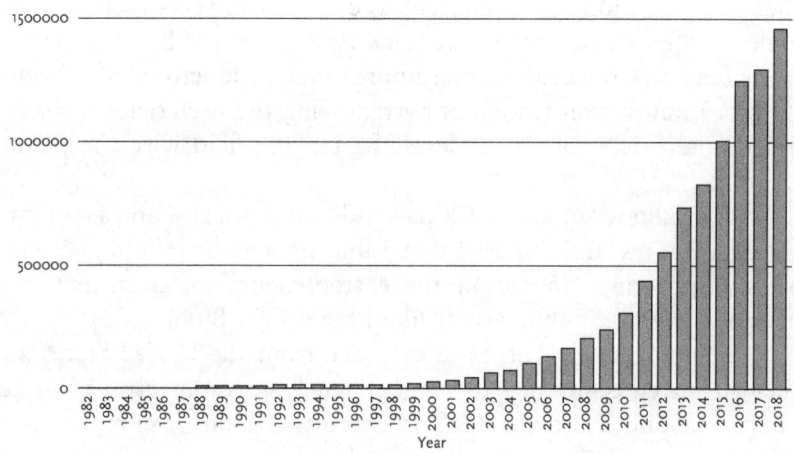

SOURCE: World Intellectual Property Organization (WIPO).

FIGURE 3.4 Patent applications by international applicants, World Intellectual Property Organization, 2014–18

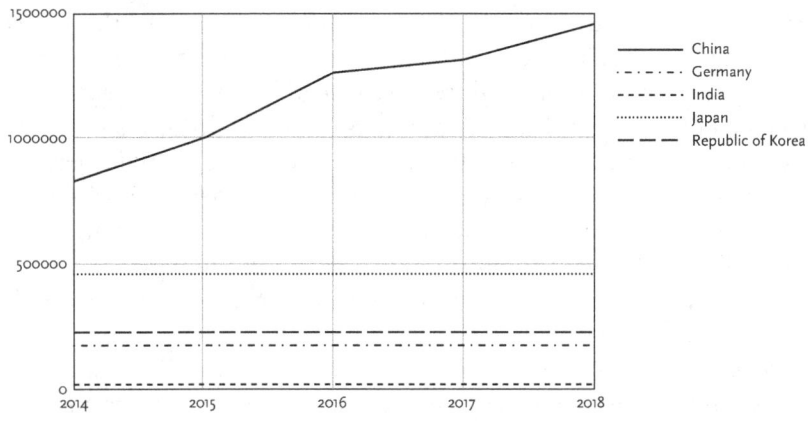

SOURCE: World Intellectual Property Organization (WIPO).

FIGURE 3.5 Number of patents granted by the United States Patent and Trademark Office to international corporate applicants, 2014–19

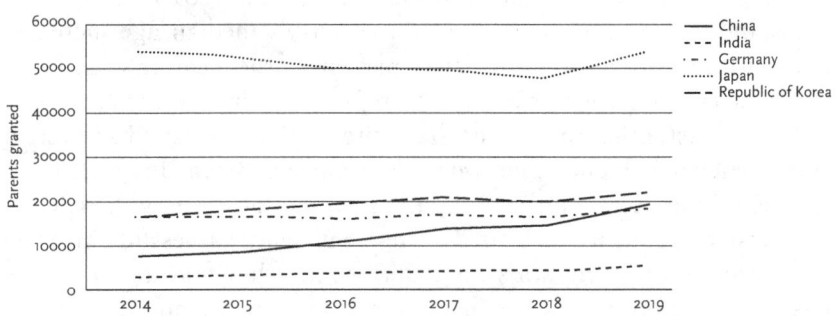

SOURCE: United States Patent and Trademark Office 2020a, 2020b, 2020c, 2020d, 2020e, 2020f.

dramatic expansion of college education, further investment in education remains vital for China's long-run improvement in living standards. Moreover, China's current leadership especially emphasizes the catalytic importance of state-led development.

While China's "local state corporatism" (Oi 1992) or "entrepreneurial state" (Mazzucato 2015) has fostered significant investments in internationally competitive firms in strategic sectors, not all of its policies to foster innovation and entrepreneurship have delivered intended effects. For example, Eesley, Li, and Yang (2016) argue that one prominent policy designed to promote entrepreneurship, the Project 985 program funding new research centers for a set of universities, actually resulted in more high-tech ventures, but in entrepreneurs not as financially successful as entrepreneurs who founded firms before the reform or from non-985 universities. They conclude that "Project 985 was institutionally inconsistent with China's broader institutional environment. An important implication is that institutional changes may alter beliefs and behavior, but they must be consistent with the broader institutional environment to improve firm performance" (Eesley, Li, and Yang 2016, 446).

Does demography determine innovation destiny? To what extent does China's demographic change trammel China's programs and policies for innovation and entrepreneurship like Project 985? Views differ. Liang, Wang, and Lazear (2018) argue that too many older workers in society slows entrepreneurship, because older workers occupy key positions and block younger workers from acquiring skills. Using data from the Global Entrepreneurship Monitor to measure entrepreneurship around the world, Liang, Wang, and Lazear (2018) find that a one-standard-deviation decrease in a country's median age increases new business formation by about 40 percent of the mean rate, and that older societies have lower rates of entrepreneurship at every age.

By contrast, other researchers have shown that the age of successful entrepreneurs is higher than one might surmise from this argument. Azoulay, Jones, Kim, and Miranda (2020) demonstrate with rich administrative data for the United States that many successful entrepreneurs are middle-aged, not young. Specifically, they find that 45 is the median age of founders for firms that go on to become the one-in-one-thousand fastest growing new ventures. One of the reasons appears to be that experience matters: industry-specific experience predicts relative success in entrepreneurship. Thus, Azoulay and coauthors might be considered to refute the hypothesis of Liang and coauthors that youth is key for entrepreneurship, although they measure entrepreneurship in different ways. Liang and coauthors discuss broad measures of entrepreneurship, whereas Azoulay and coauthors focus on high-growth entrepreneurship. Still, one wonders why the median age of a country suppresses low-growth entrepreneurship while in a relatively low-median-age country like the United States, it is middle-aged entrepreneurs who are the most successful with high-growth ventures. Ultimately, it appears that demography is important but not destiny. Other societal and economic factors shape and mediate the relationship between the age of the individual, the age structure of the economy, and success in innovation.

Moreover, while many studies might imply that innovation is a homogenous flow of products and services that can be sped up or slowed down by demographic factors, innovation can in fact be qualitatively different as well. Which technologies are invented and disseminated depends on population patterns—from the basic economics of the relative scarcity of labor to capital, to the finer details regarding cohorts at various ages. Acemoglu and Restrepo (2017) present data contradicting economic models that link population aging to slower improvement in living standards and potential secular stagnation because older workers will work less, be less productive, or save in excess of productive investment. Acemoglu and Restrepo instead argue that a compensating form of technological change has more than offset such factors, leading to greater economic growth in older societies, because countries further along in the demographic transition have invested in more rapid development and diffusion of automation technologies.

If automation is driven by aging and boosts GDP growth, as Acemoglu and Restrepo's line of reasoning suggests, then population aging may set off a virtuous cycle of innovation and automation in China, rather than a vicious cycle of ossification and stagnation. How does this square with the logic of those who claim that if robots are coming for all our jobs, surely they are coming for the jobs of the elderly first? Both can be true. Automation may substitute for brawn-based tasks that older workers are challenged to perform, but may also augment the tasks proliferating in aging societies, such as long-term care for the frail elderly. Humans have a distinct comparative advantage over machines in many of the tasks in the caring professions, including compassion, dexterity, and the human touch. Japan has for years subsidized robots for long-term care of the elderly (Eggleston ⓡ Lee ⓡ Iizuka 2021), and China's use of robots has been given a significant boost during the COVID-19 pandemic in light of their added benefits in preventing infection.

According to recent analyses of firm-level robot adoption in China's manufacturing firms by Hong Cheng, Ruixue Jia, Dandan Li, and Hongbin Li, public policies have played an important role through subsidies and other support as part of focusing on development of several strategic sectors, including robotics, artificial intelligence, and automation. The authors emphasize that these policies have been especially prominent for upgrading China's manufacturing industries and would appear to give prima facie evidence that Chinese authorities do not worry about robotics as disruptive technology for employment and social stability (Cheng, Jia, Li, and Li 2019). Their own qualitative research in which they interviewed employers and employees reinforces this perception that robotics function to augment China's strengths rather than substitute for labor or exacerbate challenges facing employment and workforce disparities. Which social interests become aware and voice their concerns and have input to policy certainly matters. For example, Cheng, Jia, Li, and Li (2019) speculate that the lack of any prominent worker voice of skepticism about job displacement from robot adoption might be because of the absence of independent unions in China.

Endogenous technological change may smooth the labor force transition toward an older age structure with longer work lives without clogging career opportunities for younger entrepreneurs or forcing older adults much healthier than earlier generations to retire at the same young ages. As emphasized by Ameriks, Briggs, Caplin, Lee, Shapiro, and Tonetti (2020), older individuals—both those still working and those retired who might prefer ongoing labor force participation— especially value flexibility in work schedules, and empirical evidence from the authors' custom survey of older Americans clearly indicates willingness to work longer if they could secure jobs with such flexibility. Thus, the empirical findings highlight the importance of demand-side factors for late-in-life labor force participation and the need to incorporate these concerns into policies designed to promote longer work lives (Ameriks et al. 2020). Although some might assert that the "gig economy" provides such flexibility already, Cook, Diamond, and Oyer (2019) note that older workers are paid less than their younger coworkers in that context, in part because such workers largely receive their own marginal product, whereas older workers in career jobs usually benefit from the latter end of an implicit contract rewarding loyalty and tenure rather than current productivity. Such implicit contracts present particular challenges for East Asian economies like Japan (which has been revising the practice, as discussed in chapter 4 by Ogawa et al.) and China, given dramatic changes in human capital across generations. If older workers not only decline in physical and cognitive abilities but also had fewer opportunities for education, then their relatively low marginal productivity may not support raising retirement ages and investing in expensive technologies to prolong their employment in the way that Japan has been undertaking (as discussed in chapter 6 by Kushida).

Many factors shape firms' demand for older workers. Allen (2019) cites empirical evidence from researchers such as Christine Milligan, Johnathan Gruber, Alicia Munnell, and April Wu that older workers have *not* crowded out young workers, in contrast to more recent studies by Guilia Bovini, Matteo Paradisi, and others who suggest the opposite. Despite this somewhat mixed message, empirical evidence consistently shows that a higher percentage of women experience age discrimination than men do. There is no reason to think that China is an exception. Indeed, the gender dynamics of age discrimination are especially fraught, given uneven follow-through on Mao's famous rhetoric of women "holding up half the sky," the gender imbalance driven by lingering son preference, and the reality of substantially lower educational attainment among older women in China compared to both older men and younger women. Moreover, the economic blow from COVID-19, and the presumption that children during school closures are women's responsibility, complicates any effort to combat labor market preferences for men.

Younger workers are also more diverse, given changing social mores, and training women and minorities and giving them opportunities to contribute to innovation through meaningful careers could be especially imperiled by old thinking and a crisis on the current scale, for economies around the world, not just China.

Another demographic factor distinctive to China arises from the legacy of historic episodes such as the Great Leap Forward famine and the Cultural Revolution. For example, Huang, Phillips, Yang, and Zhang (2020) examine the innovation of firms with CEOs who turned 18 during the Cultural Revolution, which sharply reduced their chances of attending college. They show that Chinese firms led by CEOs without a college degree spend less on R&D, generate fewer patents, and receive fewer citations to these patents.

A more basic demographic factor may ultimately be most powerful: declining "surplus labor" and aspirations to enjoy comfortable middle-class consumption while still enjoying a block of leisure at the end of life. China has introduced a rural pension for the first time in its long history, and even the rural poor and migrant labor are beginning to benefit from rising wages. Wei, Xie, and Zhang (2017) argue that, spurred by rising wages among other factors, China's entrepreneurs and policies have been rising to this challenge of increasing productivity fueled by domestic innovation. Cheng, Jia, Li, and Li (2019) echo this point about rising wages, noting that China's robotics industry development and firm-level adoption of robots have both been spurred in part by increasing manufacturing labor costs per hour in China, which are estimated to surpass those of many other Asian economies, not only India and Vietnam, but also Malaysia and Thailand. Drawing on 2016 survey data of over 1,000 manufacturing firms (with a response rate of 84 percent), Cheng, Jia, Li, and Li (2019) document that the wage bill and voluntary worker turnover are positively correlated with robot adoption, while involuntary turnover is not.

However, Wei, Xie, and Zhang (2017) highlight evidence of resource misallocation, with state-owned enterprises (SOEs) receiving more subsidies for innovation relative to their private counterparts despite the latter's vitality in innovation. Misallocation of credit and favoritism toward SOEs remain large issues, according to many observers of China (e.g., Economy 2018, Lardy 2020). For example, Lardy (2020) also argues that misallocation of credit constitutes one main source of China's economic slowdown, even before COVID-19.

As noted by multiple observers, the global geopolitical environment, and the U.S.-China relationship in particular, may also powerfully constrain or foster China's economic growth and innovation. With its rising economic and geopolitical heft, citizens of Asia and beyond can only hope that China will avoid reenacting previous historical periods of destructive competition with other powers like the United States (see, for example, Brunnermeier, Doshi, and James 2018) in pursuit of more productive cooperation to address common global challenges. Cooperative innovations will be critical for achieving or preserving global public goods such as antimicrobial effectiveness, green growth, climate resilience, and pandemic prevention.

Case Study: Innovation for Healthy Aging

As noted in Eggleston (2020b, 2020c), China's healthcare system well illustrates some of the economic and social tensions and promising possibilities inherent in China's search for innovations appropriate to its current demography. For example, one key issue will be how the authoritarian government implements public policies that leverage a market-based economy to bring innovations not only to the rich, but also to the broader populace and the vulnerable. Health services are one example. China's health service delivery system is overwhelmingly government-owned and managed. However, in recent decades authorities have not only allowed but even encouraged investment from nonstate sources, both for medical care and for long-term care services. In many regions and segments of the medical services markets, private providers constitute a nontrivial albeit definitely minority share of service. For example, the "Law of the People's Republic of China on the Promotion of Basic Medical and Health Care" and other recent measures reiterate the promotion of private-sector engagement in health services while strengthening regulation. The government has previously specifically encouraged private-sector investment and public-private partnerships for elderly care, encouraging public-private partnerships in the construction of elderly care institutions and community care. For an overview of these policies and examples of "collaborative governance, Chinese style" in long-term care, see the healthcare chapter in Eggleston, Donahue, and Zeckhauser (2021).

Public-private engagement in the health sector can be vital for addressing social needs, as is perhaps well illustrated by the current pandemic. Development of a health service and research ecosystem can be the key to an "all hands on deck" approach to developing a vaccine or innovating in social and economic policy to mitigate the costs of lockdown or physical distancing, without too deeply and permanently scarring our societies in other ways. Private connections also link the global scientific community and its cooperation. Within weeks of the first cluster of cases, Chinese researchers had released the genomic sequence of the virus. Such prompt data sharing enabled the development of vaccine candidates and unprecedented speed in their testing, approval, and distribution. None of that would have been possible without international scientists' culture of data sharing, careful but prompt review of evidence, and collaboration among public and private sectors to get the job done.

Innovations may prove life-saving not only for global supply chains to support the healthcare response (personal protective equipment, ventilators, masks, pharmaceutical ingredients, food, etc.), but also innovations that can enhance the ability of societies to leverage civil society and public-private partnerships for the broader social good, to help the poor and vulnerable, to ensure that a vaccines are widely and equitably available, to restore treatment for other urgent health conditions, and to avoid what Case and Deaton (2020) call "deaths of despair" and a devastating mental health toll. China's strengthened health system, compared to SARS or earlier public health crises, along with industry and research capacities, have enabled a more resilient response than would otherwise have been the case.

The COVID-19 pandemic has further underscored the evolution of specific technological developments. China's government and private sector have utilized many technologies in response to the crisis, which, like elsewhere, may continue to play a much larger role in the healthcare system in the future. A prime illustration is telemedicine and "internet-plus" healthcare. For example, China's WeDoctor launched a platform for doctors to provide online consultations, psychological assistance, and other services, making it possible for people to consult with a doctor at home during the pandemic (People's Daily Online 2020). Recently, Qi Xiaoxia (2020), director general of the Bureau of International Cooperation, Cyberspace Administration of China, has argued that China's leveraging of multiple technologies in the efforts to curb COVID-19 portend broader use of these technologies in the future as well, with examples including the following:

- AI: Baidu Research open-sourced LinearFold (its linear-time AI algorithm), to epidemic prevention centers, gene-testing institutions, and global scientific research institutions.
- Big data: Qihoo 360, in February 2020, released its "Big Data Migration Map," which users can access through mobile phones or computers to help understand and predict changes in the epidemic situation nationwide.
- Cloud computing: Alibaba Cloud made its AI computing power available for free to public research institutions around the world, to accelerate the development of new pneumonia drugs and vaccines.
- Blockchain: Lianfei Technology launched the nation's first blockchain epidemic monitoring platform, which can track the progress of COVID-19 in all provinces in real time and register the relevant epidemic data on the chain to make it traceable and prevent tampering.
- 5G: China Mobile opened 5G base stations at Huoshenshan and Leishenshan hospitals, providing real-time views of the construction.

In the future, China, along with other Asian nations (e.g., South Korea and Singapore), will probably continue to roll out and deepen technologies for contract tracing during the remainder of the COVID-19 pandemic and to prepare for any future one, with differing levels of social debate about the trade-offs between civil liberties and intrusiveness on privacy versus the benefits of real-time contact tracing and containment of epidemic spread. China has seen some objection to widespread technology deployment in everyday life—such as a lawsuit against requiring face scanning for annual park passes—but whether the current crisis will permanently shift that debate remains to be seen. Certainly, the integration of telemedicine and other technologies for healthcare and elderly care will continue to develop, with the potential of either increasing or ameliorating the current disparities within China's health system.

More broadly, the response to COVID-19 in China and its devastating impacts around the globe will leave an indelible mark on health policies for decades to come, not only in terms of technology adoption but also organizational innovation and, hopefully, prioritization in resource allocation to safeguard and undergird the future of the "China Dream" (or the "American Dream," for that matter). Clearly the crisis is a test of governance. Unprecedented measures have been successfully implemented to contain the virus spread, and the PRC health system is much better prepared than during SARS. Perhaps in the future renewed investment and innovation can diagnose and effectively treat health system weaknesses, just like scientific cooperation about the SARS-CoV-2 virus itself. Maybe China will champion renewed commitment to the evidence-based, scientific study of health systems—leveraging new technologies to strengthen prevention; to address the root causes of Chinese patients' ubiquitous lament, "getting healthcare is difficult and expensive" (*kan bing nan, kan bing gui*) and the sometimes tense physician-patient relationship in China; and to invest in cost-effective, high-quality primary care and two-way referral systems that can promote healthy lives for every Chinese citizen, including the rural poor and the vulnerable.

No doubt China's twenty-first century will be strongly shaped by how the country innovates, from its provision of public services to its citizens to many other aspects of its economy, society, and global position. Demography impinges upon those trajectories both in terms of supply of innovators and demand for specific kinds of technological and governance innovations. The remainder of the volume looks at other economies of Asia in more depth, with a particular focus on Japan, South Korea, and India.

References

Acemoglu, Daron, and Pascual Restrepo. 2017. "Secular Stagnation? The Effect of Aging on Economic Growth in the Age of Automation." *American Economic Review* 107, no. 5 (May): 174–79.

Agarwal, Arunika, Alyssa Lubet, Elizabeth Mitgang, Sanjay Mohanty, and David E. Bloom. 2020. "Population Aging in India: Facts, Issues, and Options." In *Population Change and Impacts in Asia and the Pacific,* edited by Jacques Poot and Matthew Roskruge, 289–311. Springer, Singapore.

Allen, Steven G. 2019. "Demand for Older Workers: What Do Economists Think? What Are Firms Doing?" Working Paper 26597. National Bureau of Economic Research, December. http://www.nber.org/papers/w26597.

Ameriks, John, Joseph Briggs, Andrew Caplin, Minjoon Lee, Matthew D. Shapiro, and Christopher Tonetti. 2020. "Older Americans Would Work Longer If Jobs Were Flexible." *American Economic Journal: Macroeconomics* 12, no. 1: 174–209.

Azoulay, Pierre, Benjamin F. Jones, J. Daniel Kim, and Javier Miranda. 2020. "Age and High-Growth Entrepreneurship." *American Economic Review: Insights* 2, no. 1: 65–82.

Babiarz, Kimberly Singer, Karen Eggleston, Grant Miller, and Qiong Zhang. 2015. "An Exploration of China's Mortality Decline Under Mao: A Provincial Analysis, 1950–80." *Population Studies* 69, no. 1: 39–56.

Bloom, David E., and David Canning. 2000. "The Health and Wealth of Nations." *Science* 287, no. 5456: 1207–09.

Bloom, Nicholas, Charles I. Jones, John Van Reenen, and Michael Webb. 2020. "Are Ideas Getting Harder to Find?" *American Economic Review,* 110, no. 4: 1104–44.

Bloom, Nicholas, John Van Reenen, and Heidi Williams. 2019. "A Toolkit of Policies to Promote Innovation." *Journal of Economic Perspectives* 33, no. 3: 163–84.

Brunnermeier, Markus, Rush Doshi, and Harold James. 2018. "Beijing's Bismarckian Ghosts: How Great Powers Compete Economically." *Washington Quarterly* 41, no. 3: 161–76.

Case, Anne, and Angus Deaton. 2020. *Deaths of Despair and the Future of Capitalism.* Princeton, NJ: Princeton University Press..

Cheng, Hong, Ruixue Jia, Dandan Li, and Hongbin Li. 2019. "The Rise of Robots in China." *Journal of Economic Perspectives* 33, no. 2: 71–88.

Cook, Cody, Rebecca Diamond, and Paul Oyer. 2019. "Older Workers and the Gig Economy." AEA Papers and Proceedings 109: 372–76.

Decker, Ryan, John Haltiwanger, Ron Jarmin, and Javier Miranda. 2014. "The Role of Entrepreneurship in US Job Creation and Economic Dynamism." *Journal of Economic Perspectives* 28, no. 3: 3–24.

Economy, Elizabeth. 2018. *The Third Revolution: Xi Jinping and the New Chinese State.* Oxford University Press.

Eesley, Charles, Jian Bai Li, and Delin Yang. 2016. "Does Institutional Change in Universities Influence High-Tech Entrepreneurship? Evidence from China's Project 985." *Organization Science* 27, no. 2: 446–61.

Eggleston, Karen, 2020a. "Demographic Challenges: Healthcare and Elder Care." In *Fateful Decisions: Choices That Will Shape China's Future,* edited by Thomas Fingar and Jean C. Oi. Stanford, CA: Stanford University Press.

Eggleston, Karen, 2020b. *Healthy Aging in Asia.* Stanford, CA: Shorenstein Asia-Pacific Research Center.

Eggleston, Karen, 2020c. *Hearing on China's Evolving Healthcare Ecosystem: Challenges and Opportunities. Hearing Before the U.S.-China Economic and Security Review Commission.* 116th Congress. Statement of Karen Eggleston. May 7, 2020. https://www.uscc.gov/hearings/chinas-evolving-healthcare-ecosystem-challenges-and-opportunities.

Eggleston, Karen, John D. Donahue, and Richard J. Zeckhauser. 2021. *The Dragon, the Eagle, and the Private Sector: Public-Private Collaboration in China and the United States.* New York, NY: Cambridge University Press.

Eggleston, Karen, and Victor R. Fuchs, 2012. "The New Demographic Transition: Most Gains in Life Expectancy Now Realized Late in Life," *Journal of Economic Perspectives* 26, no. 3: 137–56.

Eggleston, Karen ⓡ Yong Suk Lee ⓡ Toshiaki Iizuka. 2021. "Robots and Labor in the Service Sector: Evidence from Nursing Homes," NBER Working Paper 28322, available at https://www.nber.org/papers/w28322.

Feyrer, James, Bruce Sacerdote, and Ariel Dora Stern. 2008. "Will the Stork Return to Europe and Japan? Understanding Fertility Within

Developed Nations." *Journal of Economic Perspectives* 22, no. 3: 3–22.

Gordon, Robert J. 2017. *The Rise and Fall of American Growth: The US Standard of Living Since the Civil War.* Princeton, NJ: Princeton University Press.

Huang, Zhangkai, Gordon M. Phillips, Jialun Yang, and Yi Zhang. 2020. "Education and Innovation: The Long Shadow of the Cultural Revolution." Working Paper 27107. National Bureau of Economic Research (May). https://www.nber.org/papers/w27107?utm _campaign=ntwh&utm_medium=email&utm_source=ntwg15.

Jiang, Quanbao, Xiaomin Li, Shuzhuo Li, and Marcus W. Feldman. 2016. "China's Marriage Squeeze: A Decomposition into Age and Sex Structure." *Social Indicators Research* 127, no. 2: 793–807.

Kornai, János. 2014. *Dynamism, Rivalry, and the Surplus Economy: Two essays on the Nature of Capitalism.* New York, NY: Oxford University Press.

Lardy, Nicholas. 2020. "China's Economic Development: A Forty-Year Perspective." Presentation at "The PRC at 70: The Past, Present—and Future?" Shorenstein Asia-Pacific Research Center, February 5, 2020. https://fsi-live.s3.us-west-1.amazonaws.com/s3fs -public/nicholas_lardy_transcript_final_1.pdf

Lee, James, and Feng Wang. 2001. *One Quarter of Humanity: Malthusian Mythology and Chinese Realities, 1700–2000.* Cambridge, MA: Harvard University Press.

Lee, Ronald. 2003. "The Demographic Transition: Three Centuries of Fundamental Change." *Journal of Economic Perspectives* 17, no. 4: 167–190.

Liang, James. 2018. *The Demographics of Innovation: Why Demographics Is a Key to the Innovation Race.* Hoboken, NJ: John Wiley & Sons.

Liang, James, Hui Wang, and Edward P. Lazear. 2018. "Demographics and Entrepreneurship." *Journal of Political Economy* 126, S1: 140–96.

Mazzucato, Mariana. 2015. *The Entrepreneurial State: Debunking Public vs. Private Sector Myths.* Vol. 1. London: Anthem Press.

OECD. 2020a. "Gross Domestic Spending on R&D." https://data .oecd.org/rd/gross-domestic-spending-on-r-d.htm.

OECD. 2020b. "Gross Domestic Spending on R&D (Indicator)." Accessed June 6, 2020. https://doi.org/10.1787/d8b068b4-en.

OECD. 2020c. "Gross Domestic Spending on R&D as % of GDP (Indicator)." Accessed May 24, 2020. https://doi.org/10.1787/d8b068b4-en.

Oi, Jean C. 1992. "Fiscal Reform and the Economic Foundations of Local State Corporatism in China." *World Politics: A Quarterly Journal of International Relations* 45, no. 1: 99–126.

People's Daily Online. 2020. "'Internet Plus Healthcare' Platforms Assist Fight Against COVID-19 at Home and Abroad." April 8, 2020. http://en.people.cn/n3/2020/0408/c90000-9677073.html.

Qi, Xiaoxia. 2020. "How Next-Generation Information Technologies Tackled COVID-19 in China," World Economic Forum, April 8, 2020. https://www.weforum.org/agenda/2020/04/how-next-generation-information-technologies-tackled-covid-19-in-china.

Sapienza, Paola, and Luigi Zingales. 2013. "Economic Experts Versus Average Americans." *American Economic Review* 103, no. 3: 636–42.

Schumpeter, Joseph Alois. 1950. *Capitalism, Socialism and Democracy.* 3rd ed. New York: Harpe.

United States Patent and Trademark Office. 2020a. "Patent Counts by Origin and Type, Calendar Year 2014." Accessed June 6, 2020. https://www.uspto.gov/web/offices/ac/ido/oeip/taf/st_co_14.htm.

———. 2020b. "Patent Counts by Origin and Type, Calendar Year 2015." Accessed June 6, 2020. https://www.uspto.gov/web/offices/ac/ido/oeip/taf/st_co_15.htm.

———. 2020c. "Patent Counts by Origin and Type, Calendar Year 2016." Accessed June 6, 2020. https://www.uspto.gov/web/offices/ac/ido/oeip/taf/st_co_16.htm.

———. 2020d. "Patent Counts by Origin and Type, Calendar Year 2017." Accessed June 6, 2020. https://www.uspto.gov/web/offices/ac/ido/oeip/taf/st_co_17.htm.

———. 2020e. "Patent Counts by Origin and Type, Calendar Year 2018." Accessed June 6, 2020. https://www.uspto.gov/web/offices/ac/ido/oeip/taf/st_co_18.htm.

———. 2020f. "Patent Counts by Origin and Type, Calendar Year 2019." Accessed June 6, 2020. https://www.uspto.gov/web/offices/ac/ido/oeip/taf/st_co_19.htm.

Wei, Shang-Jin, and Xiaobo Zhang. 2011. "The Competitive Saving Motive: Evidence from Rising Sex Ratios and Savings Rates in China." *Journal of Political Economy* 119, no. 3: 511–64.

Wei, Shang-Jin, Zhuan Xie, and Xiaobo Zhang. 2017. "From 'Made in China' to 'Innovated in China': Necessity, Prospect, and Challenges." *Journal of Economic Perspectives* 31, no.1: 49–70.

World Bank. 2020. "GDP Per Capita." Accessed June 6, 2020. https://data.worldbank.org/indicator/NY.GDP.PCAP.CD.

World Intellectual Property Organization (WIPO).

4   Changing Cognitive Performance and the Untapped Work Capacity of Older Persons in Japan

Naohiro Ogawa, Hidehiko Ichimura,
Taiyo Fukai, and Rikiya Matsukura

Low fertility, coupled with mortality declines and prolonged lifespan, causes population aging and thereby carries the potential to bring about a decrease in a country's labor force, savings, and economic dynamism. Understanding the economic effects of these demographic transformations is absolutely essential if optimal adjustments are to be made not only by governments, but also by firms, households, and individuals.

Over the past half century, Japan has been the most rapidly aging nation in the world; right after the turn of the century, it also became the most aged society, surpassing Italy. In addition, since 2008, Japan's total population has been continuously diminishing. According to the population projection prepared by the United Nations in 2017, the declining trend of Japan's population is expected to last throughout the twenty-first century (UN 2017). Population aging has already imposed great financial pressures on Japan's social security system, pressures that are forecast to intensify further in the coming years.

In view of the aggravation of financial difficulties, which is likely to persist over the next several decades, Japan needs effective policies to substantially boost national productivity. In the present study, therefore, in search of potential policy options, we will attempt to measure to what extent the size of Japan's labor force could expand if the mandatory retirement age were entirely removed and all healthy older adults were able to participate in the labor force as gainful workers.

Authors' acknowledgment: This work has been supported by JSPS KAKENHI Grant Number 15H05692.

Besides the potential increase in the quantity of the labor force, we will shed light on potential improvements in the quality of the labor force by examining the cognitive function of Japanese workers aged 50 and over using recent data. We will also assess the future possibilities for improving the cognitive abilities of Japan's aging labor force. To address these qualitative and quantitative aspects of the labor force, we will draw upon microlevel data gathered from older persons in 10 selected Japanese cities and towns from 2007 to 2011.

This study is structured as follows. To begin, demographic and socioeconomic changes in Japan are briefly discussed to provide the context. Next, the cognitive function of Japanese people aged 50 to 79 is measured and compared with the results obtained from two selected Asian countries (China and India), the United States, and several European countries. We then estimate the untapped work capacity of older persons and compute the magnitude of its impact on the growth of Japan's per capita real gross domestic product (GDP). Finally, we discuss a few important limitations of the present study, summarize the main findings, and provide some policy implications.

Rapid Changes in the Demographic and Economic Landscape in Postwar Japan

Before proceeding any further, let us briefly discuss some unique aspects of Japanese postwar demographics.

Falling fertility and mortality

Japan's postwar fertility decline was the earliest to occur in the non-Western world and the greatest in magnitude among all industrialized countries. Subsequent to a short-lived baby boom period (1947–49), Japan's fertility plunged dramatically (Hodge and Ogawa 1991; Ogawa and Retherford 1993; Retherford and Ogawa 2006). As depicted in figure 4.1, the total fertility rate (TFR) dropped by more than 50 percent (from 4.54 to 2.04 children per woman) in just 10 years, from 1947 to 1957. This dramatic decline of fertility is unprecedented in the history of humanity. After this reduction, except for 1966,[1] there were only

---

1   In the sexagenary cycle, 1966 was a Fire-Horse year. Because of superstitions regarding girls born in such a year, many Japanese chose not to have children during the period.

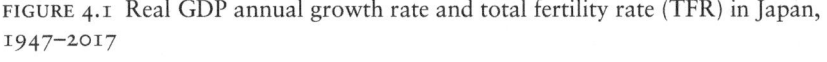

FIGURE 4.1 Real GDP annual growth rate and total fertility rate (TFR) in Japan, 1947–2017

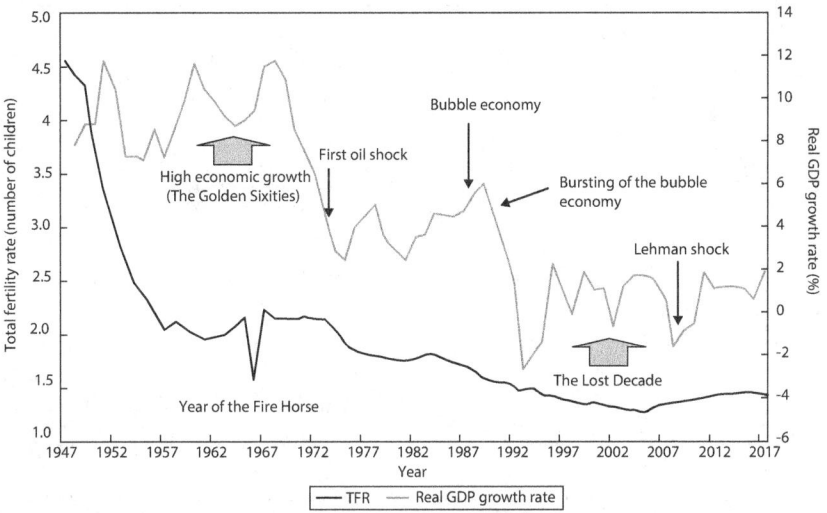

SOURCE: Real GDP growth rate calculated from Cabinet Office, *Annual Report on National Accounts*, various years; TFR gathered from the Ministry of Health, Labour and Welfare, *Vital Statistics of Japan*, various years.

minor fluctuations around the replacement level until the first oil crisis occurred in 1973, as shown in figure 4.1. Thereafter, the TFR began to decline again. In 2005, it dropped to 1.26, the lowest in the postwar period, before a considerable rebound to 1.43 in 2017. If fertility were to remain constant at the current level, the population of each successive generation in Japan would decline approximately at a rate of 31 percent per generation.

Although Japan's fertility decline has attracted a considerable amount of attention both at home and abroad, relatively little heed has been given to the rapidity with which Japan's mortality transition has occurred. From 1950 to 1952, life expectancy at birth was 59.6 years for men and 63.0 years for women. In 2017, life expectancy at birth reached 81.1 years for men and 87.3 years for women. Moreover, during the same period, life expectancy at age 65 increased to a great extent, from 11.4 years to 19.6 years for men, and from 13.4 years to 24.4 years for women, which implies a marked increase in the retirement period and in the survival to older age of both men and women.

FIGURE 4.2 The historic reversal of population: Japan, Asia, and the world total, 1950–2100

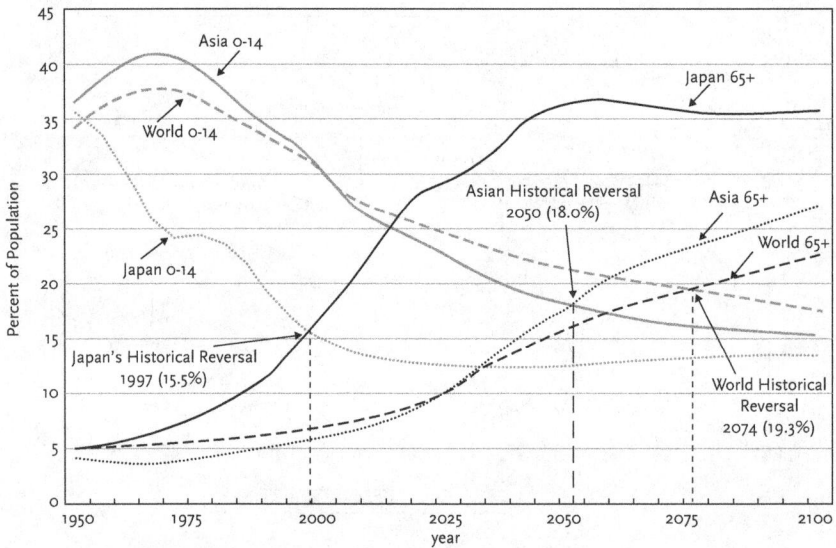

SOURCE: United Nations 2017.

As a consequence of these rapid transformations in fertility and mortality, the age distribution of the Japanese population has substantially changed over the past several decades. As displayed in figure 4.2, the proportion of the population aged 15 and younger has been declining almost continuously since the second half of the twentieth century, while the proportion of the population aged 65 and over has grown at a phenomenal rate during the corresponding period. For all of human history, the proportion of the young population had consistently exceeded that of the aged population, until the end of the twentieth century; accordingly, the index of aging, defined as {[(65 and over) / (0–14)] x 100}, had never surpassed the 100-level. However, after Italy reached this demographic turning point in 1995 for the first time in the history of humankind, Japan joined it in 1997 (see figure 4.2). This newly emerging demographic turning point was recently termed "the historic reversal of populations" (Chamie 2016). Furthermore, according to the 2017 United Nations population projection, Japan's index of aging is expected to remain the highest in Asia over the next few decades (UN 2017). By 2050, however, the values of the indices of aging for Singapore and South Korea are projected to surpass that of Japan. In addition, for Asia as a whole, the index of aging is projected to exceed the 100-level in 2050, which is considerably earlier than 2075, the year projected for the entire world.

Changing economic growth performance and two demographic dividends

Japan's postwar demographic transition has been closely linked to its economic growth performance. At the end of World War II, the Japanese economy was totally devastated. In 1950, Japan's per capita gross national product (GNP) was lower than that of Mexico or the Philippines. However, it recovered at a phenomenal pace. By 1957, Japan's per capita income had grown to the prewar level. In the 1960s, Japan's real GDP increased at the rate of 11 percent per year, and in 1968, Japan's GDP was the second largest in the free world, after the United States. Because of such miraculous economic growth performance, many economists call the 1960s Japan's Golden Sixties (see figure 4.1).

One of the major factors that contributed to this superb economic growth was the so-called first demographic dividend.[2] As described in many publications related to the system of National Transfer Accounts (NTA) (Lee and Mason 2011), when a country's fertility rate begins to decline, the first demographic dividend arises due to an increase in the number of working-age persons relative to those in the non-working-age groups. Working-age people produce more than they consume, so to be more precise, the first demographic divided is generated because of an increase in the share of population of ages when production exceeds consumption.

Figure 4.3 depicts the age-specific profiles of consumption and production in contemporary Japan, based on the National Survey of Family Income and Expenditure (NSFIE) conducted in 2009. By utilizing the computed age-specific results displayed in this graphical exposition as statistical weights to adjust for the population, we have calculated the number of age-specific effective workers and the number of age-specific effective consumers over the period 1950–2050, using the United Nations population projection prepared in 2017. The ratio of

2   Other factors that contributed to the Golden Sixties include the borrowing of advanced technology from developed nations and favorable conditions in international trade markets (Ogawa, Jones, and Williamson 1993).

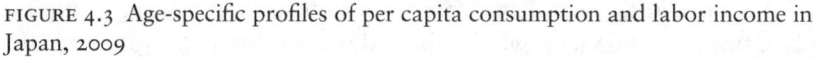

FIGURE 4.3 Age-specific profiles of per capita consumption and labor income in Japan, 2009

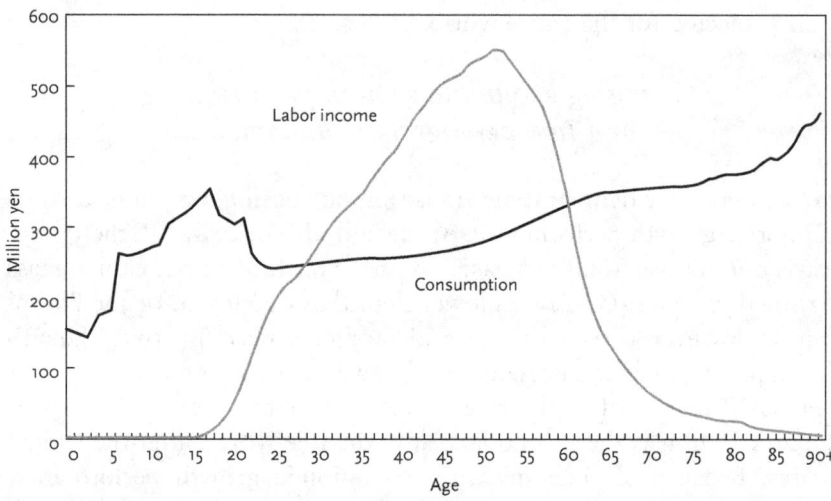

SOURCE: Authors.

effective workers to effective consumers is called the economic support ratio (ESR). When the ESR value rises, an economy is in the period of the first demographic dividend. The computed results pertaining to Japan's first demographic dividend from 1950 to 2050 are shown in figure 4.4.

Figure 4.4 reveals that Japan's first demographic dividend was positive for 46 years, from 1950 to 1996. The magnitude was especially large during the rapid economic growth of the 1960s (Ogawa, Lee, Matsukura, Tung, and Lai 2012). This result provides a piece of convincing empirical evidence pointing to the high likelihood that the unprecedented fertility reduction after the baby boom of 1947 to 1949 played an important role in boosting the growth of per capita income to phenomenal levels during this period of high economic growth. It is also conceivable that in the case of Japan, the first demographic dividend was utilized primarily for augmenting physical capital, rather than for boosting consumption.

Subsequent to the Golden Sixties, the Japanese economy entered a new stage where the tempo of real economic growth began to slow down, particularly after the oil crisis of 1973. The slower growth

FIGURE 4.4 Japan's first demographic dividend, 1950–2050

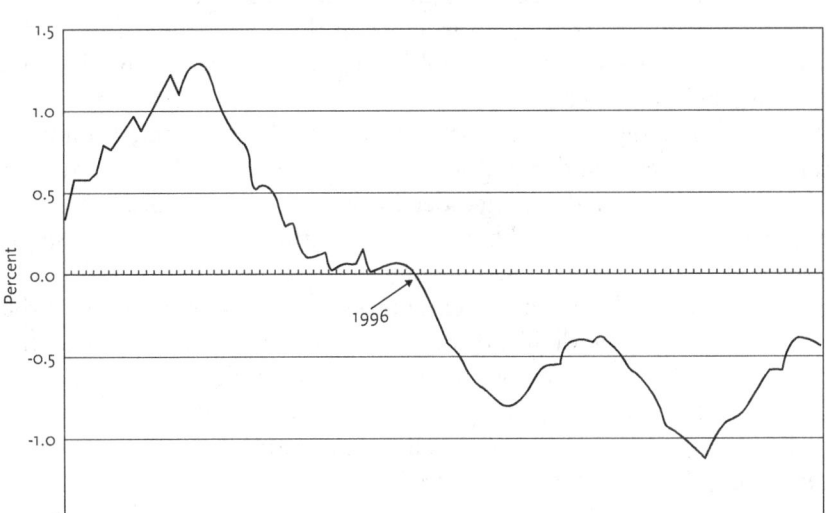

SOURCE: Authors.

continued up to the mid-1980s, when Japan stepped into the bubble economy phase, which lasted until the early 1990s. Although the Japanese government implemented a host of macroeconomic policies and programs with a view to rectifying the situation regarding the bursting of the bubble economy, these turned out to be inadequate and misguided. It took several years for the government to realize that more drastic restructuring policies were necessary to make the Japanese economy more competitive in international markets. Because of such delayed policy responses, some economists call the 1990s Japan's lost decade (Yoshikawa 2001). Due to this policy failure, by 2018, Japan's government debt accumulated to the level of approximately 2.4 times the country's GDP. Triggered by the lost decade, the ranking of Japan's international competitiveness dropped from first in 1990 to twenty-fifth in 2018 (IMD, various years).

Despite the fact that Japan's first demographic dividend ended in 1996, which coincides with the prolonged sluggishness in economic activities of the lost decade, the Japanese economy is likely to enjoy another, second demographic dividend. There are two ways in which demographic factors cause an increase in the demand for lifecycle wealth and the second demographic dividend. First, there is a compositional effect, caused by an increase in the proportion of individuals who have nearly or fully completed their productive years. Second, there is a behavioral effect, caused by an increase in life expectancy and the accompanying increase in the duration of retirement, leading in turn to an increase in demand for wealth. Demand for lifecycle wealth is mainly concentrated among older working adults who are approaching their peak earnings and have completed their child-rearing responsibilities. Mason (2007) uses the wealth held by those aged 50 and over to measure the effect of demography on lifecycle wealth and the second demographic dividend. In the case of Japan, from now to the mid-2020s, the second baby boom generation (eight million persons), born between 1971 and 1974, will reach approximately age 50 and will likely generate the second demographic dividend, which will in turn boost the country's capital stock.

Aging labor force and traditional employment practices

In parallel with these demographic evolutions and macroeconomic transformations, the labor force size and its age composition have been changing significantly in the postwar period. As the data gleaned from the Japanese population census plotted in figure 4.5 indicate, the size of the total labor force grew continuously from 1970 to 1995. After reaching its peak in 1995, however, it began to shrink. According to the population projection released in 2017 by the National Institute of Population and Social Security Research (NIPSSR 2019), Japan's working-age population (15–64 years old) is expected to dwindle continuously from 77.3 million in 2015 to 45.3 million in 2065.

In addition to the total labor force size, the overall labor force participation rate has been on a mildly downward trend, as displayed in figure 4.5. It is worth observing, however, that the labor force participation rate for men aged 65 and over has been higher than 30 percent and has been gradually rising since 2014. In sharp contrast, the male labor force participation rates in European countries have been low, around 10 percent or below, as depicted in figure 4.6. The same observation is applicable to the case of older women in Japan and industrialized countries in the West. Nevertheless, over the long term, Japan's labor force participation rate for men and women combined declined almost continuously from 32% in 1970 to 20% in 2003, after which

FIGURE 4.5 Japan's labor force size and participation rate, 1920–2015

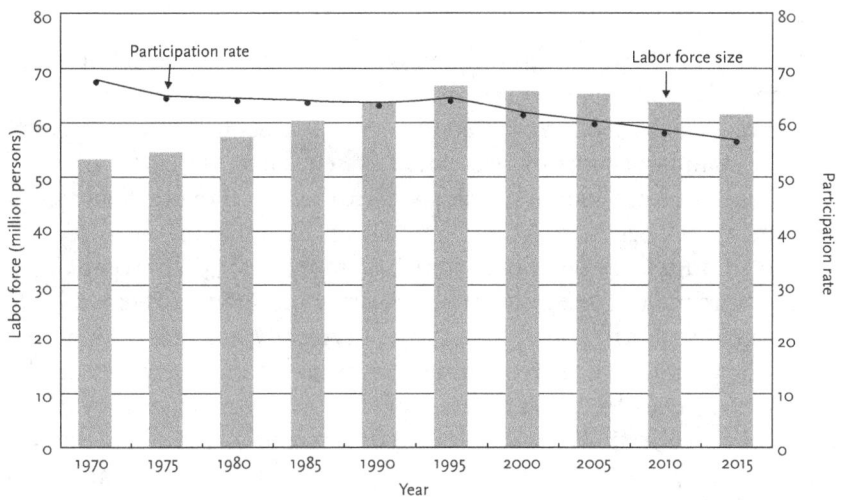

SOURCE: Statistics Bureau; various years, *Population Census*.

FIGURE 4.6 Labor force participation rates among men and women 65 and over in Japan and other industrialized countries in recent years

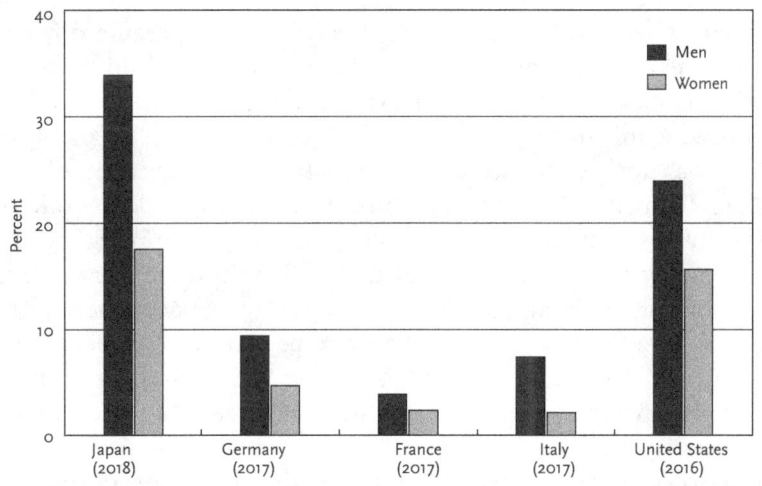

SOURCE: Statistics Bureau of Japan 2018, *Annual Labour Force Survey*; OECD 2018, database.

it marginally oscillated up to 2010. Between 2010 and 2015 it was on a slow but steadily upward trend, recording 25% in 2018 (Statistics Bureau 2019).

In spite of these substantial changes over time in the labor force size and the participation rate, Japan's well-established employment practices consisting of lifetime employment, the seniority wage system, and the mandatory age of retirement system have remained virtually intact, without any major revisions (Kato 2016). Japan's mandatory retirement policies in particular remain an extreme among the practices of industrialized nations. In 2018, more than 95 percent of all firms had mandatory retirement policies that required workers to leave the company at a relatively young age—typically at age 60. However, while the mandatory retirement age has been set relatively low, in the past several decades a sizable proportion of older Japanese workers have consistently shown stronger work preferences than their counterparts in Europe or North America (Clark, Ogawa, Lee, and Matsukura 2008; Clark, Matsukura, Ogawa, and Shimizutani 2015).

As a consequence of the rapid health improvements, as well as the very slow adjustment of institutional factors of the labor market, the constraint of the mandatory age of retirement imposed on the employment of older persons had, with time, become increasingly severe in the latter half of the twentieth century in Japan. To alleviate the constraint of the long-lasting, inflexible mandatory retirement age, the Japanese government enacted the Law Concerning the Stabilization of Employment of Older Persons in 2004. This law's passage required firms to choose one of three options for older employees: (1) completely abolish the mandatory retirement age, (2) raise it to 65, or (3) introduce a continued employment system. If the age is raised to 65, the employee's salary does not get reduced from age 60 to 65. In contrast, the continued employment system requires firms to rehire their older workers at age 60 and keep them on the payroll up to age 65, assuming they wish to continue working, but firms are given the right to drastically reduce their working hours and salaries, starting from age 60. When they are rehired at age 60, they are offered only 50 percent to 70 percent of their previous salaries. Under this law, companies were required to complete the transition in the age limit from 60 to 65 over the period of 2006 to 2013.

Due to the law's implementation, the labor force participation rate among workers in their early 60s has been considerably increasing. For instance, as shown in figure 4.7, the labor force participation rate

FIGURE 4.7 Change in the labor force participation rates for men and women aged 60–64, 2004–18

SOURCE: Statistics Bureau of Japan 2019, *Annual Labour Force Survey.*

for men aged 60 to 64 increased from 71% in 2004 to 84% in 2018. Similarly, the labor force participation rate of women in the same age group rose from 40% to 58% over the same period. Although persons in this age group who do not want to work at all are not required to submit themselves to this policy change, the size of this group is also shrinking. During 2005 to 2009, the proportion of men aged 60 to 64 who did not want to be employed declined marginally, from 15.1% to 13.4%. More important, since this law was enacted, approximately 70% of Japanese firms have chosen the continued employment system option. This implies that a considerable amount of the work capacity of workers ages 60 to 64 is neither fully utilized in terms of hours worked, nor is the work compensated at full salary.

In recent years, further enhancement of the labor participation of older people has been persistently promoted by the Japanese government and business circles as an agenda of prime importance. One of the most recent government initiatives was a plan announced on May 16, 2019 (NHK 2019). According to that plan, the government will revise the ongoing Law Concerning the Stabilization of Employment of Older Persons, enacted in 2004, and require all employers to keep their employees on the payroll until they reach age 70, if the employees want to stay on. To achieve this goal, the government is asking businesses to choose from among seven measures designed to allow older people to continue working. These measures include abolishing the retirement age, extending the retirement age to 70, and providing older employees with information about and recommendations for jobs at other firms. The legislation is expected to come in two stages: the bill submitted in 2020 simply urges businesses to retain employees until age 70, but later the measures will be made mandatory.

In view of these recent developments, the present study attempts to measure the potential work capacity of older workers, with the goal of finding effective labor-related policy options that could alleviate the adverse effects of aging and population decline on Japan's economic growth in the next few decades. In this study, there are two analytical parts. We first examine, by utilizing the microlevel data of the Japanese Study of Aging and Retirement (JSTAR) survey, how and to what extent the cognitive abilities of older Japanese workers vary with demographic, socioeconomic, and biomedical factors. Based upon the computed results, we compare the current level of the cognitive capacity of older Japanese workers with those of other countries in Asia and in the West, and then discuss the likely future trend in the cognitive functioning of older Japanese workers.

In the second part of the study, we shift the main focus of our analysis from the qualitative to the quantitative aspect. By drawing upon the microdata gathered in the five rounds of JSTAR (2007, 2009, 2011, 2013, and 2015), we estimate the relationship between health and employment among men and women aged 50 to 59, and use the estimated result, along with the actual characteristics of people aged 60 to 69, to simulate the latter's capacity to work, based on health. We then attempt to link the estimated statistical results derived from JSTAR to the NTA system,[3] constructed based on Japanese data gathered in 2009. In addition, by using the NTA framework, we quantify to what extent the economic support ratio would be enhanced through the utilization of the untapped work capacity among workers aged 60 and over.

---

3   The macroeconomic model called the system of National Transfer Accounts (NTA) has been drawing a great deal of attention from policymakers and researchers interested in tackling a wide range of policy problems related to population aging. A fuller explanation of the NTA's basic concepts, the crucial computational assumptions utilized, and definitions of other key variables can be found on the NTA global project website (http://www.ntaccounts.org).

Variation in Cognitive Functioning Among Older Japanese Workers

Let us now turn our attention to the cognitive performance of older Japanese persons.

Selected previous studies

Higher chronological age tends to be related to a host of health risks such as cardiac infarction and cerebral hemorrhage (Slomski 2014). Similarly, cognitive functioning tends to be a good predictor of future morbidity and mortality (Negashi et al. 2011). Therefore, individuals with higher cognitive abilities are more likely to be healthier and live longer than those with lower cognitive abilities. As demonstrated by numerous studies (e.g., Skirbekk, Loichinger, and Weber 2012), cognitive abilities predict individual productivity better than any other observable individual characteristic and are increasingly relevant for labor market performance. More important, this finding is applicable to many countries, both developed and developing, and to various settings, both urban and rural (Behrman, Ross, and Sabot 2008).

Over the past few decades, the number of seniors has been increasing in labor markets at an accelerating pace. Because certain cognitive abilities decline substantially at late adult ages, most of the studies previously conducted with regard to older workers have focused on the population of age 50 and over (Anderson and Craik 2000; Coe and Zamarro 2011; Bianchini and Borella 2016; Mazzonna and Peracchi 2017). An individual's potential lifetime length of stay in the labor market is partly determined by how long that individual can retain high cognitive performance.

Primarily due to the growing availability of representative surveys on the cognitive functioning of older adults in various countries and regions, an increasing number of empirical studies pertaining to the determinants of cognitive performance among the elderly have been carried out in recent years. In addition, almost all these surveys have used highly comparable questionnaires, thus making intercountry comparisons feasible. One of the salient examples is the study carried out by Maharani and Tampubolon (2016). Using data gleaned from the 2006 English Longitudinal Study of Ageing (ELSA) Wave 3 and the 2007 Indonesian Family Life Survey Wave 4, the authors examined the associations between central obesity, as measured by waist circumference, and the cognition level in adults aged 50 and over in England and Indonesia. In their regression analysis, after controlling for some selected demographic, socioeconomic, and biomedical variables, they found that centrally obese respondents had lower cognition levels than non–centrally obese respondents in England, and that this result obtained from ELSA was not comparable with Indonesia.

In addition, Weir, Lay, and Langa (2014) have analyzed data from studies similar to the Health and Retirement Study (HRS)[4] for China (China Health and Retirement Longitudinal Study [CHARLS]) and India (Longitudinal Aging Study in India [LASI]), as well as from the World Health Organization (WHO) Study of Global Aging and Adult Health (SAGE), to examine the pattern of gender inequality in cognition in these two Asian countries. They have found that, despite some notable differences in samples and measures, a strong general association of cognition in older ages with education emerges as a potential explanation for gender gaps and cohort differences. They have also found that female disadvantage in cognition is large in both China and India, before and even after controlling for education.

Doblhammer, van den Berg, and Fritze (2013) examined, by utilizing data gleaned from the Survey of Health, Ageing and Retirement in Europe (SHARE), cognitive functioning at age 60 and over. In their study, a total of 17,070 persons in 10 SHARE member countries[5] were included in the analysis of several domains of cognitive functioning, which was linked to the macroeconomic deviations in the year of birth. One of the main findings of this study is that economic conditions at birth significantly influence cognitive functioning late in life in various domains. Another finding was that economic recessions adversely affect numeracy, verbal fluency, and recall abilities, as well as the score on the omnibus cognitive indictors.

Bordone, Scherbov, and Steiber (2015) have investigated if and why individuals aged 50 and over who were born into more recent cohorts perform better in terms of cognition than their counterparts of the same age born into earlier cohorts (a phenomenon called the Flynn effect). Based on data from two waves of English (ELSA) and German

---

4   The HRS is a longitudinal survey that was carried out by the University of Michigan's Institute for Social Research and was sponsored by the U.S. National Institute on Aging and the Social Security Administration.

5   The 10 countries included in the study are Austria, Belgium, Denmark, France, Germany, Italy, the Netherlands, Spain, Sweden, and Switzerland.

(German Socio-Economic Panel [SOEP]) surveys, they show that cognitive test scores of participants aged 50 and older in the later wave are higher than those of participants aged 50 and older in the earlier wave. In addition to identifying the Flynn effect on the basis of the two cross-sectional waves, they pointed out that the reason why they used the two waves was that the use of a repeat cross-sectional design overcomes potential bias of retest effects. They also showed that, although compositional changes regarding education in the older population partly explained the Flynn effect, the increasing use of modern technology (i.e., computers and mobile phones) in the first decade of the 2000s also contributed to the explanation.

Skirbekk, Loichinger, and Weber (2012) examined the intercountry age variation in cognitive functioning, measured in terms of immediate recall score. They computed the mean age-group-specific immediate recall score, using data from the HRS, SAGE, SHARE (Northern Europe), SHARE (Continental Europe), and SHARE (Southern Europe). Caution should be exercised, however, in interpreting their computed results. For each five-year age group, the mean value of the immediate recall score for older persons falling into that age group was computed based on each relevant survey, but there are some differences between the surveys in the way in which the respondents are tested by the interviewers. That is, the respondents in as many as 18 countries were given one minute for recall, while the respondents in the United Kingdom and the United States had two minutes.[6] Furthermore, the interviewers read out 10 words to be recalled only once in all surveys except SAGE, where the interviewers read out the words three times before the survey subjects responded.[7] Despite these differences in the way that data on the immediate word recall were collected, the computed results showed a statistically significant age-related decline in all countries within the 50–84 age interval.

A brief comparison of immediate recall scores: Japan vs. selected countries

Following Skirbekk, Loichinger, and Weber (2012), to compute the mean age-group-specific immediate recall scores for various countries,

---

6   95 percent of the U.S. participants completed the task within one minute.

7   To enable international comparison, Skirbekk, Loichinger, and Weber used only the result for the first time.

we will calculate, by drawing on microlevel data from JSTAR, the mean age-group-specific immediate recall score for older Japanese persons, and then compare the computed result for Japan with those for select countries from the list in the study done by Skirbekk, Loichinger, and Weber (2012).

JSTAR is a longitudinal, interdisciplinary survey that collects internationally comparable data on Japanese who are middle-aged and older. The JSTAR project commenced in 2007, and the survey has since been implemented in two-year intervals. JSTAR is a sister survey compatible with the HRS, ELSA, SHARE, CHARLS, and LASI. JSTAR's design and sample methodology are described elsewhere (Ichimura, Hashimoto, and Shimizutani 2009). The baseline sample consists of male and female respondents aged 50 to 79 from 10 municipalities. The respondents were randomly chosen from household registries in each of the 10 cities, towns, or villages. The sample size and the average response rate at the baseline are approximately 8,000 and 60 percent, respectively. JSTAR collects a wide range of variables, including the economic, social, familial, and health conditions of the sampled respondents.

To avoid problems arising from nonrandom dropout and retest-practice effects associated with longitudinal surveys (Thorvaldsson, Hofer, Berg, and Johansson 2006; Skirbekk, Bordone, and Weber 2014), we have used only the data from the first round of JSTAR coming from the following three groups: the five municipalities surveyed in 2007 (Takikawa, Sendai, Adachi, Kanazawa, and Shirakawa), the two municipalities added in 2009 (Naha and Tosu), and the three that joined the survey in 2011 (Chofu, Tondabayashi, and Hiroshima). As is the case with most of the internationally comparable surveys such as SHARE, JSTAR respondents listened to 10 words read out by the interviewers and were given one minute to recall them.

Figure 4.8 compares Japan's mean age-group-specific immediate recall score from 2007 through 2011 with those for four SHARE countries in 2006 and 2007 (Germany, Spain, France, and Sweden), the United States from the 2006 and 2007 round of the HRS, and two Asian countries (China and India) from the 2007–09 round of the SAGE survey. A glance at this graphical exposition reveals a few interesting patterns of change among the eight countries. Germany has the highest score for the age group 50 to 54 (0.62, i.e., 6.2 words were recalled out of the 10 given words), followed by the United States (0.61), and the two countries show a comparable age-specific pattern

FIGURE 4.8 Mean age-group-specific immediate recall scores in eight selected countries including Japan, circa 2010

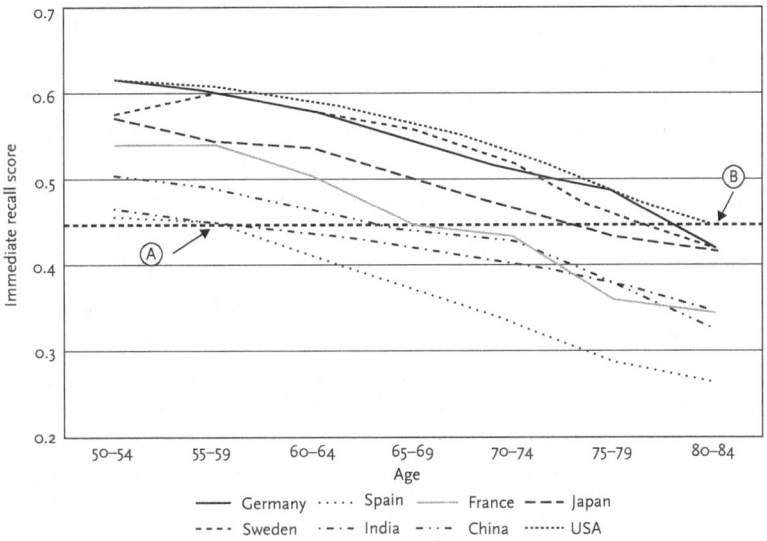

SOURCE: See main text.

of change. Immediate recall age trajectories for Japan and France are similar, although the latter shows consistently lower scores than the former. Relative to the other European countries selected for this graphical comparison, Spain has a substantially lower score, and its scores are consistently the lowest in all age groups among all the countries listed in figure 4.8.

India has a distinctively flatter age-cognition curve, compared with the others. When it comes to the age group 50 to 54, China has a higher score than India, but in the age group 80 to 84, China has been overtaken by India. This fact may reflect a selectivity mechanism in operation in India; it is conceivable that the cohorts that are presently 50 years and older in India grew up during the period of widespread poverty and high mortality, and that, as a result, the population has been positively selected in terms of cognitive performance at a more advanced age (Skirbekk, Loichinger, and Weber 2012).

In figure 4.8, we have arbitrarily drawn a dotted line at the score 0.45 for facilitating an interesting discussion. Point Ⓐ refers to a Spanish person at age 57.5 and point Ⓑ refers to an American at age

82.5. From these two points we can see that, at present, a Spanish person at age 57.5 and an American at age 82.5 have the same level of cognitive functioning, implying that a huge gap exists between the two countries in cognitive functioning. Such marked, intercountry differences in the level of cognitive functioning may pose a major stumbling block to activating the transfer of new technologies and the adoption of innovative production methods from one country to another in the future.

The foregoing comparative analysis seems to indicate that Japan's recent pattern of age-related decline in cognitive functioning is fairly comparable to that of the United States and the selected European nations. In addition, as illustrated in figure 4.8, Japan's age-specific cognitive levels seem to be comparable to the average level of the developed countries in Europe and the United States combined. This seems to suggest that although Japan's population aging level has been by far the highest in the entire world over the past 15 years, Japan's current and future prospects regarding population aging may not be as depressing as the academia and mass media in Japan and elsewhere have claimed, once age-specific cognitive abilities are included into the computation of aging indices.

Determinants of cognitive functioning

In this subsection, we will identify, by running a linear regression, the determinants of immediate recall scores among the Japanese persons aged 50 and over who were included in the first wave of JSTAR in the aforementioned 10 municipalities. The total number of observations amounts to 5,421. The dependent variable is the number of words recalled by the respondent immediately after 10 words were read out. In this regression, we have introduced the following 10 explanatory variables: age groups (50–54, 55–59, 60–64[†], 65–69, 70–74, and 75–79), sex (man, woman[†]), marital status (currently married, currently not married[†]), work status (working, not working[†]), education (junior high school[†], senior high school, junior college, university or higher), self-rated health status (excellent, very good, good, fair[†], poor), CES-D ($\geqq 16$, 16[†]), IADLs($\geqq 1$, 0[†]), height (cm), and municipalities (Takikawa, Sendai, Adachi, Chofu, Kanazawa, Shirakawa, Tondabayashi, Hiroshima[†], Tosu, Naha). Except for the height of the respondent, all the other explanatory variables are dummy variables, with the dagger notation ([†]) representing the reference group.

In this regression, the respondent's age and education have been incorporated to capture the effect of two types of intelligence—fluid intelligence and crystallized intelligence—on cognitive functioning. *Fluid intelligence* refers to the ability to reason and think flexibly, while *crystallized intelligence* refers to the accumulation of knowledge, facts, and skills that are acquired throughout life (Cattell 1978). The explanatory variable, age, is expected to capture the change in fluid intelligence, which peaks at approximately age 25. Because the respondents included in the regression are older than 50, the estimated coefficients are expected to have negative signs. The other explanatory variable is expected to capture the effect of education on crystallized intelligence, which is based on facts and rooted in experiences. As we age and accumulate new knowledge and understanding, crystallized intelligence becomes stronger. Thus, we expect the estimated coefficient for education to have a positive sign. In addition, we can anticipate that the higher the level of education, the larger the estimated coefficient will be.

The health-related explanatory variables, such as the self-rated health status, the Center for Epidemiologic Studies Depression Scale (CES-D),[8] and instrumental activities of daily living (IADLs),[9] are expected to be related to a higher cognitive performance. The respondent without a spouse is likely to be left alone without having anybody to communicate with, which should weaken their cognitive functioning. Similarly, whether the respondent holds a job is likely to affect their level of crystallized intelligence.

The respondent's height has been incorporated into the regression because adult height is closely related to childhood nutritional conditions, which in turn affect cognitive functioning and other dimensions of human capital, such as school ability (LaFave and Thomas 2017; Weir, Lay, and Langa 2014). Moreover, the same empirical studies show that women tend to perform better in terms of immediate recall scores than men.

We have also included in the regression a set of explanatory variables representing survey areas, which differ considerably in terms of the level of urbanization and lifestyles. It can be easily conceived that a

---

8   Scores on the CES-D range from 0 to 60, where higher scores suggest a greater presence of depression symptoms. A score of 16 or higher is interpreted as indicating a risk for depression.

9   In JSTAR, 15 questions pertaining to IADLs are asked, and the IADL dummy variable takes the value of 0 if the respondent has no difficulty in performing any of the 15 activities, and 1 otherwise.

TABLE 4.1 Regression analysis of immediate recall score (dependent variable = immediate recall score)

Explanatory variables	Coefficient	T-value		Explanatory variables	Coefficient	T-value	
Age				Self-rated health status			
50–54	0.203	2.83	**	Excellent	0.173	2.38	**
55–59	0.052	0.81		Very good	0.145	2.06	**
60–64[†]	—	—		Good	0.111	1.67	*
65–69	−0.228	−3.45	***	Fair[†]	—	—	
70–74	−0.481	−6.95	***	Poor	−0.381	−2.70	***
75–79	−0.781	−5.04	***	CES-D			
Sex				≥16	−0.078	−1.27	
Male	−0.562	−8.30	***	<16[†]	—	—	
Female	—	—		IADLs			
Marital status				≥1	−0.165	−3.71	***
Currently married	0.088	1.44		0[†]	—	—	
Currently not married	—	—		Height	0.007	1.69	*
Work status				Municipalities			
Working	−0.022	−0.45		Takigawa	−0.740	−7.64	***
Not working[†]	—	—		Sendai	−0.043	−0.50	
Education				Adachi	0.015	0.18	
Junior high[†]	—	—		Chofu	0.310	2.57	**
Senior high	0.341	6.04	***	Kanazawa	−0.150	−1.68	*
Junior college	0.490	6.58	***	Shirakawa	−0.167	−1.79	*
University or higher	0.686	8.92	***	Tondabayashi	−0.227	−2.04	**
				Hiroshima[†]	—	—	
				Tosu	−0.316	−3.27	***
				Naha	−0.302	−3.26	***
				Intercept	4.194	7.16	***

NOTE: Dependent variable = immediate recall score; level of statistical significance: *10%, **5%, ***1%; [†] reference group; adjusted R-squared = 0.118; number of observations = 5,421.
SOURCE: Authors.

large proportion of older persons living in Chofu, which is a relatively wealthy urban area in Tokyo, are exposed in their daily lives to modern technologies such as the internet and computers. It is plausible that those who often use these modern technologies, by doing so, stimulate their crystallized intelligence (Bordone, Scherbov, and Steiber 2015).

Table 4.1 shows the estimated results. All the explanatory variables except for the respondent's marital status, work status, and CES-D are statistically significant, with the coefficients having expected signs. One of the key findings is that education has a huge impact on immediate recall scores; the higher the educational level, the better the cognitive performance. Another important finding is that the respondent's health relates positively to the immediate word recall scores. Moreover, women show a considerably higher cognitive score than men, which is comparable to the pattern widely prevailing in developed countries. However, this JSTAR-based result pertaining to the gender cognitive gap is contrary to the pattern being observed in other Asian countries such as India and China, as previously mentioned (Weir, Lay, and Langa 2014). It is interesting that the respondent's height is positively linked to better cognitive ability, which implies that the nutritional condition in childhood plays an important role in developing cognitive functioning. It is also interesting that the coefficient for Chofu is not only statistically significant but also positive, which agrees with our *a priori* expectation.

These statistical results indicate that the cognitive ability of older Japanese persons is likely to improve in the years to come due to the following possibilities: (1) the level of education among those 50 and over is expected to rise at a phenomenal rate, as shown in figure 4.9; (2) the future generations of older Japanese persons are likely to have an advantage over past generations, because children's nutritional conditions began to improve considerably in Japan in the late 1950s, when the school lunch program started on a nationwide basis; and (3) the use of modern communication technologies among older persons is

FIGURE 4.9 Changes in the educational composition, by sex, 1920–80

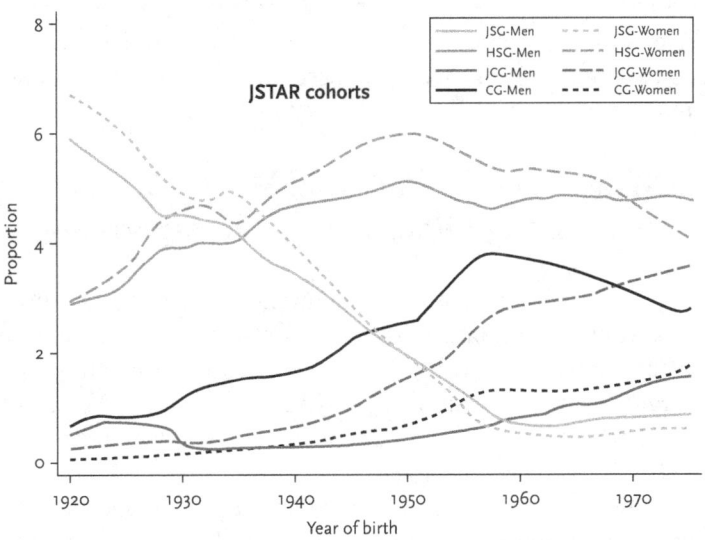

NOTE: JSG = junior high, HSG = senior high, JCG = junior college CG = university or higher.
SOURCE: Statistics Bureau; various years, *Population Census*.

FIGURE 4.10 Japanese internet use patterns by age, 2016

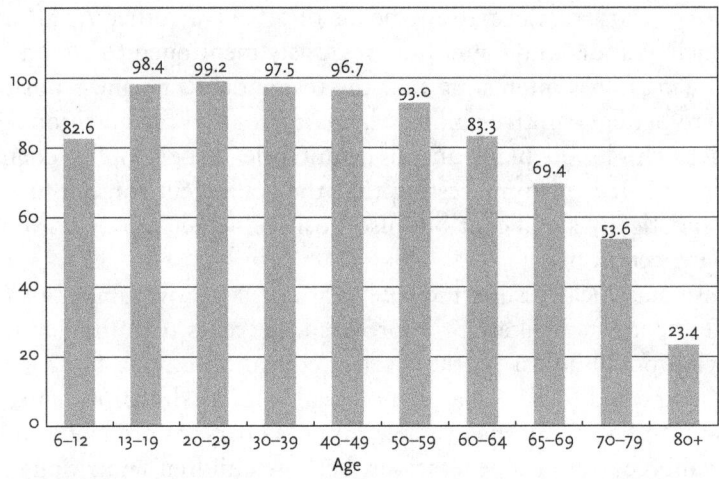

SOURCE: Ministry of Internal Affairs and Communications 2017, *Communications Usage Trend Survey*.

likely to increase at a remarkable rate, because the young cohorts have already been exposed to the use of computers and mobile phones, as illustrated in figure 4.10. In addition, judging from the long-term trends of life expectancy at age 50 in Japan, it seems safe to presume that the physical condition of older Japanese persons will continuously improve in the years ahead.

Measuring the Potential Work Capacity among Older Persons in Japan

In this section, following up on our earlier study (Matsukura et al. 2018), we attempt to quantify the potential work capacity in Japan in terms of health status among those aged 50 and over, by pooling all the observations from the first to the fifth waves of JSTAR, conducted in 2007, 2009, 2011, 2013, and 2015. In our earlier work, we covered only the first three waves of JSTAR.

In our analysis, we do not include a number of factors affecting decisions concerning labor supply (for example, wages), but focus on health disability to examine to what extent the labor supply of older persons is limited. We employ a linear probability model to regress a binary variable of employment, which is equal to 1 if the individual is in the labor force (both employed and unemployed) and 0 if the individual is out of the labor force, on the following health-related explanatory variables: (1) dummy variables for self-reported health status (five-point scale), (2) the incidence of limitations on instrumental activities of daily living (IADLs), (3) the CES-D depression scale, (4) the Nagi physical ability index (Nagi 1965, 1979), (5) limitations in sensory organs (poor eyesight, poor hearing, and difficulty chewing),[10] and (6) individual attributes, such as sex, educational attainment, and marital status. In addition, dummy variables for each municipality and for survey years are included.[11]

In the estimation, we use the sample of individuals aged 50 to 59 and combine both sexes for a baseline regression. In this analysis, we implicitly assume that adults aged 50 to 59 are likely to be in the labor force unless their health is impaired. We have a sample of 4,666 person-year observations. We do not use the longitudinal feature of the JSTAR sample, since we are interested in the prevalence of work capacity (factors that determine the level of work capacity) by age, rather than the incidence (i.e., factors that change work capacity) along with age.

Most of the explanatory variables incorporated into the regression have already been utilized in our statistical analysis of cognitive functioning in the previous section. The Nagi index and the limitation in sensory organs are the two explanatory variables that are newly added here.[12] The Nagi index in JSTAR consists of 10 items and is designed to capture difficulties in physical activities that are relevant to work capacity: (1) walking 100 meters, (2) sitting continuously for two hours,

---

10   For each of the sensory organs, we have assigned the following three numerical values: "2" denotes conditions ranging from "very good" to "not bad," "1" stands for "bad," and "0" stands for "intolerable."

11   In addition, Usui, Shimizutani, and Oshio (2016) use the following variables: incidence of limitations on physical activity and limitations on activities of daily living (ADLs), past medical history and present diagnosed diseases (from a list of about 20 diseases), being over- or underweight (using the body mass index [BMI]), and being a current or a former smoker, all of which are common in papers produced by researchers in the International Social Security Project of the National Bureau of Economic Research. However, these health variables have not been included in the present study because the incidence of physical or ADL limitations, as well as of diseases diagnosed by medical doctors, is quite low among those in their 50s. Also, in Japan, the BMI and smoking status seem to be less relevant to work capacity.

12   For a detailed description of the limitations in sensory organs, see Matsukura et al. 2018.

(3) standing up from a chair after sitting for a long time, (4) climbing several steps without using handrails, (5) climbing one step without using handrails, (6) squatting or kneeling, (7) raising hands above the shoulders, (8) pushing and pulling large objects such as chairs and sofas in a living room, (9) lifting and carrying an object weighing more than 5 kg, and (10) grasping a small object, such as a 1 yen coin, with fingers.

Estimated results

Table 4.2 shows the estimated results. First, the coefficient for males is positive and significant, indicating that males are more likely, by 23 percent, to be in the labor force than females. Moreover, the education gradient is also observed; compared with the reference group (junior high school graduates), high school graduate and university graduates are more likely to be in the labor force, by 4 percent and 7 percent respectively. The coefficient for being currently married is negative and significant, but this comes from the fact that males and females are combined in this explanatory variable.

Second, turning to the health-related variables, we see that the coefficients for the self-rated health status show that the respondents who rate their own health level higher than the reference group ("fair") are, as expected, more likely to be in the labor force. For instance, those who report that their health is "excellent" are more likely, by 10 percent, to be employed than those included in the reference group, and those who report that their health is "poor" are less likely, by 25 percent, to be employed. The coefficient for the variable representing the CES-D measure is unexpectedly positive but not statically significant. Similarly, the incidence of IADLs has a positive coefficient but is not statically significant. However, regarding the items from the Nagi index, the estimated coefficients for "sitting for two hours" and "lifting and carrying more than 5 kg" are significant and negative. The coefficients for sensory organs are mixed. The coefficient for eyesight limitations and hearing limitations are negative and statically insignificant, but the estimated coefficient for chewing is positive and statically significant. In addition, some of the estimated coefficients related to the municipalities and survey years are significant; for example, the survey site Shirakawa is an agricultural area, which is significantly different from the reference group, Hiroshima (a large city).

TABLE 4.2 Estimated regression results

Explanatory variables	Coefficient	T-value		Explanatory variables	Coefficient	T-value
Sex				**Sensory organs**		
Male	0.234	21.7 ***		Eyesight	−0.005	−0.16
Female†	—	—		Hearing	−0.059	−1.48
Education				Chewing ability	0.136	3.53 ***
Junior high†	—	—		**Municipalities**		
Senior high	0.037	2.17 **		Takigawa	0.016	0.56
Junior college	0.040	2.09 **		Sendai	−0.043	−1.83 *
University or higher	0.072	3.72		Adachi	0.044	1.84 *
Marital status				Chofu	0.031	1.15
Currently married	−0.079	−5.91 ***		Kanazawa	0.025	1.13
Currently not married	—	—		Shirakawa	0.065	2.84 ***
Self-rated health status				Tondabayashi	0.019	0.76
Excellent	0.104	5.24 ***		Hiroshima†	—	—
Very good	0.060	3.06 **		Tosu	0.016	0.67
Good	0.005	3.45 **		Naha	0.017	0.75
Fair†	—	—		**Year of survey**		
Poor	−0.247	−5.52 ***		2007	—	—
CESD				2009	−0.025	−1.68 *
≥16	0.019	1.55		2011	−0.028	−1.68 *
<16†	—	—		2013	−0.036	−1.87 *
IADL				2015	−0.023	−0.91
≥1	0.005	0.45		Constant	0.577	4.44 ***
0†	—	—				
Nagi index						
Walking 100 meters	−0.095	−1.51				
Sitting for two hours	−0.079	−1.75 *				
Standing up for a long time	0.010	0.25				
Climbing several steps without handrails	−0.060	−1.35				
Climbing one step without handrails	−0.016	−0.29				
Squatting or kneeling	−0.038	−1.12				
Raising hands above the shoulders	−0.013	−0.24				
Pushing and pulling a large object	−0.074	−1.42				
Lifting and carrying more than 5kg	−0.144	−2.75 **				
Picking up a small object with fingers	0.150	2.06 **				

NOTE: Dependent variable: 1 = in the labor force, 0 = otherwise; level of statistical significance: *10%, **5%, ***1%; † reference group; adjusted R-squared = 0.165; number of observations = 4,666.

SOURCE: Authors.

Impact of the use of untapped work capacity upon total labor income and labor supply

We simulate the untapped work capacity for Japanese adults aged 60 through 79. We use the estimated coefficient to compute predicted values for each individual in JSTAR and average them for each age. The "untapped work capacity" is defined as the difference (or slack) between the actual and the predicted employment probability. Figure 4.11 shows that the estimated untapped capacity, shown in gray, increases with age. Japan's untapped work capacity is estimated to be 4.12 million persons for ages 60 through 79.

To calculate the potential impact of these additional workers on Japan's GDP, we have set up three cases. Case I assumes that if the potential older workers are employed, they earn labor income that is in accordance with the NTA age-specific labor income profile observed in 2009, as depicted in figure 4.3; Case II assumes that potential older workers at each age can earn the same amount of labor income as their counterparts who were employed in 2014; and Case III assumes that if

FIGURE 4.11 Age-specific observed labor force participation rate and potential labor force participation rate in Japan

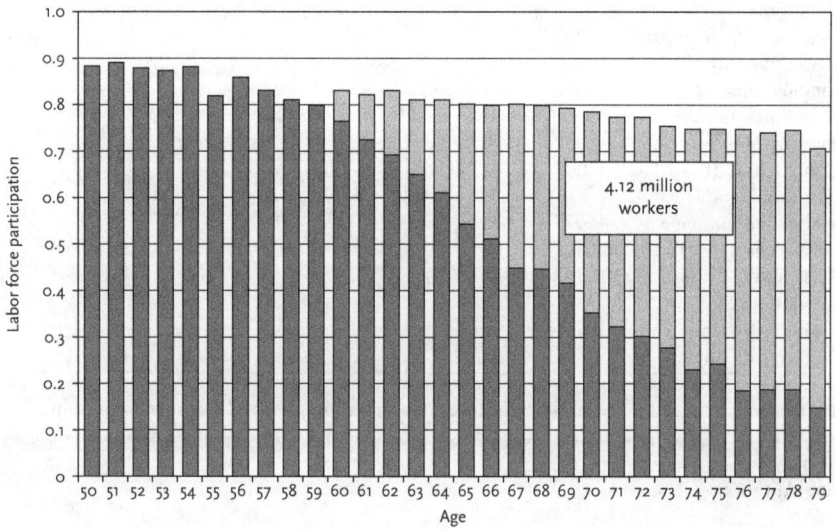

SOURCE: Authors.

the potential older workers are employed, they earn only the minimum wage set by the Japanese law. The computed results are as follows: in Case I,[13] the GDP for 2015 is 4.5% higher; in Case II, 6.0% higher; and in Case III, 3.2% higher.

Caution is important, because in the preceding simulation exercise, the age-specific consumption profile is assumed to remain unchanged. We should keep in mind that if older workers earn higher labor income, it is conceivable that they may increase their consumption. Thus, in response to increased labor income, we would have to shift the age-specific consumption profile upward among those over 60 years of age. However, the interaction between the age-specific labor income and consumption profiles is extremely complex, and thus falls outside the scope of this study.

Further Discussion

Our analyses developed above suggest that Japan's older labor force has a fairly good potential not only for improvement in quality but also for a substantial expansion in quantity over time, in spite of the country's bleak demographic prospects. However, one important institutional factor that we have not explicitly incorporated into our regression analyses is the timing of retirement from the labor market.

When we were quantifying the amount of untapped work capacity of older Japanese persons, we treated the health status among those aged 60–79 as the main determining factor, so we excluded the mandatory retirement age from the computational process. It is important to bear in mind that a relatively abundant volume of literature pertaining to the relationship between older individuals' age-related cognitive performance and the timing of their retirement from the labor market has been published.

As discussed earlier, the Japanese government has recently begun making strenuous efforts to postpone the mandatory age of retirement, possibly to 70 years old, in the hope of raising the pensionable age, with a view to maintaining the financial solvency of the social security system. As is the case with our analysis of the untapped work capacity of older persons presented in the previous section, an important question is whether continuous labor participation helps maintain

---

13   We have used the preliminary version of the age-specific profiles of per capita consumption and labor income for Japan in 2014.

high levels of cognition at older ages. To partially answer this question, we have introduced into the regression reported in table 4.1 another explanatory variable representing whether a respondent was already retired at the time of the survey.[14] The computed coefficient shows a positive sign but is statistically insignificant. To properly analyze the relationship between the two variables in question, we need additional explanatory variables, such as the cognitive score prior to retirement, the years elapsed since the time of retirement, and so on. Unfortunately, in our data set created from the first survey round for each administrative district, the required data are not available. Moreover, when we attempted to conduct an analysis utilizing data from the first two rounds of the survey, we found that a substantial proportion of the respondents who participated in the first round refused to respond to the questions related to cognitive functioning in the second round, due to their poor performance in the first round, thus yielding a statistical bias. Also, as briefly touched upon earlier, in our data set we found substantial evidence of the presence of retest effects and nonrandom dropouts among the respondents who answered the cognition-related questions when we carried out a few analyses using cohort-based individual data collected from the two successive rounds, which were only two years apart.

In contrast to this result, obtained from our analysis based upon JSTAR, past studies are more conclusive, in the sense that they have tended to find a negative effect of retirement on cognition (Rohwedder and Willis 2010; Bonsang, Adam, and Perelman 2012; Mazzonna and Peracchi 2012, 2017; Celidoni, Dal Bianco, and Weber 2017). In addition, Bonsang, Adam, and Perelman (2012) have shed light on the negative relationship between retirement from the labor market and cognitive functioning among older persons in the context of financial sustainability of social security. They demonstrated, using six waves (1998 through 2008) of the HRS, that retirement negatively affects the cognitive functioning of older Americans. This finding suggests that reforms aimed at promoting labor force participation at an older age may not only ensure the sustainability of social security systems but may also create positive health externalities for older individuals.

---

14   We have created this new explanatory variable (representing whether the respondent was already retired) by reclassifying the "work status." The new variable takes a value of 1 if the person is retired, and 0 if not retired.

Most of the existing studies are based largely on data from a selected set of countries obtained through surveys such as the HRS, ELSA, and SHARE, which is why the scope of analyses of the relationship between retirement and cognition has been limited to the United States and Europe. A recent study by Atalay, Barrett, and Staneva (2019) has added a new perspective to the literature. By heavily drawing upon data from the Household, Income and Labour Dynamics in Australia (HILDA) panel survey, the authors have estimated the short-term effect of retirement on cognitive performance of older Australians, using the exogenous variation in retirement decisions in social security eligibility rules.[15] Their estimated results show that retirement has a negative but modest effect on cognition and that the rate of cognitive decline with age is greater for men than for women. One of the unique aspects of this study is that, although the past literature has hardly focused on the relationship between retirement and cognitive functioning from a gender point of view, this study shed light on gender differences in cognitive functioning. Moreover, taking advantage of HILDA's high-quality data—obtained thanks to several unique design features of the survey that make it well suited for the measurement of the relationship between retirement and cognitive functioning—the authors have demonstrated that moving into retirement makes women spend more time on intellectual and household activities, which likely contributes to a modest positive effect observed among retired women. It is conceivable that, compared with employment, housework actually offers more autonomy to women (Bird 1999). Furthermore, Atalay and his associates have included in their analysis measures of both fluid and crystallized cognitive abilities,[16] thus providing additional evidence concerning the effect of retirement on different cognitive domains.

---

15   In the HILDA survey, a person's cognitive functioning was measured at two points in time: in 2012 and 2016. Despite the relatively short interval (four years) between the two rounds, the authors of this study did not pay much attention to the possibility of statistical bias due to retest effects and nonrandom dropouts. In the case of JSTAR, the interval between two rounds is two years, and we have identified a strong bias present due to these two factors.

16   In the present study, as mentioned earlier and as shown in table 4.1, we have introduced into the regression the respondent's age and education as proxies for capturing the effect of fluid intelligence and crystallized intelligence on cognitive functioning. In the HILDA-based study, however, the authors have used more refined assessment tasks (e.g., the Symbol-Digits-Modalities Test, Backwards Digit Span Test, and the National Adult Reading Test).

Several studies have found positive effects of retirement on cognition. For instance, Bianchini and Borella (2016) find retirement to have a beneficiary effect on verbal memory, when allowing for nonlinear effects of age on cognition. Neuman (2008) has shown based on data from the United States that retirement improves health because of the removal of the time constraint caused by labor market participation, which means that more time can be allocated to activities conducive to the enhancement of individual's health. Generally, retirement affects cognition by allowing for an increase in various mental and physical exercises and pastimes, such as reading magazines, writing, or playing board games (Wilson et al. 2013), as well as for engagement in sociocultural activities (Marquie et al. 2010).

To date, some analyses based on the panel data generated from JSTAR have encountered a number of limitations in applying some of the important observations derived from the studies conducted abroad to the context of Japan. However, we have recently completed JSTAR's work history survey, covering the respondents who participated in the 2015 round, and will soon be ready to undertake a wide range of new, in-depth statistical analyses. Cognitive functioning is one of the areas that feature high on our research agenda to be further pursued with the newly created data set.

Let us now turn the focus of our discussion to the untapped work capacity of older workers in Japan. Because the problem of labor squeeze has been deepening in the past decade, the Japanese government has recently changed its immigration policy by officially opening the doors to significant numbers of lower-skilled foreign workers. Between 2019 and 2024, a total of approximately 345,000 foreign workers are expected to come to Japan, who will be employed in one of 14 industrial sectors: nursing care, catering, construction, custodial services, agriculture, food and beverage manufacturing, hotels, raw material industries, shipbuilding, fisheries, automotive parts manufacturing, industrial machinery, electronics and electrical equipment, and aviation.

According to the Immigration Bureau, only 895 work permits were issued under the new visa system intended for skilled blue-collar workers in the seven months since the new immigration policy went into effect in April 2019 (Osumi 2019). The main reason behind the slowdown in the anticipated influx of foreign workers is the time required for introducing industrial skills tests, which are mandatory for those who are applying for the new visa. As of the end of October 2019, the tests have been conducted only in Japan and six other countries and for only six of the 14 selected industrial sectors.

Although Japan's nursing care sector, which has long suffered from a severe labor shortage, was opened up in 2017 to foreign workers wanting to work as technical trainees, as of 2019 none of the trainees taking part in the program have completed the training. Acquiring the required level of proficiency in the Japanese language is an extremely difficult stumbling block for the trainees.

At this stage, it may be too early to make a definite statement regarding the prospect of the new immigration policy adopted by the Japanese government. Nonetheless, it seems safe to say that it is highly unlikely that the country will manage to accept 345,000 foreign (mostly Asian) workers in the planned period between 2019 and 2024. In light of the fact that the untapped work capacity of older Japanese persons is huge (4.12 million potential workers) and that a large proportion of them possess both the desire to work and a solid work ethic, we feel that the Japanese government would be well advised to reconsider its newly adopted immigration policy and revise it from a more realistic point of view. In the process of revising its labor market policies, the government should take advantage of the potential offered by older Japanese workers, reexamine the recruitment procedure for foreign workers, and at the same time carefully assess the potential of a wider use of artificial intelligence and robotic technology.[17]

Concluding Remarks

In the first half of this chapter, we found that the cognitive performance of Japanese persons aged 60 to 75 is basically similar to that prevailing in a number of European countries. Moreover, in Japan, the potential for the future growth of cognitive functioning among older persons, here measured in terms of immediate word recall scores, seems to be promising, thanks to higher educational levels, better childhood

---

17   As is the case elsewhere in the world, the issue of substitutability between human resources and AI and robotic technology has been frequently discussed by Japanese mass media. A recent study by Adachi, Kainuma, Kawaguchi, and Saito (2019), who applied the same methodological approach adopted by Acemoglu and Restrepo (2017) to Japanese prefecture-level data, has not found any significant substitutability in work between the human labor supply and AI/robotic technology.

nutritional conditions, and the changes in lifestyles characteristic for the era of the fourth industrial revolution.

In the second half of this chapter, we have shown that the volume of untapped work capacity among those aged 50–79 is vast, amounting to more than four million workers at present. Partly using the NTA framework, we have also obtained computed results concerning the impact of these potential, additional workers on the Japanese economy. Japan's GDP for 2015 could have been between 3.2 percent and 6.0 percent larger had these relatively healthy older individuals joined the ranks of workers. However, in this chapter we have not examined the issue of whether the use of untapped work capacity of older persons could affect the well-being of workers belonging to other age groups. We hope to address this question in the near future.

References

Acemoglu, Daron, and Pascual Restrepo. 2017. "Secular Stagnation? The Effect of Aging on Economic Growth in the Age of Automation." *American Economic Review* 107: 174–79.

Adachi, Daisuke, Shuhei Kainuma, Daiji Kawaguchi, and Yukiko Saito. 2019. *Introduction of Automation Technologies and Labor Substitution*. RIETI Policy Discussion Paper Series 19-P-010. (In Japanese.)

Anderson, Nicole D., and Fergus I. M. Craik. 2000. "Memory in the Aging Brain." In *The Oxford Handbook of Memory*, edited by Endel Tulving and Fergus I. M. Craik, 411–25. Oxford: Oxford University Press.

Atalay, Kadir, Gary F. Barrett, and Anita Staneva. 2019. "The Effect of Retirement on Elderly Cognitive Functioning." *Journal of Health Economics* 66: 37–53.

Behrman, Jere, David Ross, and Richard Sabot. 2008. "Improving Quality Versus Increasing the Quantity of Schooling: Estimates of Rates of Return from Rural Pakistan." *Journal of Development Economics* 85: 94–104.

Bianchini, Laura, and Margherita Borella. 2016. "Retirement and Memory in Europe." *Ageing Society* 36: 1434–1458.

Bird, Chloe E. 1999. "Gender, Household Labor, and Psychological Distress: The Impact of the Amount and Division of Housework." *Journal of Health Social Behavior* 40: 32–45.

Bonsang, Eric, Stéphane Adam, and Sergio Perelman. 2012. "Does Retirement Affect Cognitive Functioning?" *Journal of Health Economics* 31: 490–501.

Bordone, Valeria, Sergei Scherbov, and Nadia Steiber. 2015. "Smarter Every Day: The Deceleration of Population Ageing in Terms of Cognition." *Intelligence* 52: 90–96.

Cattell, Raymond B. 1978. *The Scientific Use of Factor Analysis*. New York: Plenum Press.

Celidoni, Martina, Chiara Dal Bianco, and Guglielmo Weber. 2017. "Retirement and Cognitive Decline: A Longitudinal Analysis Using SHARE Data." *Journal of Health Economics* 56: 113–25.

Coe, Norma B., and Gema Zamorro. 2011. "Retirement Effects on Health in Europe." *Health Economics* 30: 77–86.

Chamie, Joseph. 2016. "The Historical Reversal of Populations."
    Inter Press Service, August 8, 2016.

Clark, Robert L., Naohiro Ogawa, Sang-Hyop Lee, and Rikiya
    Matsukura. 2008. "Older Workers and National Productivity
    in Japan." In Alexia Prskawetz, David E. Bloom, and Wolfgang
    Lutz (eds.), *Population Aging, Human Capital Accumulation, and
    Productivity Growth* (supplement to vol. 34 of *Population and
    Development Review*), 257–74. Blackwell Publishing (published on
    behalf of the Population Council).

Clark, Robert L., Rikiya Matsukura, Naohiro Ogawa, and Satoshi
    Shimizutani. 2015. "Retirement Transitions in Japan." *Public Policy
    Aging Report* 25, no. 4: 129–31.

Doblhammer, Gabriela, Gerard van den Berg, and Thomas Fritze.
    2013. "Economic Conditions at the Time of Birth and Cognitive
    Abilities Late in Life: Evidence from Ten European Countries."
    PLOS ONE 8: e74915.

Hodge, Robert W., and Naohiro Ogawa. 1991. *Fertility Change in
    Contemporary Japan*. Chicago: University of Chicago Press.

Ichimura, Hidehiko, Hideki Hashimoto, and Satoshi Shimizutani.
    2009. "Japanese Study of Aging and Retirement: First Results."
    RIETI Discussion Paper Series 09-E-047. Tokyo, Japan: The
    Research Institute of Economy, Trade and Industry.

IMD (International Institute for Management Development). Various
    years. *IMD World Competitiveness Yearbook*. Lausanne: IMD.

Madalena Osumi. 2019 "Only 895 Granted Blue-Collar Visas Since
    April, Immigration Agency Admits." *Japan Times*. November 13,
    2019.

Kato, Takao. 2016. *Productivity, Wages and Unions in Japan*. Condi-
    tions of Work and Employment Series No. 73. Geneva: Interna-
    tional Labour Office.

LaFave, Daniel, and Duncan Thomas. 2017. "Height and Cognition
    at Work: Labor Market Productivity in a Low Income Setting."
    Economic Human Biology 25: 52–64.

Lee, Ronald, and Andrew Mason. 2011. *Population Aging and
    the Generational Economy: A Global Perspective*. Cheltenham,
    Northampton, Ottawa: Edward Elgar and International Develop-
    ment Research Centre.

Maharani, Asri, and Gindo Tampubolon. 2016. "National Economic
    Development Status May Affect the Association Between Central

Adiposity and Cognition in Older Adults." *PLOS One*, February 10, 2016.

Mason, Andrew. 2007. "Demographic Transition and Demographic Dividends in Developed and Developing Countries." In *Proceedings of the United Nations Expert Group Meeting on Social and Economic Implications of Changing Population Age Structures*, edited by United Nations, Population Division, Department of Economic and Social Affairs, 81–101. New York: United Nations.

Marquié, Jean-Claude, Liliana R. Duarte, P. Bessières, C. Dalm, Catherine Gentil, and J. B. Ruidavets. 2010. "Higher Mental Stimulation at Work Is Associated with Improved Cognitive Functioning in Both Young and Older Workers." *Ergonomics* 53: 1287–1301.

Matsukura, Rikiya, Satoshi Shimizutani, Nahoko Mitsuyama, Sang-Hyop Lee, and Naohiro Ogawa. 2018. "Untapped Work Capacity Among Old Persons and Their Potential Contributions to the 'Silver Dividend' in Japan." *Journal of the Economics of Ageing* 12: 236–49.

Mazzonna, Fabrizio, and Franco Peracchi. 2012. "Ageing Cognitive Abilities and Retirement." *European Economic Review* 56: 691–710.

Mazzonna, Fabrizio, and Franco Peracchi. 2017. "Unhealthy Retirement?" *Journal of Human Resources* 52: 128–51.

Nagi, Said Z. 1965. "Some Conceptual Issues in Disability and Rehabilitation." In *Sociology and Rehabilitation*, edited by Marvin B. Sussman, 100–13. Washington, D.C.: American Sociological Association..

Nagi, Said Z. 1979. "The Concept and Measurement of Disability." In *Disability Policies and Government Programs*, edited by Edward D. Berkowitz, 1–15. New York: Praeger.

NIPSSR (National Institute of Population and Social Security Research). 2019. *Latest Demographic Statistics 2019*. Tokyo: National Institute of Population and Social Security Research.

Neuman, Kevin. 2008. "Quit Your Job and Get Healthier? The Effect of Retirement on Health." *Journal of Labor Research* 29:177–201.

Negashi, Selam, Glenn E. Smith, Shane Pankratz, Jeremiah Aakre, Yonas E. Geda, Rosebud O. Roberts, David S. Knopman, Bradley F. Boeve, Robert J. Ivnik, and Ronald C. Petersen. 2011. "Successful

Aging: Definitions, and Prediction of Longevity and Conversion to Mild Cognitive Impairment." *American Journal of Geriatric Psychiatry* 19: 581–88.

NHK (Nihon Houso Kyokai). 2019. "Government Draws Up Plan to Enable Work Until Age 70." *NHK World News*, May 15.

Ogawa, N., G. Jones, and J. Williamson, eds. 1993. *Human Resources and Development Along the Asia Pacific Rim*. Singapore: Oxford University Press.

Ogawa, Naohiro, Sang-Hyop Lee, Rikiya Matsukura, An-Chi Tung, and Mun Sim Lai. 2012. "Population Aging, Economic Growth, and Intergenerational Transfers in Japan: How Dire Are the Prospects?" In *Aging, Economic Growth, and Old-Age Security in Asia*, edited by Donghyun Park, Sang-Hyop Lee, and Andrew Mason, 231–76. London and New York: Edward Elgar.

Ogawa, Naohiro, and Robert D. Retherford. 1993. "The Resumption of Fertility Decline in Japan: 1973–92." *Population and Development Review* 19: 703–41.

Retherford, Robert D., and Naohiro Ogawa. 2006. "Japan's Baby Bust: Causes, Implications, and Policy Responses." In *The Baby Bust: Who Will Do the Work? Who Will Pay the Taxes?*, edited by Fred R. Harris, 5–47. Lanham, Maryland: Rowman & Littlefield.

Rohwedder, Susann, and Robert J. Willis. 2010. "Mental Retirement." *Journal of Economic Perspectives* 24, no. 1: 119–38.

Skirbekk, Vegard, Valeria Bordone, and Daniela Weber. 2014. "A Cross-Country Comparison of Math Achievement at Teen Age and Cognitive Performance 40 Years Later." *Demographic Research* 31: 105–18.

Skirbekk, Vegard, Elke Loichinger, and Daniela Weber. 2012. "Variation in Cognitive Functioning as a Refined Approach to Comparing Aging Across Countries." *Proceedings of the National Academy of Sciences* 109: 770–74.

Slomski, Anita. 2014. "Midlife Diabetes, Hypertension, May Affect Cognition Later in Life." *JAMA* 311: 2056.

Statistics Bureau, Ministry of Internal Affairs and Communications, Japan. 2019. *Annual Report of the Labour Force Survey*.

Thorvaldsson, Valgeir, Scott M. Hofer, Stig Berg, and Boo Johansson. 2006. "Effects of Repeated Testing in a Longitudinal Age-Homogeneous Study of Cognitive Aging." *Journals of Gerontology. Series B, Psychological Sciences and Social Sciences* 61: 348–54.

UN (United Nations, Department of Economic and Social Affairs, Population Division). 2017. *World Population Prospects: The 2017 Revision.*

Usui, Emiko, Satoshi Shimizutani, and Takashi Oshio. 2016. "Health Capacity to Work at Older Ages: Evidence from Japan." NBER Working Paper no. 21971.

Weir, David, Margaret Lay, and Kenneth Langa. 2014. "Economic Development and Gender Inequality in Cognition: A Comparison of China and India, and of SAGE and the HRS Sister Studies." *Journal of the Economics of Ageing* 4: 114–25.

Wilson, Robert S. , Patricia A. Boyle, Eisuke Segawa, Lei Yu, Christopher T. Begeny, Sophia E. Anagnos, and David A. Bennett. 2013. "The Influence of Cognitive Decline on Well-Being in Old Age." *Psychology and Aging* 28: 304–13.

Yoshikawa, Hiroshi. 2001. *Japan's Lost Decade.* Tokyo: International House of Japan.

5 Sectoral Shift, Technological Change, and Older Labor

Evidence from the United States and South Korea

Chulhee Lee

Population aging is one of the most pressing economic and social issues in many nations today. Given the rising life expectancy and declining fertility rates, the proportion of the elderly population has been rapidly increasing in most developed countries and in many emerging nations. South Korea is no exception to this global phenomenon, and in fact, its current pace of population aging is much faster than that of most countries under the Organisation of Economic Cooperation and Development (OECD). According to the most recent government statistics, the current proportion of the population aged 65 and older is 14 percent and is projected to increase to approximately 40 percent by 2040 (Statistics Korea 2019).

Population aging is anticipated to radically change the fundamental features of economies and societies. Labor shortages, lowered productivity, and increased fiscal pressure on social insurance programs are among the most frequently mentioned economic consequences of this ongoing demographic change. For economists, one of the most critical issues related to population aging is the trend and determinants of the labor force participation of older adults. As the elderly population increases, their potential work contribution becomes an increasingly

Note: This chapter is based largely on the author's previous studies on the employment and economic status of older adults in the United States and in South Korea over the last 25 years. The introduction of methods and explanations of major results are freely drawn from Lee (1998, 2002, 2004, 2005, 2010, 2015, and 2019). Additional work was supported by the Center for Distributive Justice at the SNU Economic Research Institute.

important determinant of the overall size of the labor force. Accordingly, one of the primary policy measures proposed in response to the potential labor market problems associated with an aging of society is to encourage the employment of older workers.

A potentially important trend determinant of elderly participation in the labor force is the emergence of new technologies, which is often symbolized by the development of information technology (IT), diffusion of automation, and the emergence of artificial intelligence (AI). A few studies have investigated and predicted the labor market consequences of the technological changes of the Fourth Industrial Revolution. Debates are ongoing on whether newly invented machines would radically replace human labor and on the kinds of jobs that would be vulnerable to the effects of technological changes (Autor, Levy, and Murnane 2003; Goos and Manning 2007; Graetz and Michaels 2015; Autor 2015; Frey and Osborne 2017). Recent studies have investigated the employment effects of robot adoption (Acemoglu and Restrepo 2017; Lee, Decker, and Chung 2019).

Few studies have investigated how technological changes affect young and old workers differently, compared with the attention given to the differences across workers with disparate human capital or skills. Using U.S. commuting zone data, Acemoglu and Restrepo (2018) examined whether robot adoption affects middle-aged and older workers' employment. They found that robot adoptions tend to reduce employment and earnings of middle-aged workers but have no impact on older workers. Because middle-aged workers are more likely to engage in blue-collar jobs that can be automated by robots, they explain, those workers are more susceptible to job loss due to robot adoption. They also found that countries experiencing rapid aging are more likely to invest in robots. Their estimates suggest that aging explains 40 percent to 65 percent of the cross-country variation in robot adoptions.

As marginal workers in the labor market, older adults may likely be vulnerable to radical economic changes such as the emergence of new technology. As noted by Acemoglu and Restrepo (2018), the potential disadvantages associated with aging may stem from the lower level of skills possessed by older workers, compared with younger ones. However, even with the same quality of human capital, the labor market effects of technological changes could be strongly felt among older adults. A simple model illustrates how technological changes can differently affect the employment of older workers even without any productivity and replacement effects. The probability of retirement at a point in time for the self-employed and the majority of the salaried workers who are not subject to mandatory retirement may be determined by the expected net gains from retirement, which is denoted by R^* in equation (1).

$$R_i^* = R(\bar{Z} - Z_i, N_i, X_i, B_i, \theta_i). \tag{1}$$

I hypothesize that the costs and benefits of retirement are determined by the discrepancy between the amount of minimum work efforts (such as hours and intensity of work) required by a job (denoted by $\bar{Z}$) and the desirable amount of work efforts that the individual worker i would choose under no restriction (denoted by Z_i).[1] $\bar{Z}$ is determined by various job-specific demand-side factors, such as production technology, managerial practices, and labor market condition, and Z_i is determined by the taste and productivity of the individual worker i. The value of retirement is likewise determined by the demographic and job characteristics of the worker (denoted as X_i and B_i, respectively) that are not fully captured by the term $(\bar{Z} - Z_i)$ as well as retirement incomes (denoted by vector N_i). θ_i denotes unobservable personal characteristics.

Aging diminishes a worker's physical strength, functional ability, and preferences regarding work, thus decreasing the desirable amount of work effort (Z_i). The discrepancy increases as long as the minimum work effort required by the job $(\bar{Z})$ remains fixed, thereby raising the value of retirement. Thus, the size of $(\bar{Z} - Z_i)$ depends on (1) the quality of matching between the worker and the job in terms of the desirable and required amounts of work effort, and (2) the ability of the worker to change the required work effort $(\bar{Z})$ either within the same job or by switching jobs.

Technological changes can alter the quality of matching or its relationship with aging by modifying the relative sizes of industrial sectors with varying degrees of work flexibility. As a person ages, the gradual changes in health, preferences regarding work, and other factors affecting labor force participation make it preferable for the aging person to reduce the amount of work by degrees rather than to work full time and then retire completely. This gradual retirement is a possible option in several sectors, especially among the self-employed.

Technological changes within a sector (or even within an establishment) could likewise affect the employment of older workers.

---

1   This model is drawn from the conceptual framework used in Lee (2008) and Lee and Lee (2013).

Technological progress is often associated with radical changes in job requirements and working conditions. Adoption of new technology can make it increasingly costly for older workers to continue working as the speed and intensity of work as well as the requirements for skills increase, possibly beyond their physical and mental capacities. Given their deteriorating physical strength and health, obsolete skills and knowledge, and lack of education compared with young cohorts, older workers have lower capabilities (or incentives) to learn to meet new work requirements. Returns from training generally decrease as workers age; thus employers would be unwilling to invest in the training of older workers, thereby increasing the severity of their disadvantages.

I provide two cases of historical evidence in this chapter of how rapid changes in the industrial structure and production technology affect the employment and retirement of older adults, specifically, in the United States from 1880 to 1940 and in South Korea from 1960 to 2015. Both nations experienced radical economic and social changes during these periods. The United States transformed from an agrarian society into the world's strongest industrial power as the Second Industrial Revolution occurred and matured. Similarly, South Korea transformed from a poor country recovering from a devastating war into one of the fastest-growing economies in the late twentieth century. Therefore, these two historical cases from opposite sides of the globe and during different time periods may offer useful insights into the effects of rapid and radical economic changes on aged labor.

Labor Market Status of Older Adults in the United States During the Industrial Era

The United States experienced a rapid maturing and deepening of industrialization from the late nineteenth to the early twentieth century, which is generally referred to as the Industrial Era. As a consequence, the proportion of the labor force in agriculture shrank considerably during this period. The effects of the changes in the industrial structure on the employment of older Americans during this era are well documented. Contemporary and historical studies widely acknowledge that, owing to its considerable flexibility, self-employed jobs, particularly farming, are more favorable for the employment of older workers compared with salaried jobs. The self-employed can remain in the workforce until late in life by adjusting their work efforts in accordance with their changing health, preferences, and economic needs. This reasoning led early studies on the older labor force to conclude that the decline of agriculture caused a decline in the labor market involvement of older men (Durand 1948; Long 1958; Bancroft 1958).

Manufacturing in the United States likewise went through dramatic technological transformations during this period, which is known as the Second Industrial Revolution. This period is characterized by the growth of large modern firms, the emergence of new products, power sources, and technologies, and changes in the industrial structure (Chandler 1977, 1990). It is during this period that scientific knowledge began to be systematically applied to industrial technology, mass production methods spread, and knowledge of scientific management was adopted in workplaces. In terms of the long-term impact on productivity and human well-being, the technological changes of this era are arguably the most critical in all of modern times—even more so than those of the First Industrial Revolution or the information technology revolution in recent decades (Gordon 2000).

Contemporary observers believed that older workers were reduced to "industrial scrap heaps," victimized by the consequences of technological changes. According to these accounts, older industrial workers were subject to a high probability of job loss and forced retirement because of unfavorable work conditions, such as less flexibility and increased work intensity (Squier 1912; Epstein 1928). A well-known anecdote is the exodus of older operatives from the printing industry upon the adoption of fast machines (Graebner 1980). Industrialization also brought considerable disadvantages in employment associated with aging, such as serious age discrimination and the high importance of job-specific skills that inhibited the hiring and training of older workers (Slichter 1919; Haber 1983).

This conventional view of the labor market status of older adults and reasons for retirement was challenged by later studies that suggested an optimistic portrait of old-aged life. According to this revisionist view, the labor market status of older adults is not degraded by the impact of industrialization, as previously believed. This new interpretation of the economic activity state of older persons is based on evidence that tends to reject the key theses of the traditional view. First, Ransom and Sutch (1986) reported that the labor force participation rate (LFPR) of older males was stable at a relatively low level until the enactment of the Social Security Act in 1935. Therefore, the idea that older workers were being forced out of employment is questionable.

A number of recent studies have suggested that farmers were no less likely to retire than nonfarmers in the early-twentieth century (Moen 1994; Costa 1995; Carter and Sutch 1996), which implies that the decline in agriculture could not explain the fall in the labor market activity of older males.

These new results, in turn, led to a favorable view of retirement during the turn of the century. Gratton (1986, 96) maintained that the relatively low LFPR among older men could be explained at least partly as the "voluntary action by workers who chose more leisure and some income over little leisure and more income." In support of this view, Gratton (1996) reported that the real incomes of older workers rose during the late nineteenth and early twentieth centuries and that "family economic strategies" (old-age support provided by family members) provided older adults with the promise of considerable security. Carter and Sutch (1996) asserted that the retirement pattern in the early twentieth century was modern in the sense that men planned their retirement through savings.

Labor force participation of older adult males, 1880–1940

As noted earlier, the trend of the LFPR of older adult men is one of the major issues concerning the pattern of aging and retirement during the early twentieth century. In particular, the status of the long-term unemployed is central in the debate over the definition of the labor force and the LFPR trend of older males before 1940. Although the controversy over the same trend in 1870 and 1880 stems from different sources, the main point remains: whether to include older adults who had gainful occupations but who may be practically out of the labor force (Ransom and Sutch 1986, 1989; Moen 1987). If the long-term unemployed (reporting six or more months of unemployment) is considered as "permanently unemployed" and thus excluded from the labor force, then the declining trend of the LFPR of older adult men during the Industrial Era disappears.

To resolve the disagreement, I attempted to determine whether the labor market behavior of the long-term unemployed (hereafter UNEMP) is similar to that of the employed (hereafter EMP) or to that of the retired (hereafter RET). Using a longitudinal sample of aged Union Army veterans, I found that UNEMP is distinct from EMP and RET in terms of the probability of labor force participation 10 years later and the equations governing their participation decisions (Lee

1998). The study compromised the need for a two-state classification and the behavioral difference between UNEMP and the other states by treating UNEMP as a mixed group of EMP and RET, as presented in equation (2):

$$LF|_{UNEMP} = \gamma \cdot LF|_{RET} + (1-\gamma) \cdot LF|_{EMP} \qquad (2)$$

Utilizing the relative size of the probability of remaining in the labor force, I estimated that the proportion of the retired men among UNEMP (γ) is 51 percent.

Table 5.1 reports the trend in the LFPR of men aged 60 and over and those aged 65 and over, based on three distinct definitions of the

TABLE 5.1 Estimated labor force participation rates in the United States, 1880–1940

	1880	1900	1910	1920	1930	1940
A. Age 60 and over						
Mean unemployed months[a]	6.58	5.95	4.25			
LU / U[b]	55.8	49.4	31.2			
LU / P[c]	16.9	7.1	2.2			
LFPR (including LU)[d]	84.5	73.2	69.1			54.7
LFPR (+ half of LU)[e]	76.1	69.7	68.0			
LFPR (R & S)[†]	64.3	66.1			64.5	
B. Age 65 and over						
Mean unemployed months[a]	7.28	6.28	4.69			
LU / U[b]	63.1	52.2	35.4			
LU / P[c]	17.6	6.6	2.1			
LFPR (including LU)[d]	78.6	65.2	58.9			43.5
LFPR (+ half of LU)[e]	69.8	61.9	57.9			
LFPR (Moen / Long)[‡]	78.0	65.4	58.1	60.1	58.0	43.5

NOTE: [a]Mean length of unemployment among those who had experienced unemployment.
[b]Proportion of the long-term unemployed (LU) among those with any length of unemployment (U).
[c]Proportion of the long-term unemployed (LU) among all men in the sample (P). The estimate for 1880 is upper bound. See text for the method.
[d]LFPR calculated based on the assumption that the long-term unemployed were in the labor force.
[e]LFPR calculated assuming that a half of the long-term unemployed were out of the labor force. The upper bound of the estimate of LU/P was used: LFPR (+ half of LU) = LFPR (including LU) − [(LU/P) × 0.5]
SOURCE: Lee (1998). The figures in the first five rows of each section were originally calculated from the public-use micro samples of the censuses of 1880, 1900, 1910, and 1940.
[†]Ransom and Sutch (1986).
[‡]Moen (1987) for 1880, 1900, and 1940, and Long (1958) for 1910–1930.

labor force according to the proportion of the UNEMP who are likely to be RET. The intermediate estimate in which half of the UNEMP are counted in the labor force shows a clear downward tendency for the period between 1880 and 1940. The LFPR among men aged 60 and over is 79.2% in 1880, 69.7% in 1900, and 68.0% in 1910. For men aged 65 and over, the LFPR is 69.8%, 61.9%, and 57.9% for 1880, 1900, and 1910, respectively. The fall in the LFPR among men aged 65 and over prior to 1940 accounts for nearly half of the entire decline between 1880 and 1990. This result suggests that the secular decline in the labor force participation of older males started as early as the end of the nineteenth century, as the traditional view proposes.

Sectoral shift and the labor force participation of older adult males

The traditional view of the decrease in the labor market involvement of older adult men suggests that it was in part produced by the decline of the agricultural sector. This explanation is based on the belief that farmers tend to stay in the labor force longer than those who are employed in nonagricultural occupations, owing to the considerable flexibility of farming. Indeed, many farmers in the United States during the nineteenth and early twentieth centuries gradually left the workforce because they were able to reduce the hours and intensity of work by adjusting acreage and crop mix or by adopting mechanization (Pedersen 1950). Thus, the decline of farming during industrialization likely decreased the LFPR of older adults.

However, the validity of this view is questioned in later studies. Moen (1994) reported that many older adult males living in rural nonfarming households who were not gainfully employed could have been former farmers who moved off the farm upon retirement. This finding implies that the LFPR of men living in farming households would overstate the participation rate of farmers. Using a longitudinal sample of aged Union Army veterans, Costa (1995) found that farmers and nonfarmers are not statistically different in terms of the probability of being out of the labor force between 1900 and 1910. Carter and Sutch (1996) likewise compared the hazard rate of leaving the labor force at the turn of the century between self-employed farmers and nonfarmers by applying the so-called census survivor method based on the 1900 and 1910 censuses. Farmers were found to more likely retire, compared with nonfarmers, which implies that the decline of agriculture could explain the decrease in the LFPR of older adult males around the turn of the century. That the self-employed, particularly farmers, tend to retire at earlier ages compared with industrial workers has been interpreted as evidence that retirement during the turn of the century was more voluntary than forced (Carter and Sutch 1996).

A drawback of the evidence against the sectoral shift hypothesis is that it is drawn from a single decade (from 1900 to 1910). To obtain a general picture of the Industrial Era as a whole, I estimated the hazards of the labor force participation of farmers and nonfarmers within each decade from 1880 to 1940, based on the census survivor method (Lee 2002), which is briefly introduced as follows. Let N_x and N_x^j denote, respectively, the total number of a cohort in the labor force aged x and the number of the cohort at the same age who is employed in industry j. The number of the cohort who is employed in industry j at age $x + 1$ (N_{x+1}^j) is determined by the probability of dying between x and $x + 1$ (denoted d_x^j), the probability of retirement at age $x + 1$, which is conditional on surviving until age $x + 1$ (r_x^j), and the probability of net entry from other industries, which is conditional on remaining in the labor force (m_x^j), as given in equation (3):

$$N_{x+1}^j = N_x^j (1 - d_x^j)(1 - r_x^j)(1 + m_x^j) \tag{3}$$

Using the preceding equation, the change in the share of a cohort employed in industry j between x and $x + 1$ can be presented as follows:

$$\frac{N_{x+1}^j}{N_{x+1}} - \frac{N_x^j}{N_x} = \frac{N_x^j(1-d_x^j)(1-r_x^j)(1+m_x^j)}{N_x(1-d_x)(1-r_x)(1+m_x)} - \frac{N_x^j}{N_x} = \frac{N_x^j}{N_x}\left(\frac{(1-d_x^j)(1-r_x^j)(1+m_x^j)}{(1-d_x)(1-r_x)(1+m_x)} - 1\right) \tag{4}$$

If it is assumed that the age-specific mortality is the same for all industries, that is, $d_x^j = d_x$ for all j, then the labor market survival rate between x and $x + 1$, which is conditional on remaining alive, can be defined as follows:

$$S_x^j = (1 - r_x^j)(1 + m_x^j) \tag{5}$$

Applying equation (3), the ratio of the labor force share of farmers (N_{x+1}^F / N_{x+1}) to that of nonfarmers (N_{x+1}^N / N_{x+1}) for the cohort aged $x + 1$ in a given year is presented as

$$\frac{N_{x+1}^F / N_{x+1}}{N_{x+1}^N / N_{x+1}} = \frac{N_{x+1}^F}{N_{x+1}^N} = \frac{N_x^F(1-d_x^F)(1-r_x^F)(1+m_x^F)}{N_x^N(1-d_x^N)(1-r_x^N)(1+m_x^N)} \tag{6}$$

where F and N stand for farmers and nonfarmers, respectively. If we assume that the age-specific mortality rate is the same for farmers and nonfarmers, and we apply the definition of the labor market survival rate, which is presented in equation (5), the ratio of the labor market survival rate of nonfarmers to that of farmers, which is denoted by α, is given as follows

$$\alpha = \frac{S^N}{S^F} = \frac{(N^N_{x+1} / N^F_{x+1})}{(N^N_x / N^F_x)} \tag{7}$$

The labor market survival rate for the entire labor force can be calculated as the weighted average of the survival rates for farmers and nonfarmers, as follows:

$$S = \omega^F S^F + (1 - \omega^F)S^F \tag{8}$$

If a rather strong assumption is imposed that the rate of net transitions between agriculture and nonagriculture is zero (that is, $m^F = m^N = 0$), then S is the hazard LFPR within a given period.

The results on occupation-specific labor market survival rates suggest that older adult farmers are more likely to remain in the labor force 10 years later than nonfarmers for all decades, except in the years between 1900 and 1910. The evidence against the agricultural decline hypothesis (Costa 1995; Carter and Sutch 1996) is mainly drawn from the first decade of the twentieth century, when the retirement rate of farmers relative to nonfarmers was unusually high. This peculiarity of the decade may be explained by the unusually rapid growth in the value of farm property during the period of 1895 to 1915. In another study, I found that the average farm value of a county shows a strong positive effect on the odds of the retirement of farm owners during the first decade of the twentieth century (Lee 1999). In addition, farm owners in counties that experienced a rapid growth in farm value between 1900 and 1910 were more likely to retire by 1910. The overall results from all six decades largely support the traditional view that farmers were less likely than nonfarmers to retire during the industrialization era.

I further examined the percentage decline of the LFPR of aged men between 1880 and 1940, which can be attributed to the decline in the relative size of agriculture. First, I calculated a counterfactual hazard rate of participation (S^*) that would have resulted if the percentage of farmers in the male labor force remained unchanged since 1820, by replacing the weight of farmers (ω^F) with the value as of 1820 in equation (6). Second, the LFPR at a certain age (P_{50+k}) can be presented in terms of the LFPR at the initial age, which is defined here as 50 (P_{50}), and the hazard rate of participation within each age interval (S_j), as shown in the following equation:

$$P_{50+k} = \prod_{i=50}^{50+k-1} P_{50}S_i. \qquad (9)$$

Applying the counterfactual hazard rate (S_j^*) to equation (9) instead of the actual rate, I estimated the counterfactual LFPR of each cohort at ages 60 through 69 and 70 through 79 that would have resulted if the share of farmers in the labor force had remained unchanged since 1820.

Columns 1 through 5 in table 5.2 report the actual and counterfactual LFPR at ages 50 through 59, 60 through 69, and 70 through 79 between 1880 and 1940. The final two columns in table 5.2 compare the actual and counterfactual LFPR of males at ages 60 through 79. These rates are the weighted averages of the LFPRs for ages 60 through 69 and for ages 70 through 79, which are reported in columns 2 through 4. The actual LFPR of men aged 60 through 79 fell from 86.7% in 1880 to 59.4% in 1940. This result indicates that the LFPR of older males in 1940 would have been 65.5% instead of 59.4% had there been no decline in agriculture since 1820. Therefore,

TABLE 5.2 Actual and counterfactual labor force participation rate of men 60–79, 1880–1940

Year	(1) P_{50-59}	(2) P_{60-69}	(3) P_{60-69}^*	(4) P_{70-79}	(5) P_{70-79}^*	(6) ω_{60-69}	(7) P_{60-79}	(8) P_{60-79}^*
1880	0.967	0.913	—	0.757	—	0.705	0.867	—
1890	0.947	0.882	0.870	0.703	—	0.699	0.828	—
1900	0.938	0.843	0.864	0.596	0.723	0.692	0.767	0.821
1910	0.951	0.812	0.779	0.528	0.536	0.700	0.727	0.706
1920	0.938	0.834	0.782	0.521	0.508	0.708	0.743	0.701
1930	0.945	0.821	0.825	0.454	0.461	0.692	0.708	0.713
1940	0.903	0.712	0.770	0.341	0.408	0.682	0.594	0.655

NOTE: P_a denotes the labor force participation rate at age a. ω_{60-69} denotes the share of men aged 60–69 among the entire male population between 60 and 79. P_a^* stands for the estimated counterfactual labor force participation rate at age a that would have occurred had the farmers' share in the male work force remained unchanged since 1820.
SOURCE: Lee (2002). Actual figures reported in columns (1), (2), (4), (6), and (7) were originally calculated from IPUMS of the censuses for 1880, 1900, 1910, 1920, and 1940, and the published census for 1930 (U.S. Bureau of the Census 1933). Counterfactual figures reported in columns (3), (5), and (8) are estimated using the actual labor force participation rate at ages 50–59 and counterfactual hazard rates of labor force participation.

the decline in the relative size of the labor force that was employed in agriculture explains approximately 22% of the fall in the LFPR of older males between 1880 and 1940. The effect of sectoral shift was particularly strong from 1880 to 1900, which explains more than half of the decline in LFPR.

Technological changes and employment of older manufacturing workers

Manufacturing industries in the United States underwent tremendous transformations in production technologies, work organizations, and managerial practices in the late nineteenth and early twentieth centuries. The key features of these technological changes are the application of scientific knowledge to industrial production and the adoption of scientific management in the workplace. Firms rapidly grew in size, labor productivity soared, and production became heavily dependent on materials and energy, especially electric power. The prevailing workings hours decreased during this period, particularly after 1909, though the prevalence of shorter workdays probably came with strengthened intensity of work (Whaples 1990). In addition, the numbers of managers and clerks per worker appeared to increase.

I explored how industry-specific technological, organizational, and managerial characteristics affected the labor market status of older male manufacturing workers in the United States during the early twentieth century (Lee 2015). For that purpose, I compiled industry-level data from the 1899 and 1909 manufacturing censuses and linked them to the 1910 census of the Integrated Public Use Microdata Series (IPUMS USA) and a longitudinal sample of Union Army veterans. The obtained results showed several industrial characteristics that are favorably related to the labor market status of older industrial workers, including high labor productivity, less capital- or material-intensive production technologies, short workdays, low work intensity, considerable job flexibility, and formalized employment relationship. These industrial characteristics accounted for the observed interindustry differences in the incidence of long-term unemployment among older adult male workers.

These results suggest that the transformations in the U.S. industry probably brought about favorable and adverse consequences to the labor market status of older manufacturing workers. Technical progress and organizational modifications may have improved their employment prospects by improving labor productivity, diminishing working hours, and formalizing employment relations. However, technical innovations that led to capital- and material-intensive productions may have forced older workers out of their jobs by augmenting the requirements for physical strength, mental agility, and ability to acquire new skills. Given that the pace and features of technological changes differed across industries and possibly across firms within the same industry, the experiences of individual older workers were presumably highly heterogeneous. In certain industries, a few older adult workers were probably relegated to the state of "industrial scrap heap," as claimed by contemporary critics. However, such a pessimistic view of aged workers may not be generalized for all manufacturing industries.

I attempted to investigate which of the two opposite effects is stronger. The question is related to the issue of whether the "industrial scrap heap" argument describes the experiences of a typical industrial worker a hundred years ago. A rough means of addressing this question is to investigate whether older manufacturing workers are likely to be employed in industries in which the negative influences of technological changes are stronger than the positive effects. For this purpose, I estimated the industry-specific probability of long-term unemployment that is predicted by the industry variables used in the regression analyses. The estimated regression coefficient of each industry variable was then applied to the industry average of the variable. A relatively high predicted probability of long-term unemployment in a given industry indicates that the technological features of the industry are relatively unfavorable for the employment of older workers.

I then explored how this industry-specific measure of long-term unemployment risk (denoted as "prob_unemp") is related to the industry's share of male workers aged 50 and older (denoted as "share_age50"). The result presented in figure 5.1 shows that the industry share of aged workers is positively associated with the predicted probability of long-term unemployment. The regression coefficient is 5.2996 (p-value = 0.0053), which suggests that aged manufacturing workers are heavily concentrated in "unfavorable" industries. Approximately 67 percent of manufacturing workers aged 50 and older are employed in industries in which the predicted unemployment risk is above the average of the entire manufacturing sector. Although circumstantial, the evidence suggests that the contemporary argument of the "industrial scrap heap" was applicable for most of the manufacturing workers in the United States in the early twentieth century.

FIGURE 5.1 Relationship between industry share of male workers aged 50 and older and the predicted risk of long-term unemployment across industries

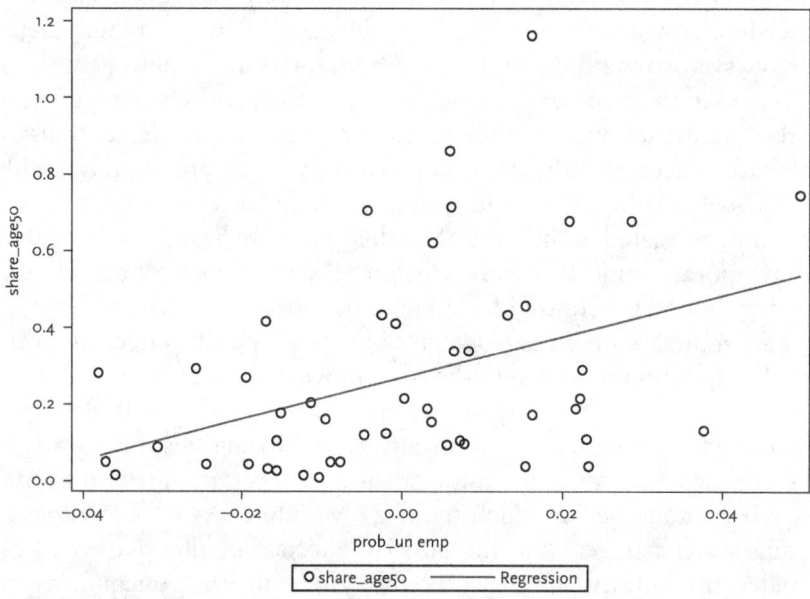

NOTE: Each industry's share of employment of male workers aged 50 and older was computed from the IPUMS of the 1910 census. The predicted probability of long-term unemployment was computed based on the result of logistic regression reported in table 4 of Lee (2015).
SOURCE: Lee (2015).

Long-term Change in the Labor Force Participation of Older Males in South Korea

Similar to the case of the United States in the past, the long-term tendency of retirement is a useful starting point for examining how economic changes in South Korea affect the labor-market status of the older adult population. Figure 5.2 shows how the LFPR of males aged 60 and over in South Korea has changed over time since the early 1960s based on the Population Census and the Economically Active Population (EAP) Survey.[2] In a comparative perspective, the most remarkable

2   The EAP is the most widely used microlevel labor survey that provides basic information on employment and unemployment in South Korea. One advantage

FIGURE 5.2 Labor force participation rate of males aged 60 and older in Korea, 1963–2015

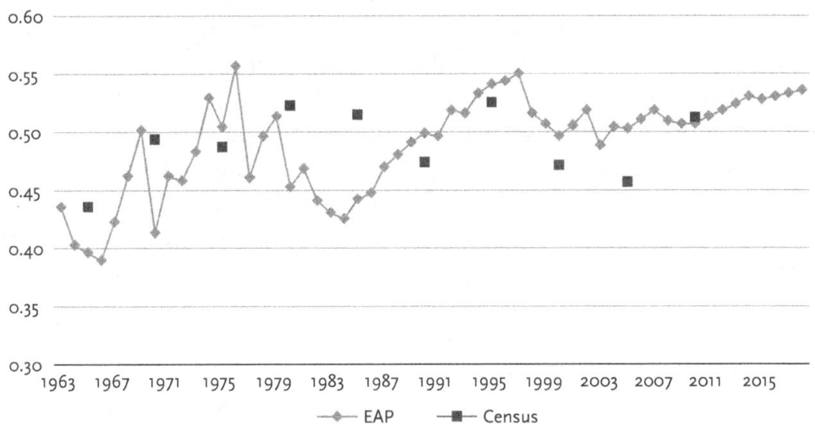

SOURCE: South Korea Population Census and Economically Active Population Survey (EAP).

feature of the observed trend is that the LFPR of older men in South Korea *increased* rather than decreased between the mid-1960s and the late 1990s. According to the results based on the EAP, the LFPR rose from 40% in 1965 to 55% in 1997. The estimate from the census shows a similar trend, with the LFPR rising from 44% to 53% between 1965 and 1995. This pattern is sharply distinct from the historical experience of most OECD countries, where there was a rapid decline in the labor force participation of older males during the entire or second half of the twentieth century. The LFPR of older males fell dramatically after 1997, presumably because of the adverse labor market effect of the financial crisis.

Why is South Korea highly different from other countries in terms of the labor market involvement of the older adult population? One

of this source over the census data is that the continuous yearly estimate of the LFPR from 1963 until the present can be obtained from the data. In addition, the most widely used definition of *employed* and *unemployed* persons as labor force participants can be consistently applied each year using this survey. *The employed is defined as all persons working at least one hour or more for pay or profits, including those working 18 hours or more as unpaid family workers during the reference week. I defined *labor force participation* as close as possible to that of the EAP when the census was used. See Lee (2010) for the differences in the definition of *participation* between the census and the EAP.

clue is the finding that the LFPR increase of older males in South Korea between 1965 and 1995 can be explained largely by the increase in the labor market activity of the older adult population in rural areas (Lee 2010).[3] The LFPR of older males is higher among the rural population compared with city dwellers, and the proportion of the older adult male population living in urban areas has rapidly increased since 1960. Therefore, other things being equal, the LFPR of aged men would have declined owing to the shift toward the urban and nonfarming sectors, as in the case of the United States in the past. However, in South Korea, the dramatic increase in the LFPR of aged men in rural areas more than offsets this countervailing force resulting from urbanization and agricultural decline.

A possible explanation for the LFPR increase among the rural elderly population is the effect of the mass migration of the rural population to the urban and nonagricultural sectors (Yoon 1984; Moon et al. 1991; E. Lee 1993; Kim et al. 1997). The selective out-migration of young people accelerated population aging in rural areas, which in turn may have produced a rise in the LFPR of older men for the following reasons. First, if young and aged workers are substitutes in the labor market, then the out-migration of the young may have increased the value of the aged workers' marginal labor productivity, thereby raising the opportunity cost of retirement. Second, the self-employed, particularly farmers, may have been forced to work for prolonged periods owing to the loss of family labor. In support of this hypothesis, I found that the percentage of males aged 60 and over in each city or county, which is an indicator of the degree of population aging in the locality, shows a strong positive effect on the odds of labor force participation, especially in rural areas (Lee 2010).

An intriguing question that is related to the rising LFPR of the rural older adult population is why the South Korean case is very different from the historical experiences of other developed nations that likewise experienced a large-scale population movement from rural to urban areas that brought about population aging in countryside. In the United States during the early twentieth century, as in the case of South Korea,

---

3   The LFPR in rural areas increased by 30 percentage points, from 46 percent in 1965 to 70 percent in 1995, which is in sharp contrast to a rise of only 4 percentage points among urban dwellers. Within the rural areas, the older men in the countryside (*myon* areas) experienced a much greater increase in participation compared to those living in towns (*eup* areas).

farmers remained in the labor force longer than nonfarmers, owing to the considerable flexibility of farming. However, the pace of the decline in the LFPR of older males in the United States was not significantly different between farmers and nonfarmers from 1880 to 1940 (Lee 2002). It was quite common for an older farmer to sell his farm, move to a nearby town, and lead a relatively independent retirement (Moen 1994; Lee 1999).

A possible answer could be that the relative decline of the rural economy during the course of industrialization made it increasingly difficult for the rural older adult population to save for retirement. The ratio of the income of farm households to the income of urban households shows a long-term decreasing trend. Rural farmers and residents possessed a smaller amount of wealth and were less prepared for retirement compared with city dwellers in the late 1990s.[4] Statistics on wealth holdings suggested that the majority of older farmers may have encountered difficulties in financing their retirement by selling their farm properties. In 1995, for instance, the average value of wealth held by farm households was 150 million KRW, which was approximately 10 times the average farm household expenditure (Korea National Statistical Office 1995). Given the highly skewed wealth distribution in rural areas, the median value of wealth possessed by farm households should be much lower than the average.

Sectoral shift and aged labor

I investigated the effects of long-term changes in the industrial structure in South Korea on the economic activity of older males on the basis of similar methods used in analyzing the case of the United States (described earlier, in "Sectoral Shift and the Labor Force Participation of Older Adult Males"). The analysis used a 2 percent random sample of the population and housing censuses for 1980, 1985, 1990, 1995, and 2000 (Lee 2004). The percentage of the labor force that is employed in

---

4   By the early 2000s, farm households received 78% of the income earned by urban households. According to the 1996 National Survey of Family Income and Expenditure, the average amount of net savings of rural households was only 76% of the net wealth held by urban households (Korea National Statistical Office 2000, 3–13). The result of the 1994 Social Statistics Survey indicates that people living in rural areas are much less prepared financially for retirement than city dwellers. While 57% of urban respondents have made preparations for retirement, only 41% of rural respondents have done so (Korea National Statistical Office 2000, 3–13).

agriculture has considerably declined since 1980, and the relative sizes of most manufacturing industries have slightly decreased or remained stable. In contrast to these rather traditional industries, most service industries have remarkably expanded. If the degree of disadvantages associated with old age in the labor market differs across industries, then such a radical shift in the industrial structure should have exerted a strong impact on the overall pressure toward leaving the labor force at an old age by altering the relative proportion of jobs that are favorable or unfavorable to the employment of older adults.

A comparison of the relative labor market survival rate (defined in equation 5) from 1980 to 2000 across industries shows that the strength of pressure to leave the labor market at an old age considerably differed across industries. Employment at old age was relatively stable for those in agriculture, insurance, real estate, and business services, as indicated by the positive sign and the relatively high labor market survival rate for those sectors. By contrast, male workers who were employed in most manufacturing industries, especially textiles, wood and lumber, pulp and paper, and primary metal, began to face strong pressure to leave their jobs as early as the age of 45. Men who were employed in a number of service sectors, such as retail, restaurant and accommodation, transportation, telecommunication, and finance, began to be pushed out of the labor market from the ages of 50 to 54.

I examined how the long-term decline of agriculture affected the LFPR of aged men between 1980 and 2000. Applying the same methods that are explained earlier, I compared the actual LFPR with the counterfactual LFPR that would have resulted had there been no relative decline in agriculture since 1980. The results reported in table 5.3 suggest that the decline of agriculture has a strong negative effect on the overall LFPR of older males. The sectoral shift played a powerful role of offsetting the increase in the actual LFPR of aged men between 1985 and 1995 and became the major factor in the sharp decline in the LFPR from 1995 to 2000.

A comparison of the changes in the actual and counterfactual LFPRs, which are 12.5% points and –6.7% points, respectively, suggests that the decline of agriculture can explain nearly half (46%) of the fall in the labor market activity of men aged 55 to 69.[5] The effect of the shrinkage of agriculture can explain 84% of the actual fall in the

---

5   The decline in the LFPR would have been 6.7% points had there been no agricultural decline, and thus the fall in the LFPR that can be explained by the sectoral

TABLE 5.3 Actual and counterfactual labor force participation rates of men aged 55–69, 1985–2000

Year	(1) P_{55-59}	(2) P^*_{55-59}	(3) P_{60-64}	(4) P^*_{60-64}	(5) P_{65-69}	(6) P^*_{65-69}	(7) P_{55-69}	(8) P^*_{55-69}
1985	0.815	0.815	0.679	0.679	0.531	0.531	0.703	0.703
1990	0.817	0.822	0.642	0.649	0.494	0.500	0.689	0.695
1995	0.853	0.865	0.698	0.728	0.525	0.559	0.732	0.755
2000	0.719	0.774	0.581	0.684	0.467	0.556	0.607	0.688

NOTE: P_a denotes the actual labor force participation rate at age a. P^*_a stands for the estimated counterfactual labor force participation rate at age a that would have occurred had the farmers' share in the male work force remained unchanged since 1980.
SOURCE: Lee (2004). Actual figures were originally calculated from the 2 percent samples of the censuses from 1980 to 2000. Counterfactual figures were estimated using the actual labor force participation rate at ages 50–54 and counterfactual hazard rates of labor force participation.

LFPR of men aged 55 to 69 (9.6% points) if the entire 15-year period from 1985 to 2000 is considered. This result strongly suggests that the relative decline in the population that was employed in agriculture is probably the single most important cause of the overall decline in the labor force participation rate of older males in South Korea since 1980.

In addition, I estimated how changing the industrial structure affected the average employment stability of older workers. For this purpose, I calculated the weighted average of the estimated labor market survival rates, using the percentage of the labor force employed in each industry each year. This weighted average of the relative survival rate for a cohort aged x, which is computed based on the industry weights for year t (S^t_x), can be presented as

$$S^j_x = \sum_j \omega^{j,t}_x S^{j,85-95}_x, \qquad (10)$$

where t denotes the baseline year, $\omega^{j,t}_x$ is the weight of industry j in year t, and $S^{j,85-95}_x$ is the relative labor market survival rate of industry j for the period 1985–95. The outcome of the computation shows the counterfactual labor market survival rate that would have resulted if the industrial structure in a given year had remained unchanged throughout the study period.

The results of this analysis suggest that the shift in the industrial structure negatively affects the labor market prospects of male workers

---

shift is 5.8% points (12.5% less 6.7%), which is 46% of the actual decline in the LFPR (12.5% points).

aged 55 and over. The average labor market survival rate, which is computed based on the 1980 industrial composition, is 0.0525, whereas the survival rate, which is calculated by applying the 2000 industry weights, is 0.0036. This result indicates that, during these two decades, the industrial structure shifted in direction to decrease the relative sizes of industries that are favorable to the employment of older workers. A similar analysis based on data for the years 2000 to 2010 shows that the industrial structure changed in direction to decrease the average labor market survival rate of older males in the subsequent decade (Lee 2012).

Technological change and older adult labor

How will new advances in technology, which are often symbolized by AI and automations in production, change the labor market in the future? Growing evidence suggests that the labor market consequences of technological changes, if any, would probably be heterogeneous across jobs with disparate human capital requirements and workplace characteristics. Older adult workers tend to have more obsolete skills, are less efficient in learning, and are less mobile across jobs compared with young people. As such, their labor market status could be strongly influenced by rapid changes in production methods and managerial practices. The mechanism or causal chain underlying these observed patterns appears related to technological changes that can affect the employment of aged workers by changing their relative productivity and by altering the quality of the matching with their jobs.

I investigated how the adoption of new production technologies affects the employment of older South Korean workers by using establishment-level panel data that are newly linked with administrative records (Lee 2019). The Workplace Panel Survey (WPS) series, conducted by the Korean Labor Research Institute in 2005, 2007, 2009, 2011, 2013, and 2015, provides detailed information on each establishment, including variables pertaining to workplace innovations in production, organization, and human resource management (see Lee 2019 for details). The Korean Employment Insurance records were matched with the WPS, and offer information on wages, labor market transitions, and personal characteristics of the individuals employed in workplaces included in the WPS.

For constructing variables pertaining to the adoption of technological innovations, I utilized responses to the following three questions:

(1) whether the firm used new automation processes in 2015, (2) how much the investments in IT sectors increased in 2015, and (3) how much the purchase of IT equipment increased in 2015. I examined how the adoption of new technologies affects the probabilities of employees leaving their jobs and how the effects differ between old and young workers by estimating the equation

$$P_{ij} = \alpha + \beta_1 A_{ij} T_j + \beta_2 A_{ij} + \beta_3 T_j + \gamma X_{ij} + \delta Z_j + \varepsilon_{ij}, \qquad (11)$$

where P denotes the probability that worker i, who is employed at establishment j at the beginning of the year 2015, leaves the job by the end of the year; A is a dummy variable for workers aged 50 and older; T is a dummy variable for the adoption of new technology; X represents a worker's personal characteristics such as age, gender, tenure, and wage; and Z represents establishment characteristics such as the number of employees and industry. The variables for the extent of automation completed by the end of 2015 are included in the regression for the effect of automation.

The regression results suggest that the adoption of automation and IT tends to reduce the overall probability of leaving a job among all workers. This result perhaps captures the effect of increased productivity on labor demand. However, the estimated coefficients for the interaction term between aged workers and technological changes are all significantly negative. Furthermore, if an industry fixed effect is included, then the absolute size of the interaction term is larger than the coefficient for technological changes. These results show that technological changes in the form of increased automation and additional investments in IT adversely affect the employment of aged workers.

Additional regression results show that the unfavorable effects of technological changes on the employment of older workers are largely observed among those employed in large establishments with at least 300 employees. However, technological changes in small establishments actually reduce the probability of job separation among older workers. The differences in the results according to firm size may be due to different labor market conditions. For instance, strong pressure toward (informal) forced retirement in large firms exists owing to inflexible pay schemes and strictly hierarchical organizations. Alternatively, the features of newly adopted technology may differ between large and small firms.

Conclusion

The evidence drawn from the United States during the Industrial Era and South Korea during the last several decades suggests that technological changes and sectoral shifts negatively affect the employment and labor market status of older workers. The industrial structure in both countries changed in direction to reduce sectors that are favorable for the employment of older adults. In particular, the shrinkage of agriculture significantly contributed to the decline of the labor force participation of older males. The majority of older manufacturing workers in the United States were adversely affected by the emergence and diffusion of new production technologies and managerial practices during the Second Industrial Revolution. Similarly, increased automation and investments in IT tended to increase the probability of job separation among older workers in South Korea.

Of course, previous events do not necessarily predict the future, and the features of ongoing technological progress may differ from past ones. Certain types of new technologies may help people become active and productive until a very old age by alleviating the impairments to productivity associated with aging. However, the remarkably parallel findings obtained from the two countries at different times strongly suggest that radical changes in technology may bring unfavorable labor market consequences for older people, at least compared with the young. In this sense, technological changes would likely produce an additional challenge for rapidly aging societies.

References

Acemoglu, Daron, and Pascual Restrepo. 2017. "Robots and Jobs: Evidence from US Labor Markets." NBER Working Paper No. 23285.

———. 2018. "Demographics and Automation." NBER Working Paper 24421.

Autor, David H. 2015. "Why Are There Still So Many Jobs? The History and Future of Workplace Automation." *Journal of Economic Perspectives* 29, no. 3: 3–30.

Autor, David H., Frank Levy, and Richard J. Murnane. 2003. "The Skill Content of Recent Technological Change: An Empirical Exploration." *Quarterly Journal of Economics* 118, no. 4: 1279–333.

Bancroft, Gertrude. 1958. *The American Labor Force: Its Growth and Changing Composition.* New York: John Wiley and Sons.

Carter, Susan B. and Richard Sutch. 1996. "Myth of the Industrial Scrap Heap: A Revisionist View of Turn-of-the-Century American Retirement." *Journal of Economic History* 56, no. 1: 5–38.

Chandler, Alfred D. 1977. *The Visible Hand: The Managerial Revolution in American Business.* Cambridge, MA: Belknap Press of the Harvard University Press.

———. 1990. *Scale and Scope.* Cambridge, MA: Belknap Press of the Harvard University Press.

Costa, Dora L. 1995. "Agricultural Decline and the Secular Rise in Male Retirement Rates." *Explorations in Economic History* 32, no. 4: 540–52.

Durand, John D. 1948. *The Labor Force in the United States, 1890–1960.* New York: Social Science Research Council.

Epstein, Abraham. 1928. *The Challenge of the Aged.* New York: Vanguard Press.

Frey, Carl B., and Michael A. Osborne. 2017. "The Future of Employment: How Susceptible Are Jobs to Computerization?" *Technological Forecasting and Social Change* 114: 254–80.

Goos, Maarten, and Alan Manning. 2007. "Lousy and Lovely Jobs: The Rising Polarization of Work in Britain." *Review of Economics and Statistics* 89, no. 1: 118–33.

Gordon, Robert J. 2000. "Does the 'New Economy' Measure Up to the Great Inventions of the Past?" *Journal of Economic Perspectives* 14, no. 1: 49–74.

Graebner, William. 1980. *A History of Retirement: The Meaning and Function of an American Institution*. New Haven: Yale University Press.

Graetz, Georg, and Guy Michaels. 2015. "Robots at Work." CEPR Discussion Paper 1335.

Gratton, Brian. 1986. *Urban Elders*. Philadelphia: Temple University Press.

———. 1996. "The Poverty of Impoverishment Theory: The Economic Well-Being of the Elderly, 1890–1950." *Journal of Economic History* 56, no. 1: 39–61.

Haber, Carole. 1983. *Beyond Sixty-Five: The Dilemma of Old Age in America's Past*. New York: Cambridge University Press.

Kim, Namil, S. Choi, W. Park, and K. Yang. 1997. *Population Movement and Changes in the Characteristics of the Rural Population in Korea*. [In Korean.] Korea National Statistical Office.

Korea National Statistical Office. 1995. *Farm Household Economy Survey Report*.

Korea National Statistical Office. 2000. *Population and Housing Census Report*.

Lee, Chulhee. 1998. "Long-Term Unemployment and Retirement in Early-Twentieth-Century America." *Journal of Economic History* 58, no. 3: 844–56.

———. 1999. "Farm Value and Retirement of Farm Owners in Early-Twentieth-Century America." *Explorations in Economic History* 36, no. 4: 387–408.

———. 2002. "Sectoral Shift and the Labor-Force Participation of Older Males in the United States, 1880–1940." *Journal of Economic History* 62, no. 2: 512–23.

———. 2004. "Changing Industrial Structure and Economic Activity of Older Males in Korea: 1980–2000." *Seoul Journal of Economics* 17, no. 2: 181–234.

———. 2005. "Labor Market Status of Older Males in the United States, 1880–1940." *Social Science History* 29, no. 1: 77–105.

———. 2008. "Retirement Expectations of Older Self-Employed Workers in Korea: Comparisons with Wage and Salary Workers." *Korean Economic Review* 24, no. 1: 33–71.

————. 2010. "Labor-Force Participation of Older Males in Korea: 1955–2005." In *Economic Consequences of Demographic Change in East Asia*, edited by Takahashi Ito and Andrew K. Rose, 281–313. *NBER-EASE 19*.

————. 2012. "Changing Industrial Structure and Employment of Older Workers." *Korean Journal of Labor Economics* 35, no. 1: 55–88. [In Korean.]

————. 2015. "Industrial Characteristics and Employment of Older Manufacturing Workers in the Early-Twentieth-Century United States." *Social Science History* 39, no. 4: 551–79.

————. 2019. "Technological Change and Employment of Older Workers: Evidence from South Korea." Working paper.

Lee, Chulhee, and Jinkook Lee. 2013. "Employment Status, Quality of Matching, and Retirement in Korea: Evidence from Korean Longitudinal Study of Aging." *Journal of Population Ageing* 6, nos. 1–2: 59–83.

Lee, Eunwoo. 1993. "A Study on Rural-Urban Migration in Korea." [In Korean.] PhD diss., Department of Economics, Seoul National University.

Lee, Yong Suk, Ryan Decker, and John Chung. 2019. "Robots and Jobs: More Evidence from US Labor Markets." Working paper, Stanford University.

Long, Clarence D. 1958. *The Labor Force Under Changing Income and Employment*. Princeton, NJ: Princeton University Press.

Moen, Jon R. 1987. "Essays on the Labor Force and Labor Force Participation Rates: The United States from 1860 through 1950." PhD diss., University of Chicago.

————. 1994. "Rural Nonfarm Households: Leaving the Farm and the Retirement of Older Men, 1860–1980." *Social Science History* 18, no. 1: 55–75.

Moon, Hyunsang, Y. Hahn, H. Jun, and Y. Byun. 1991. *A Study of Migration*. [In Korean.] Seoul: Korea Institute for Health Social Affairs.

Pedersen, Harald A. 1950. "A Cultural Evaluation of the Family Farm Concept." *Land Economics* 26, 52–64.

Ransom, Roger L., and Richard Sutch. 1986. "The Labor of Older Americans: Retirement of Men On and Off the Job, 1870–1937." *Journal of Economic History* 46, no. 1: 1–30.

————. 1989. "The Trend in the Rate of Labor Force Participation of Older Men, 1870–1930. A Reply to Moen." *Journal of Economic History* 49, no. 1: 170–83.

Slichter, Sumner H. 1919. *The Turnover of Factory Labor*. New York: D. Appleton.

Squier, Lee W. 1912. *Old Age Dependency in the United States*. New York: Macmillan.

Statistics Korea. 2019. *Population Projections for Korea (2017–2067)*.

Whaples, Robert. 1990. "Winning the Eight-Hour Day, 1909–1919." *Journal of Economic History* 50, no. 2: 393–406.

Yoon, Soojong. 1984. "Changes in the Rural Society Caused by the Migration of Labor." [In Korean.] PhD diss., Department of Sociology, Seoul National University.

Technology, Age Structure, and the Political Economy of Innovation

6 How Japan's Aging Demographics Have Affected Pathways of Technological Development

Opportunities in AI, IA, and New IT Services

Kenji E. Kushida

Japan has been facing an extreme aging and shrinking population, which is beginning to drive various aspects of its social, political, and economic development. In order to sustain a high standard of living, Japan's working population must increase its productivity, and productivity increases are usually best accomplished through technological progress. Given that Japan remains at the technological frontier in a wide range of industries, this chapter investigates how Japan's demographics have affected its pathways of technological development in recent years.

In a recent influential study, economists Acemoglu and Restrepo (2017) find that, across a large range of countries, population aging is often associated with rising gross domestic product (GDP) per capita; contrary to the assumption of many studies and popular opinion, aging populations have not been driving down economic growth. They suggest that industrial robots are responsible for driving productivity increases, and they put forth a model in which countries with a scarcity of younger and middle-age labor, especially where capital is abundant vis-à-vis labor, are likely to adopt labor-replacing technology. Japan perfectly fits these conditions of scarce young and middle-age labor deficiency, low interest rates, and capital abundance. Acemoglu and Restrepo's findings would lead us to expect that Japan would aggressively adopt industrial

This study draws material from the Silicon Valley–New Japan project at the Japan Program at Stanford University, which is supported by generous contributions of numerous companies. Komatsu is among the contributors but was not involved in any way with the research or production of this chapter. The author offers sincerest thanks to Elin Matsumae for assisting with this research.

robotics and artificial intelligence (AI) to overcome its labor shortages, make use of its capital abundance, and continue to grow.

Yet, even when technological and economic conditions seem poised to foster economic growth, and despite an acute need for such growth, neither technological adoption nor economic growth occur automatically. Across the world and throughout history, we can find countless examples of countries whose economic fundamentals suggest the potential for rapid growth, but where factors such as domestic politics, global trade and security contexts, and external and internal shocks prevent them from taking economically optimal actions. Moreover, national economies are shaped by corporations, and it is corporations that are directly responsible for employing labor, providing capital and services, and working with rules and regulations to shape technologies, how they are used, and how the economic gains are distributed. Firms compete intensely with one another in domestic and global arenas, and it is firms, not technologies, who are the winners and losers in competition; the best technologies by no means ensure that the firms developing or deploying them will emerge as winners (David 1985). What happens to the wealth created by successful firms, as well as the labor force of unsuccessful firms, depends largely on national political bargains and regulatory structures (Zysman 1983; Esping-Andersen 1990).

Technological progress often follows particular *trajectories*—numerous actors exerting effort and deploying resources to pursue certain technological opportunities rather than others (Dosi 1982). These trajectories can differ across countries and have profound effects on how technologies progress and diffuse.[1] For example, in the 1970s and 1980s, Japanese firms pursued hardware and manufacturing solutions in sectors such as automobiles, semiconductors, and factory automation robotics, and displaced competitors around the world, including Silicon Valley (Borrus 1988). Then, in the late 1980s and 1990s, a new

---

1   For example, historically, in its early days as a nation the United States faced extreme labor shortages coupled with resource abundance, leading to Alexis de Tocqueville lamenting the wasteful use of wood in creating houses—a contrast with Europe, where timber was scarce and labor was abundant, leading to labor-intensive craftsman production that conserved wood. During World War II, the United States concentrated its efforts on aviation technologies, such as jet engines, as well as on the development of nuclear weapons. In the Cold War era, the United States and the Soviet Union were concerned with ballistic missiles and the "space race," leading to the rapid development of transistors and semiconductors to handle massive computational needs.

wave of Silicon Valley firms moved to create value in ways that did not rely on electro-mechanical hardware manufacturing capabilities, instead providing functionality through software, utilizing outsourced manufacturing, and creating de facto standards that commodified much of the hardware that Japanese firms excelled at producing (Zysman and Newman 2006). In the 1990s and 2000s, many of the trajectories that Japan pursued in the area of information technology (IT) ended up with Japan running in a direction where much of the world was headed, but then the world shifted to a different trajectory, leaving Japan "leading without followers" (Kushida 2011).

The national political bargains in which the corporations were embedded mattered for their respective societies in how they mobilized labor and dealt with societal distributions of the gains. Japanese firms through the 1990s accumulated vast wealth, ensuring that their employees, who were guaranteed long-term employment, had stable jobs. Japan built its social protections around stable large-firm employment. This was later seen to constrain Japan's adjustment to the new technological trajectories of software and services developed by Silicon Valley. Silicon Valley's adjustment in the 1980s and 1990s gave rise to new firms but also entailed massive layoffs at large companies such as Intel and IBM. It produced a continual churning of both high-end and low-skilled employees, with limited social protections for low-end employees, many of whom had to exit the local labor market as the local cost of living rose beyond their means.

From a narrow perspective of aggregate economic productivity, the national origin of firms may not matter, since improvements in local labor utilization and technology adoption driven by non-local corporations can be just as effective in raising local productivity as local firms—e.g., whether the software and services used in Japan are created by a Japanese firm or a foreign firm to raise productivity in Japan. However, the location of the companies' primary base of operations, and where it develops the technologies and consolidates profit, can matter. For example, if Japanese firms create services that raise the productivity of Japanese workers, the profits may more likely remain in Japan to employ people living in Japan, compared to a firm such as Google, based in Silicon Valley and employing the bulk of its high-end employees there. Better yet, if Japanese firms create technologies and services that are deployed in various parts of the world, the benefits might be more likely to disproportionately benefit Japan. This does not hold true for all countries, but historical literature on multinational corporations tends to portray Japanese corporate profits benefiting Japan even if firms are multinational (Pauly and Reich 1997), and this is certainly a Japanese policy motivation; who creates the wealth matters.

Japan's Demographics as Opportunity

Japan leads the world in its demographic trajectory of aging, but there are plenty of followers, as advanced industrialized countries, China, and others such as Thailand are poised to age rapidly. The critical implication is that if technologies developed or deployed within Japan to solve domestic demographic problems are applicable elsewhere, then Japan's demographic challenge can be an opportunity to cultivate competitive products and services in global markets. Given that the Japanese economy is far more open since the late 1990s than in most of the postwar period (Kushida 2010; Kushida 2014; Vogel 2006), the opportunity to capture value from Japan's demographic shifts is not limited to Japanese firms; non-Japanese firms can gather data and provide solutions within Japan, which may then be applied in other international markets. This is another reason to examine developments within Japan.

The trajectory of technological development throughout history has not been driven simply by market opportunities or needs, but also by political and social factors (Perez 2010). In particular, regulatory structures and government policies have actively shaped the directions of technological development, as well as influenced the patterns of diffusion.

Japan's population aging and shrinking has led to three primary interrelated drivers of significance to shaping technological trajectories: (1) Demographics as a *market opportunity* of an entirely unprecedented scale to serve the needs of a rapidly aging society; (2) demographic change creating an *acute labor shortage*; and (3) *favorable political and regulatory dynamics* for pursuing the development and diffusion of new technological trajectories to solve social and economic challenges caused by demographic change.

The backdrop of these drivers is Japan's political choice to not pursue truly large-scale immigration or foreign worker inflows to attempt filling the labor shortage gap. While new worker visa programs are opening the door to substantial and significant inflows of blue-collar workers in areas such as restaurants, nursing, construction, and over a dozen other sectors, the government's projections for labor shortages in the short, medium, and long term far exceeds the new inflows.

The core finding of this chapter is that the demographics of Japan's aging society has galvanized a wide range of corporate efforts, supported both directly and indirectly by the government, to aggressively develop artificial intelligence–driven technologies and systems to perform work for which labor shortages are accelerating. We are beginning to see concrete corporate offerings to address shortages of specific types of skilled and unskilled labor, as well as numerous efforts underway to develop systems to cope with geographic regions that are sparsely populated and have a high proportion of older adults, and the with the logistics surrounding eldercare more generally.

Many of the trajectories examined in this chapter are still in an early stage of development. Examining the early signals of how technological development and diffusion are occurring in Japan reveals several underlying general dynamics of technology development and diffusion applicable anywhere that are often forgotten; politics matter, rules and regulations matter, and national contexts matter because these factors can critically determine the trajectories of how technologies develop, which technologies are deployed, and how they diffuse.

This chapter first provides a brief overview of Japan's demographic challenges going beyond typical aggregate data. It then moves to sections addressing labor shortages in the sectors of construction, agriculture, and transportation; digitalization in health care; robotics-assisted mobility; human-machine interactions; and digitization of land and housing records.

Japan's Demographic Challenges: Economic, Political, and Social Issues

The degree of Japan's demographic challenges is extreme, with the population rapidly shrinking and aging, and an increasing number of older adults living alone or in multigenerational households.

Population shrinking and aging

Japan's population growth declined sharply after 1980, with the national census recording a peak population of approximately 128 million in 2010. Between 2010 and 2015, Japan lost almost 1 million people, and government estimates show that population decline will accelerate (Statistics Bureau 2018) (see figures 6.1 and 6.2). No other

FIGURE 6.1 Japan's actual and projected population growth rate, 1960–2060

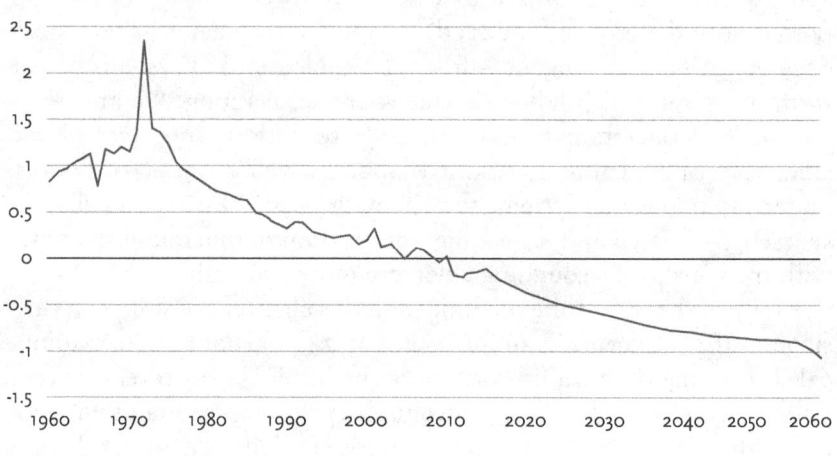

SOURCE: National Institute of Population and Social Security Research.

FIGURE 6.2 Japan's fertility rate, total, 1960–2017

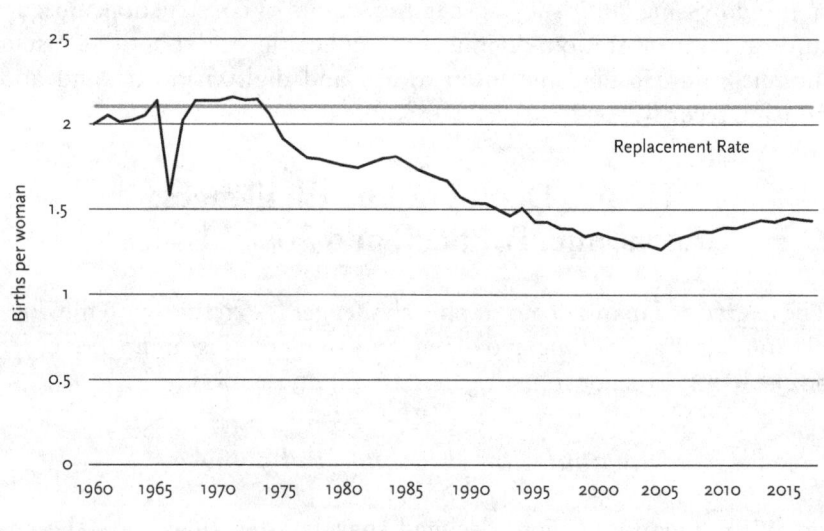

SOURCE: National Institute of Population and Social Security Research.

advanced industrialized nation has experienced a population decline of this magnitude.

In addition to shrinking, Japan's population is aging. Japan currently has the highest percentage of people over age 65, according to Japanese government and United Nations statistics. Just over one quarter of the population, at 26.6 percent, was over 65 in 2015, and the Japanese government's projection is 38 percent by 2050 (Statistics Bureau 2018).

A shrinking and aging population strains the tax base, because a high proportion of retirees are supported by a decreasing number of workers. It also creates *pressure to increase workers' productivity* to achieve economic growth, as well as *acute labor shortages*.

Political dynamics within Japan have not led to large-scale immigration policies or an attempt to aggressively increase the number of foreign workers at a level necessary to substantially decrease labor shortages. A new set of foreign worker programs enacted in April 2019 enables approximately 340,000 blue-collar workers to enter 14 sectors in Japan, including nursing, restaurants, retail, construction, and others (Koizumi, Kazuaki, and Satoshi 2019). A separate trainee program brought around 480,000 people to Japan between 2013 and 2017. Cabinet Office estimates place the current worker shortages at around 1.2 million people in sectors such as agriculture, construction, hotels, and restaurants (Obe 2019). However, these efforts are not sufficient to fill the gap of millions of workers projected to fill labor needs; one estimate from a survey by a consulting firm and Chuo University puts the number at 6.4 million workers by 2030 (Kamei 2018).

This continued labor shortage not only creates technological opportunities to develop and deploy labor-productivity-enhancing technologies, but it also provides critical political support. Replacing workers is not politically contentious in a form experienced elsewhere—such as unions in Germany concerned about firms introducing artificial intelligence (AI) to replace jobs. In Japan, AI and robotics are welcome to replace peoples' jobs, since there are not enough people to fill the jobs.

Healthcare costs are also estimated to spiral upward, given Japan's universal healthcare scheme. Healthcare costs for people over 65 are four times that of people under 65, and the medical costs as a proportion of gross domestic product (GDP), which held at around 5 percent from 1980 until 1993, increased sharply to above 8 percent in 2011 (Hsu and Yamada 2019).

The need to reduce government expenditures in the context of massive fiscal deficits also creates political tailwinds for regulatory structures and government policies to accelerate the deployment of labor force augmenting technologies.

Aging households, households with older adult residents, and older adults living alone

When examining potential markets serving older adults, one needs to look beyond aggregate population age distributions. For example, there can be significantly different needs for households in which the entire household is older, one or two older adults live in a household consisting of multiple generations, and those which consist of older adults living alone. In Japan, the number of each of these types of households is growing rapidly.

Data that is currently available does not distinguish between households with one or more senior member in multigenerational households and households in which the entire household of more than one person are older adults. However, the sum of these two—the number of households with one or more member over age 65—accounted for 41 percent of all households in 2015—or 22 million households.

Multigenerational households with one or more senior resident are likely to face a variety of needs for home eldercare. Family members taking care of older adults usually do not start out as eldercare professionals, and have significant *information needs* about caring for seniors, as well as the need to *physically support movements* of seniors, despite lacking training. The desire or need to *pursue employment* while taking care of older members of the household also leads to the *need for workplace arrangements* that enable this situation.

According to the "Aging Society White Paper" published by the Cabinet Office, the proportion of older adults (defined as 65 and older) living alone has risen dramatically. In 2015, 21% of women over 65 and 13% of men over 65 were living alone. This was an increase from 11% (women) and 4% (men) in 1980, and 16% (women) and 6% (men) in 1995. The white paper projects that, by 2040, 25% of women and 21% of men over 65 will be living alone (Cabinet Office 2018). This is around 9.5 million women and 8 million men over age 65 living alone, creating a wide range of needs for *healthcare, communications* with family or relatives, and *logistics* management of home care, physicians, and assistance in daily life including *mobility* within the home and around in the community, as well as *entertainment* and pastimes for *mental and emotional well-being*.

Moreover, the aging of Japan is more acute in prefectures that are predominantly rural. The data for the proportion of the population above 65 by prefecture shows that, in 2017, Akita Prefecture and Kochi Prefecture had the highest populations of senior citizens, at 35.6% and 34.2%, respectively, followed by Shimane Prefecture (33.6%) and Yamaguchi Prefecture (33.4%). In comparison, Tokyo was 23% and Osaka 27%. The Ministry of Internal Affairs and Communications (MIC) estimate for 2045 is that the proportion of residents over age 65 will reach 50.1% in Akita Prefecture and 46.8% in Aomori Prefecture, while Tokyo and Osaka's proportions rise to 30% and 36%, respectively.

The scale and magnitude of Japan's aging, especially when considered at a household and regional level, are truly extreme.

Addressing Labor Shortages and Skill Deficiencies: Construction, Agriculture, and Transportation

The rapidly decreasing availability of skilled labor, and the geographic mismatch between where labor is needed and potential providers of labor, are driving one trajectory of technological development and deployment in Japan that leads the world.

Construction: Upskilling to allow inexperienced workers to perform high-skilled jobs

Construction equipment manufacturer Komatsu has been a leader in the development of IT-enabled systems that enable low-skilled workers to perform construction tasks that would normally require considerably training and experience. These systems are already commercialized within Japan and are beginning to be implemented in other countries. Reducing skill requirements for particular tasks can free up the skilled workers to perform even more difficult tasks, while inexperienced workers can manage tasks that they previously had been unable to perform. This type of "intelligence augmentation" (IA) system has broad implications for a variety of political and economic conditions globally and is already gaining the attention of policymakers and industries outside of Japan and industries unrelated to construction.

In 2013, Komatsu introduced a line of "information and communications technology (ICT) Construction Equipment" that enabled unskilled operators to effectively perform tasks that previously had required around 10 years of experience. Excavators, in particular, require extensive experience to create a precise slope. Since the operator sits perpendicularly to face the slope, it is difficult to gauge the angle that is being dug, and the several joints in the arm of the digger are awkward and difficult to control to get a precise dig.

The ICT excavator, introduced in 2014, uses sensors embedded in several places in the machine to accurately and precisely sense where the joints are in relation to the desired angle to dig. The operator simply positions the end-piece in the position that the dig will start and pushes the "semi-auto" mode button on the console. The digger then performs a cut on its own. This operation is certainly not fully automated, because the operator must position the bucket to the desired location before commencing the cut. The operator also needs to determine whether potential debris is in the way, or whether large rocks or anything else might interfere with the slope carving—something that is technologically not simple to train a machine to recognize automatically, but easy for a human to identify.

Similarly, ICT bulldozers, introduced in 2013, removed the substantial skill needed to create flat surfaces. Traditionally, years of experience were necessary to make small adjustments to the blade, because the weight load and resistance of dirt shifts according to the amount of dirt being pushed, the relative texture of the dirt, and so on. However, Komatsu's IA system in its bulldozers allows the blade to be controlled by a computer, requiring the operator to only move the bulldozer itself, with the blade adjusting automatically to create a surface with just a few centimeters of variation—flatter than most experienced professionals can achieve.

These ICT-enabled diggers and bulldozers are sold ubiquitously throughout Japan, as well as in the large number of countries where Komatsu sells its equipment. A Japanese company solving domestic problems, but with global reach to diffuse the technologies it develops, is an important mechanism of how Japan's demographic changes are influencing global technological trajectories.

Partnering with Silicon Valley to rapidly deploy labor-saving site assessments

Komatsu also partnered with a Silicon Valley company providing a platform for drones to create three-dimensional maps for construction sites throughout Japan. This use of drones dramatically reduced the time and labor intensity of taking measurements of construction sites, typically from several weeks with numerous workers using tripod-mounted measurement devices, to just a few hours by sending up a drone. Komatsu met Skycatch, the drone company, in late 2014. By early 2015 they had moved to do a demo of the project in front of Komatsu's top management, and in 2016, Komatsu began using the drones (Togashi 2016). Using the ICT-enabled machinery and drone-based surveying, Komatsu introduced a "smart construction" process, which generates construction plans based on a drone-produced site survey; the construction is carried out by intelligent equipment, which allows for a visualization of daily progress and streamlined inspection and maintenance of machines.

While construction site measurement is an industry employing significant numbers of people, the lack of labor was severe enough that industry members did not engage in a significant political strategy to try to block the adoption of this technology and solution.

Agriculture: Rice paddies as flexibly deployable assets

The average age of Japanese farmers is climbing rapidly, with the proportion of agricultural workers over 65 climbing from 62 percent in 2013 to 69 percent in 2018, with an average age of 66 in 2013 and rising to 67 in 2015, as shown in table 6.1. For workers whose primary job was farming, the figures were almost identical.

The amount of cultivated agricultural land in Japan has been decreasing, as shown in table 6.2. While a shrinking population might suggest that more land could be freed up for agriculture, that has not been the case.

TABLE 6.1 Age of agricultural workers in Japan, 2013–18

	2013	2015	2016	2017	2018
Agricultural Workers					
Proportion over 65	61.6%	63.5%	65%	66.5%	68.5%
Average Age	65.8	66.4	66.8	66.7	66.8
Primary Farmers*					
Proportion over 65	61.1%	64.5%	65.0%	66.4%	68.0%
Average Age	66.1	67.0	66.8	66.6	66.6

NOTE: *Primary farmers is defined as those whose primary occupation is farming.
SOURCE: Ministry of Agriculture, Forestry and Fisheries.

TABLE 6.2 Total cultivated agricultural land in Japan

Year	Millions of Hectares
2018	4.42
2017	4.44
2016	4.47
2015	4.50
2014	4.52
2013	4.54

SOURCE: Ministry of Agriculture, Forestry and Fisheries.

Komatsu has been undertaking efforts in agriculture to deal with the need to increase the productivity of agricultural workers, as well as to better utilize the land—a surprising proportion of which is being abandoned. According to data gathered by the Ministry of Agriculture, Forestry, and Fisheries in 2016, about 930,000 hectares, or approximately 20 percent of total farmland area in Japan, is either unregistered or thought to be unregistered. Out of this land, approximately 54,000 hectares is not being utilized (MAFF 2016).

Initially, as part of its corporate social responsibility efforts to give back to Ishikawa Prefecture, where Komatsu was first founded and which is experiencing rapid aging and depopulation, Komatsu began applying industrial thought processes to the problem of how to raise the incomes, and therefore productivity, of farmers. Upon studying the cost structure of rice farming, they found that transplanting seedlings into water-drenched rice paddies was the highest cost and most labor-intensive process. The reason for transplanting was that water-drenched paddies were not productive for raising rice from seeds; the seeds would not remain in neat lines, and birds often ate the seeds, leading to low and uneven yields. (The purpose of having rice paddies water-drenched in the first place is to keep out most types of weeds.)

Komatsu's experiments showed that their industrial ICT-enabled bulldozers could make the ground in the rice paddies almost completely flat—something not previously possible. By doing so, with a groove at a particular angle cut into the paddy, rice could be planted from seeds without production loss. The cost savings were approximately 40 percent. The idea of taking bulldozers into rice paddies was not one that the agricultural sector would have thought of on its own. Moreover, compared to small agricultural tractors, industrial bulldozers turned out to be lower in cost and more durable, with little skill necessary to operate them, since the blade was automatically controlled.

The next step in this line of deployment is for rice paddies to be converted to dry fields for a variety of other crops, depending on relative market prices. Flooded rice paddies need not remain rice paddies if they are maintained by bulldozers, and can be converted to wheat, barley, soba, potatoes, or other fields, depending on weather patterns and relative prices.

Within Japan, the problem of unused agricultural land that has been abandoned is also a product of population aging and shrinking. With the use of bulldozers to maintain fields, the tasks can be scaled up.

Finally, the chairman of Komatsu announced at the Nikkei Agricultural Technology Summit in 2018 that it was taking the agricultural business into Indonesia—a very large country with many islands, small-scale farmland, and crops that include flooded rice paddies (Noji 2018).

Transportation: Coping with shortage and aging of drivers through automation

Japan's commercial drivers are aging, creating pressure to automate driving, as well as to devise methods to increase the productivity of existing drivers. The rising average age of commercial transportation drivers is a serious concern.

As table 6.3 shows, the average ages for bus, taxi, and truck drivers in Japan in 2015 were 50, 59, and 48 (2017), respectively. They worked long hours—eight hours a day for five days a week, for four weeks is 160 hours—with truck drivers working 217 hours, bus drivers 210, and taxi drivers 189 hours a month. Their incomes are not high, all below Japan's average GDP per capita (purchasing power parity) of approximately ¥43,876 in 2017, according to the World Bank. The proportion of women in all three categories is below 3 percent.

TABLE 6.3 Commercial transportation workers in Japan

	Bus	Taxi	Truck
Total number of drivers and maintenance personnel	130,000 (2015)	340,000 (2015)	830,000 (2017)
Average age (as of 2017)	50	59	48
Proportion of women	1.7%	2.7%	2.4%
Hours worked per month	210	189	217
Average annual income	¥4,570K (US$41,700)	¥3,320,000 (US$30,300)	¥4,540,000 (US$41,500)

SOURCE: Ministry of Land, Infrastructure, Transportation and Tourism.

FIGURE 6.3 Age composition of drivers in the Japanese freight transportation industry, 2012–17

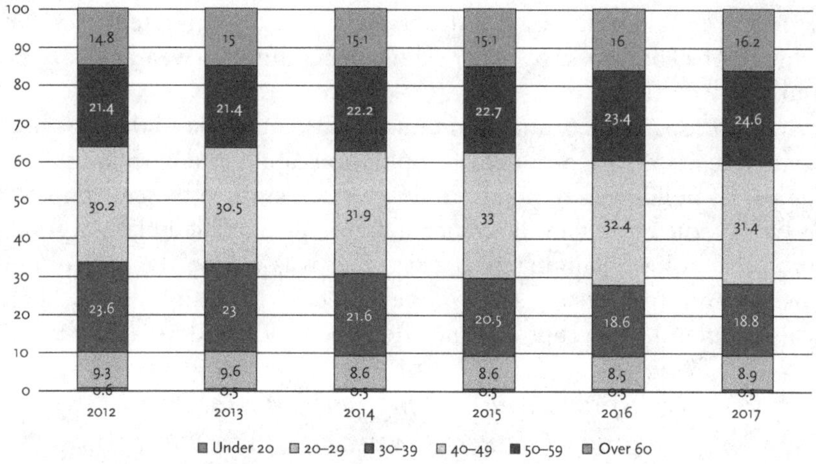

SOURCE: Japan Trucking Association.

The lack of interest in these professions, which entail long, grueling hours and vast amounts of time away from home, have led to a reported lack of drivers as a significant challenge for operators—especially trucks and buses. As shown in the age composition of the freight transportation industry (see figure 6.3), the proportion of drivers in their 20s is less than 10 percent, while over 15 percent of the drivers are over 60.

Truck Convoys

Consortia of major industry players, with the full support of government, have been developing trucking "convoy" technology, allowing one or more autonomous trucks to follow a human-driven lead truck.

In late 2018, Hino Motors and Isuzu Motors, along with Volvo Group's UD Trucks and Mitsubishi Fuso Truck and Bus, now a subsidiary of Daimler, engaged in tests on expressways west of Tokyo. Toyota Tsusho, a trading company subsidiary of Toyota, coordinated the tests, with the full support of the Ministry of Economy, Trade and Industry (METI). Large 12-meter trucks were driven 35 meters apart, at 80 kph. According to the MLIT Transportation Policy White Paper 2018, the goal of commercial deployments of driverless trucks following a driver-operated truck is planned for 2022, with a goal to have the technology created by 2020. With an array of sensors, the driverless truck could follow the driver-operated truck very closely, reducing air resistance to improve fuel efficiency (Nikkei Asian Review 2018).

Self-Driving Buses

Self-driving vehicles are a focus in Silicon Valley, largely because of the potential of transforming transportation at a global scale and the resulting financial gains. In Japan, some of the most noteworthy efforts to create automated driving solutions are motivated by demographic challenges—the mobility needs of older adults and the shortage of bus drivers.

Odakyu, best known for operating trains and buses, but also a significant commercial/residential real estate developer and operator, partnered with Kanagawa Prefecture and Keio University to develop autonomously driven buses. SB Drive, a startup, equipped buses from Hino Motors with sensors such as GPS and millimeter wave radar. As part of Kanagawa Prefecture's "Promotion of Robots in Society" initiative, Odakyu first tested the autonomous buses on Keio University's Shonan Fujisawa campus in June 2018 (Keio University 2017). Three months later, Odakyu, in collaboration with Enoshima Electric Railway, an Odakyu group company, began testing the buses on public roads in the Enoshima area; Enoshima, an island connected to the mainland by a bridge, is a popular tourist destination (Odakyu 2018). In February 2019, around 700 residents took part in a test drive of the buses on 1.4 km of residential streets in Tama City, a suburb of Tokyo, where Odakyu has a major presence (Kiyoshima 2019). Tama City is well known for a major bedroom community built in the postwar rapid growth era, Tama New Town, which is now one of the fastest aging areas in Tokyo.

Autonomous Taxis in Real-World Conditions

A partnership between Nissan and the Japanese internet company DeNA to develop a driverless taxi service in 2017 led to Japan's first field tests on public roads in March 2018.

In 2017, DeNA and Nissan began developing a robo-vehicle ride-share service, called Easy Ride. Much like popular ride-share apps such as Uber and Lyft, users can request rides by using the Easy Ride smartphone app; the vehicles that come to pick them up, however, are driverless. The service also allows users to ask for suggestions about local sightseeing destinations and download available coupons through the mobile app. Operations are monitored from a 24/7 remote control room.

DeNA and Nissan Motors have conducted two field tests so far. In the initial field test, conducted in March 2018, 300 riders were picked up and driven around a 4.5 km course in the Minatomirai district of Yokohama (Tsuruhara 2018). This was the first test in Japan of driverless vehicles on public roads with the participation of consumers. The companies have announced intentions to launch full service in the early 2020s, with limited rollout before then.

DeNA originally had been developing a similar service with the robotics company ZMP, establishing Robot Taxi as a joint venture in May 2015. However, the companies dissolved their partnership in 2017, citing disagreements in management policies. DeNA announced that it would instead be partnering with Nissan (Okuma 2017).

Cargo and Buses: Funding Transportation in Depopulated Areas—Regulatory Support

The pathway from economic necessity or potential economic benefit, to the creation of regulatory frameworks that enable industry and technology solutions to address the problem, is not automatic. Often, especially in the context of Japanese regulatory reform, vested interest groups successfully pressuring political leaders to maintain bureaucratically driven restrictions on new services or new competitors is cited as a barrier to flexible economic adjustment in the face of new global competitive realities (Katz 1998).

For example, despite the aging drivers of taxis, and the scarcity of taxis in nonurban areas, services such as Uber and Lyft have been, in effect, shut out of Japan. Under current regulations, only licensed taxi operators are allowed to take passengers.

Likewise, until 2017, passenger buses and cargo delivery vehicles were classified differently according to MLIT, and hybrid services in which buses could hold and deliver cargo were not permitted. A regulatory shift in 2017, however, enabled buses that met certain criteria for approval to carry over 350 kg of cargo. In the following two years, eight bus operators in six prefectures made use of this new regulatory environment (Nikkei 2018b).

Even before the regulatory shift, Japan's largest cargo operator, Yamato, had pioneered working with local bus companies in sparsely populated areas in Iwate and Miyazaki prefectures, both facing significant depopulation. Citing difficulties for bus operators to finance local operations that depopulated and aging communities relied on, and the difficulty and costs of finding enough bus drivers and truck drivers in rural areas, Yamato proved that they could reliably help finance local bus operations by arranging cargo sharing in buses that had some seats removed (Nikkei 2015).

After the regulatory shift of 2017, not only Yamato, but also its competitor Sagawa Kyubin, and even Japan Post, the partially privatized postal operator, joined in cargo sharing with local bus lines. The Japan Agricultural Cooperative, the powerful centralized entity handling everything from financing to logistics for much of Japan's agriculture, also began utilizing space on express buses from regional areas to Tokyo to take agriculture produce. In addition, Yamato has expanded into using refrigerated boxes on buses in Miyazaki to deliver freshly caught salmon to airports, which are then sent to Hong Kong (Nikkei 2018b). These examples show how regulatory shifts in previously strictly regulated and segmented business areas are now actively enabling new corporate partnerships to pool resources to better utilize their limited labor forces and serve sparsely populated and rapidly aging areas.

Digitalization in healthcare: Opening the door to transforming medical care and physician labor markets

The adoption of IT in Japan's healthcare system has been relatively slow. Often blamed is the large number of small-scale clinics and hospitals that are atomized. They exert political power through the Japan Medical Association (JMA), long recognized as one of Japan's most powerful interest groups.

The diffusion of electronic health records has remained at around 30%, with online systems for reservations limited to 40% of all hospitals and clinics in 2017. Moreover, government estimates cited in a Nikkei news article showed 40% of the 40 trillion yen of Japan's healthcare expenditures to be labor costs (Nikkei 2017). An internal breakdown of the digital health record adoption figures according to hospital size is revealing. As shown in figure 6.4, while the adoption of digital records at large hospitals, with over 400 beds, rose rapidly

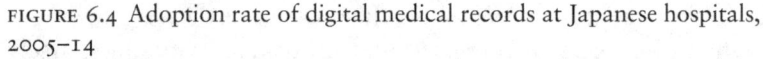

FIGURE 6.4 Adoption rate of digital medical records at Japanese hospitals, 2005–14

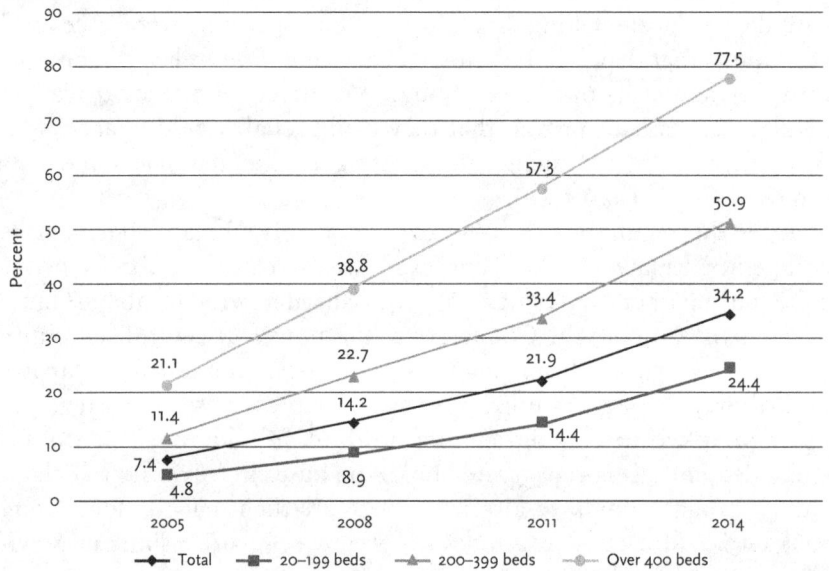

NOTE: Excludes specialized psychiatric hospitals.
SOURCE: Ministry of Health.

from 20% in 2005 to 77.5% in 2014, adoption at hospitals with 20 to 199 beds rose from 4.8% to only 24.4% during the same period.

With the advent of global-scale cloud computing as a new, low-cost global infrastructure providing abundant computing resources at ever lower prices, the costs to digitize information is decreasing rapidly (Kushida, Murray, and Zysman 2015). This has allowed a number of startups to offer digital patient record information to smaller clinics at low prices, enabling smaller hospitals and clinics to offer digital patient records.

Once medical records are digitized, the path for offering a wide array of related services opens up.

Medical imaging and remote diagnosis: Transforming both diagnosis and physician labor markets

One critical medical area where automation can have a large impact is cloud-based medical imaging services that share medical imaging data among hospitals and clinics for remote diagnosis. A startup, Medical Network Systems (MNES) provides such a system, called Lookrec. Clinics and hospitals who contract with Lookrec upload patient medical images to a system built on top of a Google cloud platform. The images are then diagnosed by medical doctors employed by MNES.

Japan has one of the highest per-capita installations of medical imaging hardware—MRIs, CT scan machines, etc.—but it faces an imbalance of having far more machines than radiology and pathology specialists who can make diagnoses. MNES founder Naoyuki Kitamura was motivated by one of his patients, a woman in her late thirties whom he diagnosed with late-stage, terminal pancreatic cancer. She had brought an MRI that was scanned six months earlier but was marked as "no abnormality." Upon research, however, Kitamura realized that the small, rural hospital where the patient had received the MRI and the diagnosis had no specialist, whereas Kitamura could easily identify the signs of cancer developing (Kitamura 2018).

Lookrec, given its cloud architecture and web front end, is low-cost, enabling medical institutions to easily share and maintain medical data, while also enabling patients to retrieve their own medical data. Because it is on a Google platform, it can be accessed overseas as well, if people require attention or treatment abroad.

Critically, services like MNES can address a mismatch between the workforce of doctors and the patients they need to serve. MNES employee physicians do not have to live near the patients they diagnose and are not constrained by hospital working hours. According to Kitamura, a significant cause of the shortage of diagnostic radiologists and pathologists is that female physicians tend to leave the field after marriage and childbirth—largely due to the extremely long and unpredictable working hours. Moreover, according to Kitamura, these female physicians with children tended to prefer living in urban areas to send their children to the best schools, making them even less likely to practice medicine in rural areas. When employed by MNES, however, working physician mothers have the job hours and locational flexibility that would enable them to continue working (Kitamura 2018).

Healthcare and eldercare logistics optimization

Japan's demographic shift creates an acute need to optimize the coordination of logistics among caregivers. Kanamic Network provides an IT service that enables information sharing between municipalities, medical associations, hospitals, home care physicians, and collaboration between medical practitioners and nursing staff, eldercare givers, and care-plan managers through a task management system. Because coordination between all these actors is necessary for eldercare, Kanamic provides a centralized location for all of them to share information and coordinate services.

The service offered by Kanamic Network became highly popular, enabling the company to list on the small-market capitalization Mothers Market in 2016, moving up to the first section of the Tokyo Stock Exchange in 2018; since then its profits have been growing robustly. In September 2018 the company reported that its systems were being used in over 22,000 offices nationwide, by over 89,000 professionals (according to the Kanamic home page).

Kanamic's cloud service was developed based on joint research with the University of Tokyo's Institute of Gerontology. Kanamic has worked on projects for major customers such as the Ministry of Health, Labour and Welfare, and the Ministry of Internal Affairs and Communications. The company has also provided consultation services for regional revitalization projects (Japan Exchange Group 2016b). Kanamic Network was founded by Minoru Yamamoto in 2000. Yamamoto was producing commercials for healthcare insurance when he developed an administrative system for more efficient nursing care at home and built a network of medical and care workers. Yamamoto's eldest son, Takuma Yamamoto, took over as CEO and president in 2005. Takuma began his career as a software engineer at Fujitsu in 2000, before eventually joining his mother and father at Kanamic.

He was initially uninterested in joining his father's company, but he quickly saw the massive level of inefficiency in the industries and processes around eldercare. Incredible amounts of paper were being used and the use of "hanko" seals to stamp them was required; eldercare home helpers were unable to go from one client to the next, instead having to return to the office between each visit to fill out paperwork. He also saw care managers needing to log in and manually input data into multiple systems for various entities, such as eldercare facilities, clinics, pharmacies, insurance, and local government.

The first major opportunity came in 2006, when local government created integrated regional assistance centers, which were tasked with creating care plans for individual elderly. Private companies were subcontracted to create care plans, but there was a severe lack of care plan managers, and the companies were mostly old-fashioned, non-IT–utilizing companies. This provided Kanamic's first spurt of growth, initially focused on Chiba Prefecture. Then, in 2011, a model known as the Kashiwa Model was created from a partnership between the University of Tokyo, Kashiwa City, and a few other entities, to deploy an online system to connect home care, medical care delivery, eldercare, nursing and others, with the objective of delivering as much healthcare and eldercare as possible at home rather than in hospital facilities—ultimately a cost issue in Japan's universal healthcare since a reliance on hospital facilities costs the government more than care provided at home (Japan Exchange Group 2016a).

Yamamoto has since become a committee member at the Ministry of Internal Affairs and Communications, and Ministry of Health, Labour and Welfare, and is also a researcher at the University of Tokyo and National Cancer Center.

Japan's need for optimizing caregiving and healthcare logics has also attracted the attention of top international researchers in artificial intelligence. The Stanford AI Vision Lab began conducting experiments with the city of Toyohashi in 2017 to collect data and to optimize for healthcare provider logistics. It also partnered with several government-funded entities to run data-gathering and logistics-optimization projects (Activity Recognition Healthcare n.d.).

Robotics-assisted mobility and communications

Japanese companies are also partnering with Silicon Valley startups to offer solutions to the aging and shrinking manual labor workforce. Obayashi, one of Japan's largest construction companies, is tying up with Seismic, which develops apparel integrated with unnoticeable robotics and sensor technology. Seismic's "Powered Clothing" offering is designed to augment human strength and give mobility to muscles and joints while looking like normal clothes. The suits provide up to 30 watts of power to each hip and the lower back to support activities such as sitting, standing, lifting, and carrying. The company was founded in 2016 by the former director of robotics at SRI International.

The technology was originally developed at SRI International for a DARPA-funded program to reduce injury risk and enhance endurance for soldiers. Seismic spun out of SRI to explore Powered Clothing for a wider range of applications. Seismic first debuted its Power Clothing in 2018 and is now looking to extend applications of the clothing to the occupational safety, wellness and lifestyle, and healthcare fields (Draper 2019).

The 2019 announcement of Seismic's strategic partnership with Obayashi, among others, was aimed at the mass deployment of Seismic in multiple industries. The collaboration with Obayashi focuses on developing industry-specific clothing worn by the construction workforce, which still relies on pervasive manual labor with considerable physical exertion. Seismic and Obayashi are working to develop suits that support workers' core muscles, help augment strength, and alleviate worksite fatigue (Seismic 2019).

Human-Machine Interactions in Eldercare

There is another active area for active ICT applications in Japan that addresses the special needs of older patients with neurocognitive disorders, as well as the increasing isolation of older Japanese citizens.

Paro: Therapeutic robotic seal for dementia—research platform

Paro is a therapeutic robotic seal modeled after a baby harp seal in both looks and sounds. Paro is covered in soft white (artificial) fur, and it has been used as a form of therapy, especially for dementia patients. The benefits of animal-assisted therapy are well documented; Paro is administered to patients in environments where live animals would present logistical difficulties. Paro is a "mental commitment robot"[2] that is designed to provide psychological effects such as patient stress reduction and comfort, physiological effects such as improvements in vital signs, and social effects, such as improvement of socialization between patients and with their caregivers.

Paro is equipped with five kinds of sensors: tactile, light, auditory, temperature, and posture sensors, with which it can perceive people and the environment. Paro has some artificial intelligence and is able to learn a new name a patient may give it and respond in a way that patients prefer. For example, if a patient continuously strokes Paro, the

---

2 See "What is a Mental Commitment Robot?" Paro, http://paro.jp/?page_id =1044.

seal wiggles and makes seal-like noises and then will remember and try to repeat this action when stroked.

Paro was created by Takenori Shibata, a senior research scientist at the Human Research Institute at the National Institute of Advanced Industrial Science (AIST). He first developed Paro in 1993, and in 2004 established Intelligent System Co., Ltd., to commercially distribute Paro (Shibata 2004).

Numerous Paro studies have been conducted in Japan, Sweden, the United States, Germany, Italy, and the United Kingdom, among other countries, according to the company's website (PARO Robots U.S.).

Telenoid: Simplified communications, especially for dementia

The Telenoid is a human-like remote-controlled android created by esteemed Japanese roboticist Dr. Hiroshi Ishiguro. Although Dr. Ishiguro, who is the director of the Intelligent Robotics Laboratory at the Graduate School of Engineering Science at Osaka University, is known for creating incredibly human-like robots, the Telenoid is minimalistic in design. The robot is the size of a small child, made of silicone rubber, with a bald head, simplified facial features, and stump-like limbs. The idea was to create a robot that could appear male or female, old or young, designed to "transmit the presence" of people in a distant place. Studies have shown that when there is insufficient information, patients with dementia are convinced of Telenoid's human qualities (Telenoid Healthcare Company).

An operator sits at a computer with a webcam and special teleoperation software, and cameras and microphones embedded into the Telenoid then project the voice and movements of the operator. The robot has a number of applications as a new communication device. In eldercare, the hope is that family members can better connect to older adult relatives.

The Telenoid was first released in 2010. In 2015, the Telenoid Healthcare Company was established with backing from the Advanced Telecommunication Research Institute International (ATR) and Nippon Venture Capital (NVCC), to begin offering Telenoid services specifically for eldercare. In 2016, five nursing facilities in Miyagi Prefecture began using Telenoid for treatment. In 2017, Telenoid teamed up with Miyagi University to begin more systematically studying the effects of the Telenoid.

Aibo: Companionship, entertainment, and security monitoring

Aibo is a companion robotic dog that is designed and manufactured by Sony. Aibo was initially developed as a research project out of Sony's Computer Science Laboratory that began in 1994, headed by Toshitada Doi, an electrical engineer at Sony who had also played a key role in developing the compact disc player in the early 1980s (Johnstone 2000). When Sony began to sell Aibo commercially in 1999, it became the first consumer robot product available to the mass consumer market.

Aibo is programmed to exhibit emotions and interact with its owners and surroundings. Aibo has intelligence and responds to training as it develops from a newborn puppy into an adult. Although Aibo was initially a success and led to several generations of Aibo robots, Sony discontinued Aibo in 2006 and ended customer support for Aibo in 2014. For a time, Japanese media featured numerous news segments and mini-documentaries showing how some seniors had become emotionally attached to their Aibo, giving rise to independent repair personnel who would service the broken Aibo, often with parts salvaged from other units, or put together in makeshift ways, to sustain Aibo even after Sony had discontinued customer support (Mochizuki and Pfanner 2015).

Eleven years after discontinuing the robot, Sony announced a new generation of Aibo in 2017, one that is more intelligent, with an ability to learn faces, develop familiarity with its owners, and recognize its environment. The robot is equipped with a camera to take pictures and has Wi-Fi and LTE connectivity to upload records of its experiences to the cloud. Users are also able to download new capabilities and new tricks via their smartphones.

The use of Aibo for treatment of elderly people, especially for patients with dementia, has been studied to some degree in the past (Tamura et al. 2004; Kimura, Yokoyama, and Naganuma 2013). Results have shown that it is an effective rehabilitation tool that helps patients relax, have fun, and be more communicative. In 2018, Sony initiated a robot therapy trial, introducing Aibo units to a nursing home run by the Sony group, along with the three other nursing facilities (Sankei Shimbun 2018b).

In February 2019, Sony announced that it was adding a new "watchdog" feature for Aibo. Aibo will patrol the house and produce a report of its findings, providing photos with its camera feature. This service could provide a layer of security for homeowners away from home and could also prove to be an especially useful feature in homes of elderly residents. Sony announced a partnership with Japanese home security company, Secom, to enhance Aibo's security offerings (Nikkei 2019b).

Digitizing Land and Housing Ownership: Improving Traceability and Inheritance

A surprising proportion of land in Japan has unknown ownership. Since all land ownership must be registered at the local government office, transfers of ownership that are not recorded—especially through inheritance—lead to incorrect land ownership documents. In some cases, people are unaware that they inherited land from a relative and are not notified that this was the case. In other cases, those who inherit the land do not want it and do not want to pay inheritance tax on the land, so they willfully neglect to register the transfer of ownership.

A 2016 estimate by the Ministry of Land, Infrastructure, Transport and Tourism (MLIT) found that 4.1 million hectares of property, 20 percent of land in Japan, has unknown ownership—as defined by the official records not matching known, live people. Put into perspective, the amount of land with unknown legal ownership is larger than the total area of Kyushu (3.68 million hectares) (MAFF 2016). In many of these cases, an investigation by the local government office can yield the identity of the rightful owner, such as the next of kin, who simply failed to register the land in their name. However, in some cases, ownership is truly unknown (Nikkei 2018a).

Blockchain technology—simply, a distributed transaction history held and updated by many parties simultaneously—is one of several promising solutions. IT systems in Japan were updated into a cloud computing architecture after the March 11, 2011 earthquake and tsunami destroyed many local government buildings, taking their documents and local computer servers along with them. Several startups are offering blockchain solutions to keep track of real estate transactions, and test trials have been undertaken with several local governments (Sankei 2018a).

Large firms are beginning to move as well. In March 2019, Hitachi, Sekisui House, and KDDI announced a new partnership to develop a secure information-sharing platform that uses blockchain technology

(Nikkei 2019a). The pilot project, which began in April 2019, aims to streamline administrative procedures for real estate rentals. The three companies have plans to create a consortium with financial institutes, local government bodies, and other companies.

Other Areas: Automating Drink Viscosity Enhancement to Avoid Dysphagia

There are also several emerging areas in which technological solutions to challenges facing the growing older adult population promises to be a growth market worthy of investment. One such area is transforming food into safer forms for the elderly to chew and swallow.

Dysphagia, the medical term for disruptions in the swallowing process, is a growing health concern for Japan's aging population. Dysphagia can cause aspiration when foods or liquids enter the airway or lungs. Aspiration pneumonia can occur when swallowed materials in the airways release bacteria, resulting in lung infection (Sura et al. 2012). Doctors recommend increasing the viscosity of thin liquids to help slow the transit of fluid substances, reducing the chance of them going down the airway and causing aspiration (Sakashita et al. 2015).

A rehabilitation and nursing home in Gifu Prefecture recently debuted a vending machine that adds viscosity to coffee and tea drinks. Previously, nursing homes would add thickeners to drinks by hand; the vending machine instead automates the process while giving patients the ability to choose whether or not to add thickener, and how thick they want their drinks (Yahoo! News Japan 2019). With this type of user-needs–based technology making headlines in Japan, other companies are likely to follow suit by developing technological, labor-saving solutions to a wide variety of needs facing nursing homes, eldercare facilities, and households with older adults.

Conclusion

Japan's current emerging technological trajectories are driven primarily by the private sector, which sees a large potential demand for products and services, given the depth and scale of the tangible social problems that must be solved to deal with labor shortages and address eldercare needs.

In many instances of private sector solutions aimed at these problems, government support has been important. The "Abenomics" reforms promulgated by Prime Minister Abe, who came to power in 2011, have provided legitimization and an indicator of preferred pathways. Abenomics' "three arrows" consist of expansionary monetary policy, massive fiscal expenditures, and economic reform (Kushida 2018; Pekkanen et al. 2018).[3] In the third arrow, economic reform, over 100 specific areas of reform have been put forth annually, with key performance indicators (KPIs) for most of them. Several specific indicators are supportive of areas such as digital health records and robotics in nursing, as well as general targets such as extending the "healthy" life expectancy (see appendix A).

This government support, however, differs from traditional "industrial policy," as seen in the heyday of Japan's rapid postwar growth. These KPIs do not entail massive subsidies and the use of financial institutions to strategically guide areas of development; instead, they are guidelines, which are sometimes removed when they are not on track to being achieved.

Looking forward, we are likely to see electoral dynamics supporting eldercare and increasing the productivity of Japanese workers to pay for social security and healthcare. It is worth looking at the electoral dynamics of Tokyo to see how far the electorate is tilted in favor of older adults, who tend to vote more often and with higher turnouts than the young. The average age of residents in Tokyo was 45 in 2018, making it one of the younger prefectures. Yet, in the local government elections for 11 of Tokyo's 23 wards in April 2019, the average age of ward mayors was 66.6. A majority of mayors were in their 70s. After the election, the average age of mayors decreased to 65.5, with a median age of 66. The youngest mayor was 47, while the oldest was 84. There was one woman before and after the election, whose seat was not contested, and she was age 60.

Technological development can sometimes be influenced by politically driven regulations that arise from key events, such as tragic accidents. For example, in April 2019, a former METI official in his late 80s lost control of his car and struck several pedestrians in a crosswalk, killing a young mother and her three-year-old daughter. National news

---

3 For more on Abenomics' Third Arrow reforms, see Kushida (2021) and Kushida (2018).

coverage of the accident led to discussions about tightening manda-tory rescreening of drivers over age 70 (Asahi 2019).[4] While young males are statistically far more likely to cause fatal traffic accidents, this type of demographically worst-case-scenario accident can galva-nize the public to move toward technical solutions, in place of enabling seniors to drive as long as possible. Japan's taxi industry has lobbied successfully to keep out ride-sharing services such as Uber and Lyft, but the needs of seniors for mobility, coupled with sensational news of such accidents, can lead to political tipping points. Yet, rather than pitting one interest group against another pervasive voting bloc, regulations supporting technical solutions such as assistive and autonomous driv-ing can be accelerated.

Japan is undoubtedly in uncharted demographic territory. If firms inside and outside Japan can use the country's aging and shrinking as an opportunity, while the nation remains wealthy overall, with firms capable of devising technological solutions along the pathways that we have identified in this chapter and given the political and regulatory moves to support these trajectories, we may end this inquiry on a note of cautious optimism.

---

4   Another accident, involving an elderly and fatigued bus driver and resulting in the death of 15 university students, was also prominent in Japan's national news. See Sankei Shinbun (2017).

References

Activity Recognition Healthcare. n.d. "Improving Senior Health Care through Powerful A.I." Accessed March 22, 2021. http:// activityrecognition.com.

Acemoglu, Daron, and Pascual Restrepo. 2017. "Secular Stagnation? The Effect of Aging on Economic Growth in the Age of Automation." *American Economic Review* 107, no. 5: 174–79.

Asahi Shimbun. 2019. "Ikebukuro jiko, shibou wa oyako unten no 87 sai 'akuseru modorazu'" [Ikebukuro accident leads to death of mother and daughter. Driver claims that the accelerator pedal got stuck.]. April 19, 2019. https://www.asahi.com/articles / ASM4M5CQSM4MUTIL036.html.

Borrus, Michael. 1988. *Competing for Control: America's Stake in Microelectronics*. Cambridge, MA: Ballinger.

Cabinet Office. 2018. *Heisei 30nen ban korei shakai hakusho* [Aging society white paper 2018]. https://www8.cao.go.jp/kourei/ whitepaper/w-2018/zenbun /30pdf_index.html.

David, Paul A. 1985. "Clio and the Economics of QWERTY." *American Economic Review* 75, no. 2: 332–37.

Dosi, Giovanni. 1982. "Technological Paradigms and Technological Trajectories: A Suggested Interpretation of the Determinants and Directions of Technical Change." *Research Policy* 11, no. 3: 147–62.

Draper, Sam. 2019. "Seismic Powered Clothing: Fashionable Clothing Fused with Robotics and Sensor Technology." Wearable Technologies (blog), January 18, 2019. https://www.wearable-technologies .com/2019/01/seismic-powered-clothing-fashionable-clothing-fused -with-robotics-and-sensor-technology/.

Esping-Andersen, Gøsta. 1990. *The Three Worlds of Welfare Capitalism*. Princeton, NJ: Princeton University Press.

Hsu, Minchung, and Tomoaki Yamada. 2019. "Population Aging, Health Care, and Fiscal Policy Reform: The Challenges for Japan." *Scandinavian Journal of Economics* 121, no. 2: 547–77.

Japan Exchange Group. 2016a. "Joujougaisha toppu intabyū 'Sou'" [Listed company interview]. https://www.jpx.co.jp/listing/ir-clips/ interview/detail/3939.html.

———. 2016b. *Shinki joujou shinsei no tame no yūka shouken houkokusho: Kanamic Network* [Securities report for new listing

application: Kanamic Network]. https://www.jpx.co.jp/listing/
stocks/new/nlsgeu000001tgee-att /09KanamicNetwork-1s.pdf.

Johnstone, Bob. 2000. "California Dreamin' Sony Style." *MIT Technology Review,* January 1. https://www.technologyreview.com/s/
400610/california-dreamin-sony-style/.

Kamei, Keiichi. 2018. "Worker Shortage in Japan to Hit 6.4m by
2030, Survey Finds." *Nikkei Asian Review,* October 25, 2018.
https://asia.nikkei.com/Spotlight/Japan-immigration/Worker
-shortage-in-Japan-to-hit-6.4m-by-2030-survey-finds2.

Katz, Richard. 1998. *Japan: The System That Soured: The Rise and
Fall of the Japanese Economic Miracle.* New York, NY: ME Sharpe.

Keio University. 2017. "Odakyūdentetsu Kanagawachūoukoutsū to
Keiogijuku to no renkei kyouryoku kyoutei no teiketsu" [Odakyu
Railway Kanagawa Central Transportation Agency and Keio University enter into a partnership agreement]. Press release, December 19, 2017.

Kimura, Ryuhei, Akimitsu Yokoyama, and Mitsuru Naganuma.
2013. "Ninchishou koureisha wo taishou ni shita robotto kaizai
katsudou no nouhasokutei ni yoru teiryouteki hyouka" [Quantitative evaluation by EEG measurement of robot therapy for elderly
people with dementia]. *Teikyo University Departmental Bulletin
Paper* 9: 7–13.

Kitamura, Naoyuki. 2018. "Mezasu no ha 'iryou no minshuka'"
[Toward the democratization of medical care]. *Huffington Post
Japan,* September 7, 2018. https://www.huffingtonpost.jp/kitamura
-naoyuki/google-20180907_a_23519814/.

Kiyoshima, Naoki. 2019. "Jikki mākā 600 ki de basu yūdou,
Odakyūdentetsu ga jidou unten de hitodebusoku kaishou he"
[Odakyu Electric Railway to eliminate labor shortage with autonomous buses]. *Nikkei x Tech,* March 14, 2019. https://tech.nikkeibp
.co.jp/atcl/nxt/column/18/00606/030400003/.

Koizumi, Masumi, Kazuaki Nagata, and Satoshi Sugiyama. 2019.
"Foreign Workers Are On the Way, But Are Japanese Businesses
Ready?" *Japan Times,* March 31, 2019. https://www.japantimes
.co.jp/news/2019/03/31/national/foreign-workers-way-japanese
-businesses-ready/.

Kushida, Kenji E. 2010. "Inside the Castle Gates: How Foreign
Companies Navigate Japan's Policymaking Processes." Ph.D dissertation, Department of Political Science, University of California
Berkeley.

―――. 2011. "Leading Without Followers: How Politics and Market Dynamics Trapped Innovations in Japan's Domestic 'Galapagos' Telecommunications Sector." *Journal of Industry, Competition and Trade* 11, no. 3: 279–307. https://doi.org /10.1007/ s10842-011-0106-5.

―――. 2014. "Foreign Multinational Corporations and Systemic Change in Japan." In *Syncretization: Corporate Restructuring and Political Reform in Japan*, edited by Kenji E. Kushida, Kay Shimizu, and Jean Oi, 199–246. Stanford, CA: Shorenstein Asia-Pacific Research Center.

―――. 2018. "Abenomics' Third Arrow: Fostering Future Competitiveness?" In *Japan Decides 2017: The Japanese General Election*, edited by Robert J. Pekkanen, Steven R. Reed, Ethan Scheiner, and Daniel M. Smith. Springer International Publishing.

―――. 2021. "Abenomics and Japan's Entrepreneurship and Innovation: Is the Third Arrow Pointed in the Right Direction for Global Competition in the Silicon Valley Era?" In *The Political Economy of the Abe Government and Abenomics Reforms*, edited by Takeo Hoshi, Phillip Y. Lipscy. Cambridge University Press.

Kushida, Kenji E., Jonathan Murray, and John Zysman. 2015. "Cloud Computing: From Scarcity to Abundance." *Journal of Industry, Competition and Trade* 15, no. 1: 5–19. https://doi.org/10.1007/ s10842-014-0188-y.

MAFF (Ministry of Agriculture, Forestry and Fisheries). 2016. "Shoyūsha fumei tochi no jittai haaku no joukyou ni tsuite" [Regarding land whose ownership is unknown]. https://www.mlit.go .jp/common/001201304.pdf.

Mochizuki, Takashi, and Eric Pfanner. 2015. "In Japan, Dog Owners Feel Abandoned as Sony Stops Supporting 'Aibo.'" *Wall Street Journal*. February 11, 2015. https://www.wsj.com /articles/ in-japan-dog-owners-feel-abandoned-as-sony-stops-supporting-aibo-1423609536.

Nikkei (Nihon Keizai Shimbun). 2015 "Miyazaki kotsu to yamato unyu, takuhai ni rosen basu wo katsuyo" [Miyazaki Kotsu and Yamato Unyu utilize local bus lines for package delivery]. September 25, 2015. https://www.nikkei.com/article/ DGXLZO92050610U5A920C1LX0000/.

―――. 2017. "IT ka okure, jinken hi omoni" [Slow IT adoption, labor cost weighs heavy]. December 18, 2017. https://www.nikkei .com/article/DGKKZO24728300V11C17A2TJE000/

———. 2018a. "410 man hekutāru: shoyūsha fumei no tochi hirogaru" [4.1 million hectares: land where ownership is unknown increases]. June 30, 2018. https://www.nikkei.com/article/ DGKKZO32439080Z20C18A6EA5000/.

———. 2018b. "Hirogaru kakyaku konsai Sagawa nado, koutsūmou kara sangyou shinkou" [Companies such as Sagawa begin to partner with local transportation to assist in transportation network maintenance and boost in industry efficiency]. October 26, 2018. https://www.nikkei.com/article/ DGXMZO36970170W8A021C1EA6000/.

———. 2019a. "Hitachi, Sekisui, KDDI ga dēta renkei burokkuchēn de" [Hitachi, Sekisui, and KDDI form data sharing partnership using blockchain]. March 19, 2019. https://www.nikkei.com/article/ DGXMZO42656140Z10C19A3X20000/.

———. 2019b. "Mimamori mo dekiru wan Sonī, aibo de shin sābisu" [Sony launches new Watchdog Aibo service]." January 23, 2019. https://www.nikkei.com/article/DGXMZO40355020T20 C19A1X12000/.

Nikkei Asian Review. 2018. "Japan Launches Test of Self-Driving Truck Convoys: Labor-Saving Tech Would Let One Driver Direct Multiple Vehicles," January 24, 2018. https://asia.nikkei.com/Editor -s-Picks/Japan-Update/Japan-launches-test-of-self-driving-truck -convoys.

Noji, Kunio. 2018. "Agricultural Innovation." Presented at the Nikkei Agritech Summit 2018 (AG/SUM 2018), June 12, 2018. https:// agsum.jp/en/symposium.html.

Obe, Mitsuru. 2019. "Five Things to Know About Japan's Revised Immigration Law." *Nikkei Asian Review*. April 1, 2019. https://asia .nikkei.com/Spotlight/Japan-immigration/Worker-shortage-in-Japan -to-hit-6.4m-by-2030-survey-finds2.

Odakyu. 2018. "9 gatsu 6 ka - 16 nichi enoshima shūhen koudou de jidou unten basu no jisshou jikken wo jisshi" [Autonomous buses tested on public roads in Enoshima area on September 6 to 16]. News release, August 14, 2018. https://www.odakyu.jp/news/ 050aa1000001bwk7-att/050aa1000001bwke.pdf.

Okuma, Nozomi. 2017. "DeNA ga jidou unten de ZMP to no teikei wo kaishou, aratani Nissan tono kyougyou ga akiraka ni" [DeNA dissolves autonomous driving partnership with ZMP, reveals new collaboration with Nissan]. *TechCrunch Japan*. January 6, 2017.

https://jp.techcrunch.com/2017/01/06/dena-zmp-dissolve-robot
-taxi/.

PARO Robots U.S., Inc. n.d. "Research Papers." http://www
.parorobots.com/whitepapers.asp.

Pauly, Louis W, and Simon Reich. 1997. "National Structures and
Multinational Corporate Behavior: Enduring Differences in the Age
of Globalization." *International Organization* 51, no. 1: 1–30.

Pekkanen, Robert J., Steven R. Reed, Ethan Scheiner, and Daniel M.
Smith, eds. 2018. *Japan Decides 2017: The Japanese General Election.* Springer International Publishing.

Perez, Carlota. 2010. "Technological Revolutions and Techno-
economic Paradigms." *Cambridge Journal of Economics* 34, no. 1:
185–202.

Sakashita, Reiko, Miho Takami, Hiroshi Ono, Tomoko Nishihira,
Takuichi Sato, and Misao Hamada. 2015. "Preventing Aspiration
Pneumonia Among the Elderly: A Review Focused on the Impact
of the Consistency of Food Substances." In *Interface Oral Health
Science 2014,* edited by Keiichi Sasaki, Osamu Suzuki, and Nobu-
hiro Takahashi, 335–51. Tokyo: Springer Japan. https://doi.org/10
.1007/978-4-431-55192-8.

Sankei Shimbun. 2017. "Jikochō 'unten misu gen'in' unkō kaisha ga
anzen keishi, chōsa hōkoku-sho kōhyō." July 5, 2017. https://www
.sankei.com/affairs/news/170705/afr1707050031-n1.html.

———. 2018a. "Sekai hatsu nihon no houjin touki (kaisha touki
jyouhou) no burokkuchēn touki sābisu, fudousan burokkuchēn
gijutsu no tokkyo hoyū nihon houjin ga sābisu kaishi" [World's
first blockchain corporate registration service, patented real estate
blockchain service commences]. June 6, 2018. https://www.sankei
.com /economy/news/180606/prl1806060315-n1.html.

———. 2018b. "Sonī-kei koureisha shisetsu de 'aibo' no robotto
serapī hajimaru" [Aibo robot therapy commences at Sony Group
elderly facility]. May 17, 2018. https://www.sankei.com/economy/
news/180517/ecn1805170052-n1.html.

Seismic. 2019. "Seismic Announces Strategic Partnerships with
Cintas Corporation, Obayashi Corporation, Transforming Age
and Solid Biosciences at CES 2019." https://www.myseismic.com/
wp-content/uploads/2019/04/Seismic-Strategic-Partnerships-Press
-Release.pdf.

Shibata, Takenori. 2004. "Serapī robotto, kaigo no mirai wo kaeru"
[Therapy robots changing the future of caregiving]. Interview. *AIST*

TMB: Tech Meets Business. January 10, 2004. https://unit.aist.go
.jp/ictes/tmb/interview09.html.

Statistics Bureau, Ministry of Internal Affairs and Communications.
2018. *Statistical Handbook of Japan 2018.* https://www.stat.go.jp/
english/data/handbook/pdf/2018all.pdf#page=17.

Sura, Livia, Aarthi Madhavan, Giselle Carnaby, and Michael A Crary.
2012. "Dysphagia in the Elderly: Management and Nutritional
Considerations." *Clinical Interventions in Aging* 7: 287–98. https://
doi.org/10.2147/CIA.S23404.

Tamura, Toshiyo, Satomi Yonemitsu, Akiko Itoh, Daisuke Oikawa,
Akiko Kawakami, Yuji Higashi, Toshiro Fujimoto, and Kazuki
Nakajima. 2004. "Is an Entertainment Robot Useful in the Care of
Elderly People with Severe Dementia?" *Journals of Gerontology.
Series A, Biological Sciences and Medical Sciences* 59, no. 1: 83–85.
https://doi.org/10.1093/gerona/59.1.m83.

Telenoid Healthcare Company. n.d. "Terenoido tte nani? | Sutōrī"
[What Is the Telenoid? Story]. https://telenoid.co.jp/story/telenoid.

Togashi, Ryoichi. 2016. "Earth and Sky: New Frontiers in Construc-
tion/Mining and Drones." Presented at the Silicon Valley – New
Japan Summit 2016, October 4, 2016. https://event.techblitz.com/
event2016/.

Vogel, Steven K. 2006. *Japan Remodeled: How Government and
Industry Are Reforming Japanese Capitalism.* Ithaca, NY: Cornell
University Press.

Yahoo! News Japan. 2019. "Shin toujou 'toromi' wo tsukeru jidou
hanbaiki, dounyū no ura ni wa Nihon ga kakaeru dai mondai ga"
[Newly introduced vending machines with 'Toromi' option reveal
a big challenge for Japan]. May 4, 2019. https://headlines.yahoo.co
.jp/hl?a=20190504-00010001-sp_ctv-bus_all.

Tsuruhara, Yoshiro. 2018. "Nissan DeNA 'Mujin takushī' no houn-
tou no sugosa" [The true value of Nissan and DeNA's "unmanned
taxi"]. *Nikkei Business Publications,* February 27, 2018. https://
business.nikkei.com/atcl/report/15/264450/022600085/.

Zysman, John. 1983. *Governments, Markets, and Growth: Financial
Systems and the Politics of Industrial Change.* Ithaca, NY: Cornell
University Press.

Zysman, John, and Abraham Newman. 2006. *How Revolutionary
Was the Digital Revolution? National Responses, Market Transi-
tions, and Global Technology, Innovation and Technology in the
World Economy.* Stanford, CA: Stanford Business Books.

Appendix A

TABLE A.1 Selected Abenomics' Third Arrow KPIs and progress so far

Target year (year introduced)	Key performance indicator	Progress as of 12/2020
	Health, medicine, and caregiving	
2020 (2013)	Extend the "healthy life expectancy" from the 2010 level (male=70.42, female=73.63) by one year. (Revised in 2017 to extend by two years by 2020, in 2019 to extend by three years by 2040.)	Initial KPI achieved 2016.
FY2020 (2013)	Increase the proportion of large hospitals (with over 400 beds) utilizing electronic medical records to 90%.	On track as of FY2019.*
2020 (2013)	Increase the market size for robotic devices in nursing care to ¥50 billion.	2015: ¥2.47 billion. Not on track.
2030 (2015)	Increase the number of robotic devices for nursing care to 8,000 units.	On track as of FY2000.
	Advancement of mobility services, eliminating "mobility disadvantaged" people, and transforming logistics	
2020 (2017)	Increase the share of new passenger cars equipped with automated braking system to over 90%.	Achieved
2020 (2018)	Commence operation of autonomous vehicles on public roads in designated regions.	Achieved
2030 (2018)	Commence operation of driverless autonomous vehicle services in more than 100 areas nationwide.	Unclear
2025 (2020)	Enable "level 4" autonomous driving on all freeways	—
2022 (2020)	Enable package delivery using drones beyond "line of sight"	—

SOURCE: Cabinet Office; *Japan Agency for Medical Research and Development.

7 Technology for Agriculture Productivity in India

Innovation to Harness the Demographic Dividend

Aparajita Goyal and Karen Eggleston

Economic development, demographic transition, and productivity growth are intricately linked, and the understanding of agriculture's place in this relationship continues to change.[1] For the early thinkers on economic development, agriculture—unlike more "modern" sectors—was identified with large families and low productivity. It was a deep pool of cheap labor, and as an economy's structure transformed, labor would flow from agriculture into more productive sectors like manufacturing and services (see, for example, Clark 1951; Lewis 1954; Kuznets 1955; Chenery and Syrquin 1975).

Since then, perceptions of agriculture's understated role in structural transformation and economy-wide productivity growth have evolved. Agricultural productivity is understood to be a powerful driver of growth that raises people out of poverty.[2] Three-quarters of the world's poor are rural people, and most derive their livelihoods from farming. Clearly, if any development strategy is to "move the needle" toward the goals of reducing poverty and boosting shared prosperity, it must catalyze growth where the majority of poor people live and work.

---

[1] For a discussion of the relationship between economic development and demographic transition, see, for example, Bloom, Canning, and Fink (2010) and Eggleston and Fuchs (2012) and sources cited therein.

[2] See a sample of studies by Schultz (1975); Timmer (2002); Gollin, Parente, and Rogerson (2002); Christiaensen, Demery, and Kuhl (2011); Goyal and Nash (2017); de Janvry and Sadoulet (2019).

India is home to the world's largest rural population (893 million).[3] Compared to the other economies analyzed in this volume, India is relatively young; it is at an earlier stage in the demographic transition—the transition from birth and death rates that are high and fluctuating, to ones that are relatively low and stable.[4] This stage in its demographic transition leads to the challenge and opportunity of a large working-age population: the challenge to productively employ its 600 million workforce.[5] Moreover, according to India's 2011 Census, 71 percent of the elderly live in rural India, so that policies to adjust to demographic change—i.e., support older Indians and their families, promote healthy aging and reduce functional dependency—necessarily disproportionately involve agricultural-based communities (Singh and Prabhakaran 2019).

In this chapter, we discuss the need for innovation to raise agricultural productivity in India so that India can reduce poverty and reap the "demographic dividend" that earlier spurred the economic development of its now aging East Asian neighbors (as mentioned in the book's introduction). We first briefly discuss India's demographic challenges and then turn to elements of a system for promoting agriculture productivity and innovation. We next focus on strengthening both public and private sector research, and end with a discussion of key features of rural incomes and the potential for digital technologies to harness productivity growth.

India's Demographic Challenge

India is the second most populous country in the world, and within the next decade or so will surpass China as the most populous. India's population is steadily aging, although it is much younger than that of East Asia, Europe, and North America (figure 7.1). The median age—the age at which half the population is older and half is

---

3 China's rural population is about 578 million. According to the UN *World Urbanization Prospects: The 2018 Revision*, globally the rural population has grown slowly since 1950 and currently is about 3.4 billion. In the coming years, it is projected to increase slightly before decreasing to around 3.1 billion in 2050.

4 See Lee (2003) for a discussion of three centuries of demographic transition and its economic significance.

5 According to the International Labor Organization, India's 2018 employment-to-population ratio was 45.42 percent, implying a workforce of slightly more than 600 million.

FIGURE 7.1 Median age in India, compared to China, Europe, Japan, and North America, 1990–2050

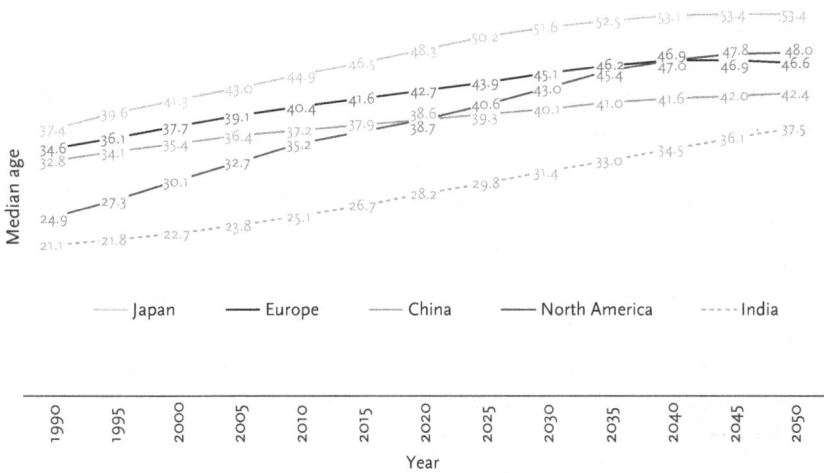

SOURCE: United Nations, *World Population Prospects: The 2017 Revision*. Medium variant.

younger—increased from 21.1 years old in 1990 to about 28 years old currently, and is projected to increase to 37.5 by the year 2050. That increase in India's median age over a 60-year period is similar to the increase projected for Japan (gaining 16 years in median age), and quite a bit larger than the increase in North America (9.5 years) or Europe (12 years). Of course, India starts from a much younger base and experiences a gentler increase than in China, which is aging rapidly. India's median age in 2050 is expected to be similar to that of Japan in 1990, Europe in 2000, North America in 2010, and China currently.

The change in population age structure derives from longer lives and fewer births. India's life expectancy at birth increased by 28 years between 1950 and 2012 (from 37 to 65) and is projected to be 74 by 2050. Over the same period, fertility declined from 6 to 2.6 children per woman (Arokiasamy et al. 2012). Although it is aging at a slower pace than many other parts of Asia, India still has a large overall "dependency ratio" (ratio of nonworkers to workers) because of large cohorts of youth as well as a growing population of older adults. In the chapter appendix, we also provide the UN projections of India's demographic future, including its total population (figure B.1), its age 60 and older population (figure B.2), and its old-age dependency ratio (figure B.3). According to the UN's median estimates, India's total population will peak around the year 2060 at over 1.6 billion; at that time, almost 400 million Indians will be age 60 or older, and those old-age dependents will number 40 per 100 population aged 15 to 59.

Only if they are productively employed will the younger generations be able to support higher living standards for themselves and for their parents and grandparents—whose incomes, healthcare, and other needs rely on younger family members. Since residents in rural areas tend to be older than in urban areas, agriculture and its associated rural livelihoods are key to supporting India's growing cohorts of older individuals. In all states (except two smaller states, Goa and Mizoram), a higher proportion of the elderly lives in rural areas than in urban areas (Singh and Prabhakaran 2019). India also has large regional heterogeneity. As Singh and Prabhakaran emphasize, the southern states are the front-runners in population aging.

The key challenge for India at the nexus of demographic change and innovation is how best to provide the working-age population with productive livelihoods to contribute to fully realizing the growth-enhancing demographic dividend. Indeed, even before the economic and social distress caused by the coronavirus pandemic, estimates suggested that India would have to create 20 percent more jobs in 2010–30 than were created in 1990–2010 (Bloom, McKenna, Prettner 2018, 12). We will come back to discussing the labor force after describing in more detail why innovation to meet India's demographic and growth challenges will need to focus on raising agricultural productivity.

Agricultural Productivity, Poverty Reduction, and Sustainable Development

Evidence shows that growth in agriculture reduces poverty more than growth elsewhere in an economy, especially in the earlier stages of structural transformation (Ivanic and Martin 2018; Ligon and Sadoulet 2018). Agriculture's poverty-reducing advantage disappears as countries (and people) get richer (see figure 7.2), but the evidence affirms that improvements in agricultural productivity are vital for structural transformation and a smooth transition toward more urbanized economies, because growth in agricultural productivity leads to higher incomes, promotes nonfarm jobs, and enables people to move out of agriculture over time (Gollin, Parente, and Rogerson 2002; McMillan

FIGURE 7-2 The relationship between per capita GDP and poverty changes from a productivity increase equal to 1 percent of GDP

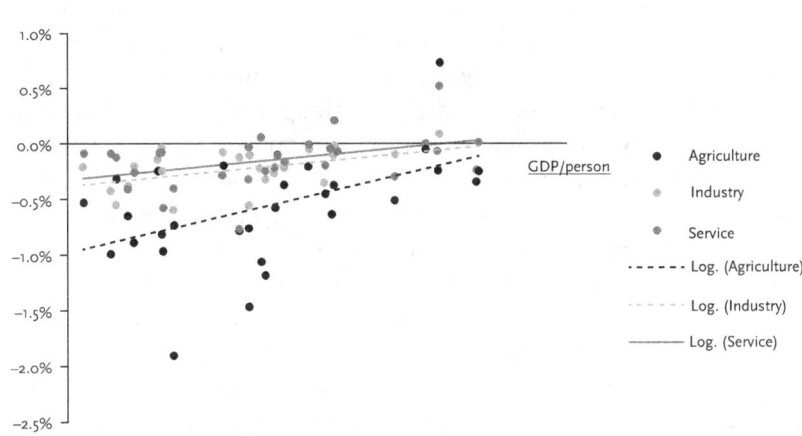

SOURCE: Ivanic and Martin (2018).

and Harttgen 2014). Investments and policies to stimulate growth in the rural economy are critical for accelerating the transition out of poverty and fostering inclusive growth.

Agricultural productivity growth, most visible in the spread of the "Green Revolution" across many parts of the world (especially South and East Asia), has helped to ward off the Malthusian catastrophe predicted in the 1960s, when the world's population was soaring, extreme poverty was widespread, agricultural productivity (particularly in food crops) was very low, and land for agriculture was limited in many areas (Timmer 2002; Gollin 2010). Productivity growth, driven by science, technology, and innovation with supportive policies and substantial institutional investments, led to significant increases in overall food production. Moreover, crop varieties bred to withstand various forms of biotic and abiotic stress made food production less volatile.

Recent trends strongly caution against complacency based on achievements to date. On the contrary, they show the urgency of sustaining past success while pushing for faster growth in agricultural productivity in the regions that are still lagging. For the third consecutive year since reaching its nadir in 2015, global undernourishment is on the rise, reaching 821 million in 2017 (FAO et al. 2018). Conflicts in various parts of the world have contributed to this problem, but a more widespread contributor is climate change. Even as the impacts of climate change are felt worldwide, the Intergovernmental Panel on Climate Change (IPCC 2018) released further sobering news: climate impacts are occurring faster than previously estimated, and will be much worse at 2°C than previously projected. These impacts, together with a deteriorating natural resource base, will hit agriculture especially hard. As it is, food security remains a persistent concern for policymakers, not only in rural Africa—the only major region where the rise in the absolute number of undernourished people is concentrated, and where agricultural growth remains driven mostly by factor accumulation—but also in South Asia, and parts of Latin America and the Caribbean, where the effects of climate change are expected to be felt most severely and large numbers of poor and vulnerable people remain. All of these trends speak to the compelling need for policies and options to accelerate agricultural productivity growth, in the interest not only of food security and incomes, but also of sustainability.

An important factor behind the large divergence in standards of living across countries, and across sectors within countries, is that agriculture in poor countries appears to be much less productive—either in cross-country comparisons or compared to other sectors where labor productivity is found to be much higher. A number of reasons have been put forward to explain these differences. A common reason is that developing country agriculture is dominated by small-scale producers who have limited access to technology, credit, insurance, and transport, and are subject to markets that discourage the adoption of modern technologies and other productivity-enhancing investments. Another reason is that low levels of human capital put rural labor at a disadvantage (Caselli and Coleman 2001). Furthermore, policies result in a misallocation of resources, which (if rectified) could potentially narrow the divergence in agricultural productivity between rich and poor countries (Adamopoulos and Restuccia 2014). Given the importance of agricultural productivity to development outcomes, it is not surprising that agriculture remains high on the agendas of policymakers, making it imperative to understand the drivers of productivity growth in specific circumstances and regions.

In this regard, success in countries throughout the world provides important lessons. Evidence shows that investments in rural public goods, combined with better policies and institutions, have driven agricultural productivity growth globally (Goyal and Nash 2017). The dividends from investments to develop and disseminate improved technologies, strengthen markets, expand access to water, and improve water management can be enormous, including the encouragement of greater private investment. Improvements in the policy environment through reforms in trade and regulatory policy further enhance the incentives for producers and innovators to invest, or to take advantage of public goods that attract or "crowd in" private investment. Research from Latin America and the Caribbean, for instance, finds that it is crucial to shift public investment away from providing goods and services to specific groups of producers and toward an increased provision of public goods. On average, 51 percent of all government spending in rural areas during 1985–2001 was for subsidies to private goods. A reallocation of 10 percentage points of public expenditures to public goods increased per capita agricultural income by about 2.3 percent without increasing total spending (Lopez and Galinato 2007). These findings from cross-country analysis of Latin America are consistent with the analysis for Asia, where spending on rural infrastructure, agricultural research and development (R&D), and technology dissemination had large poverty alleviation effects. In India, the relative performance of subsidies evolved over time: returns were somewhat higher in the early years of the Green Revolution but declined rapidly thereafter. Fertilizer, power, and irrigation subsidies were among the least significant contributors to poverty alleviation over the four decades studied (Fan, Gulati, and Thorat 2009).

The Rationale for Agricultural Innovation Policy

Many countries have viewed agricultural innovation policy, particularly investments in R&D, as a key component of their food security and economic development strategies. But despite evidence that agricultural R&D investments have yielded high returns, agricultural R&D continues to be significantly underfunded (Fuglie et al. 2019). The reasons for this underfunding include both market and political failures. Market failure, which leads to underinvestment by the private sector, arises for several reasons:

- The new knowledge embodied in innovations has characteristics of public goods. It is often difficult for innovators to protect their intellectual property and profit from their innovations. The fixed cost of creating an innovation is much higher than the marginal cost of replicating it, and marketing a biological innovation (an improved variety of seed, for example) often provides the means for replicating it.

- The small-holder structure of agriculture and its inherent risks limits the ability and willingness of farmers to invest in innovation, and gives rise to the high transaction costs of transmitting information on innovations among the farm population.
- The technological needs of farmers tend to be location-specific, meaning that technologies developed elsewhere cannot be readily applied locally.

The presence of significant market failures provides a rational for government action. However, political failures may also cause governments to underinvest in agricultural innovation. One source of political failure is the difficulty of dispersed farm populations to organize themselves effectively to lobby governments to act in their interests. Even when political systems are responsive to farm interests, agricultural research may be a low priority because of a relatively long time lag for R&D investments to yield noticeable value to their beneficiaries. Furthermore, although agricultural R&D has yielded impressive returns on average, many public agricultural research institutes have been poorly managed, lack critical mass, and have underperformed, giving rise to "donor fatigue" toward support for agricultural research.

Strengthening the Capacity and Performance of Public Agricultural Research Systems

Public agricultural research systems, including government and university research stations and laboratories, have languished in many developing countries where spending on agricultural R&D remains very low relative to the size of their agricultural sectors. But it is not just underinvestment that plagues many of these systems. Other common problems include unstable funding from year to year, low education levels of research staff, low staff retention and/or aging scientists, few operational funds available after salaries and other fixed costs are met, low performance incentives, and limited means of performance evaluation.

Public agricultural research institutions have historically relied heavily on general government revenues for funding, usually as institutional block grants for staff salaries, facility maintenance, and research programs. Some national research institutions in low- and lower-middle-income countries have also relied heavily on donor support from bilateral or multilateral aid programs. Many institutions have suffered from low and unstable funding. To increase total funding and also to reduce budget volatility, public research institutions have experimented with ways of diversifying their sources of funding. One source of additional funding for research is through producer levies. Levies are assessments made on the value of sales or exports of commodities. Revenues from the levies are typically channeled through producer organizations and used to fund a range of cooperative activities, including research, extension, and market promotion. Governments may give statutory authority to the producer associations to impose mandatory levies on producers when a majority of its members are in favor. Levies are mostly used for commodities that are grown commercially and for export, and that are marketed through a limited number of outlets, such as processing mills or ports (which reduces the transaction cost of collecting the levy).

Some public research institutes have tried to raise financial support by investing some of their assets in business ventures unrelated to research, such as for hotels or office parks. This can result in diversion of resources away from research. It also creates considerable liabilities for the institutes if these ventures fail. One way of economizing on the use of public resources in the development and dissemination of agricultural innovations is through partnerships with the private sector. In such a partnership, the private sector partner may share some of the R&D costs but focuses most of its effort on market development and promotion. It will typically have an exclusive license to the new product for a limited period of time. Such a licensing arrangement is designed to allow the company to recoup its fixed costs of research and market development.

An example of public-private joint ventures in food and agriculture is the use of Cooperative Research and Development Agreements (CRADAs) by the United States Department of Agriculture (USDA). A CRADA typically involves a government laboratory collaborating with a company to develop a technology for commercialization. Both parties commit in-house resources to R&D, and the private-sector collaborator may provide the government laboratory with some research funds. Government laboratories may provide personnel, equipment, and laboratory privileges to the private partner. Patents resulting from a CRADA may be jointly owned, and the private partner has first rights to negotiate an exclusive license for patents resulting from the CRADA. Some research data also may not be publicly disclosed for a certain period of time (Day-Rubenstein and Fuglie 2000).

One area where public-private joint ventures are common is in the seed industry. While the public sector usually assumes the major role in crop breeding, the tasks of seed multiplication and marketing often involve private seed companies. Once a new variety has been developed and approved for release, the public research institute makes available a limited amount of "foundation seed" to seed companies. Companies then multiply the seed under government oversight to ensure quality and purity. The companies then sell this "certified seed" to producers. Farmers in turn may save some of their harvest as seed for their following crop or for selling or sharing with other farmers. The specific roles of the public and private partners in seed development, multiplication, and marketing vary by crop, depending on the characteristics of the crop and seed market. Private companies often play a dominant role in breeding crop varieties grown using hybrid seed (which cannot be saved by farmers because the progeny does not maintain the characteristics of the parent seed), while public-private partnerships are typical for most other field crops. For some crops, the public sector may need to take a dominant role in both varietal development and seed multiplication and distribution—for example, when the market for improved seed is small but where the crops are being promoted to advance a public goal such as food and nutrition security (such as highly nutritious or locally important indigenous crops in low-income countries).[6]

At the heart of any research system is its cadre of scientific and technical staff. Maximizing the performance of a research system requires that its staff are properly motivated and incentivized to produce quality and relevant science and technology for its clients, namely, the farm and agribusinesses in its home region or country. One of the key factors behind the success of Brazil's Embrapa, the Brazilian Agricultural Research Corporation, was the significant attention it gave to human capital development of its staff, providing them with attractive career paths that rewarded performance, and achieving staff retention by offering salary and benefit packages competitive with the private sector. In its early years, Embrapa was investing as much as 20 percent of its budget in training and staff development, including support for degree programs (Martha, Contini, and Alves 2012). Because of its status as

---

6   For an excellent discussion of public-private roles in seed development for different types of crop and country circumstances, see "Early Generation Seed Study" by Monitor Deloitte (April 2015), a study supported by the United States Agency for International Development and the Bill and Melinda Gates Foundation.

a public corporation, it could offer greater flexibility in its human re-source policies than a government agency, where staff rank and salary are often tied more closely to length of service than to performance.

Although agricultural technologies must be tailored to location-specific conditions, the pool of agricultural science and technology knowledge and genetic resources that scientists draw upon to make these adaptations are generally supplied from advanced research in-stitutes. Broad and accessible collections of crop genetic resources are maintained by the CGIAR agricultural research centers, which con-tinue to make major methodological advances in the tools for agri-cultural sciences. Over the past couple of decades, for example, major advances have been made in the science of crop and animal breeding. The use of the haploid method in maize breeding has reduced the time necessary to develop improved parent lines from ten to two genera-tions. Using genetic testing in animal breeding now enables scientists to predict the performance of dairy calves as soon as they are born (as opposed to waiting four to five years for the animals to mature and produce). The merger of molecular biological and information tech-nologies has dramatically improved the rate of genetic progress pos-sible through breeding. To make use of these scientific advances and resources, agricultural scientists in developing countries need to form networks and collaborative relationships with scientists in leading ag-ricultural research centers and universities.

The establishment of international agricultural research centers like the CGIAR was designed to facilitate the transfer for agricultural tech-nology from developed to developing countries (and from temperate to tropical zones) and among countries in tropical zones through the transfer of research capacity. International centers can also achieve sig-nificant economies of scale in scientific activities that produce global public goods, like crop genetic conservation, characterization, and pre-breeding (moving genetic traits from wild relatives to crop-breeding parent lines). By linking their national research programs with the CGIAR and agricultural research institutes in other countries, devel-oping countries can gain access to these scientific developments. Espe-cially important for small countries, they can then focus their limited research resources on adaptation to local conditions.

Over the past couple of decades, countries like India, Brazil, and China have significantly strengthened their national agricultural re-search systems and are becoming important sources of advances in agri-cultural technology. An additional characteristic of a viable agricultural research system is integral involvement of education and training for research. This is essential if developing countries are to remove the scientific human capital constraints that limit their capacity to move to productivity-based agricultural growth. Graduate-level education in agricultural sciences is most effective when it occurs in association with a significant research program. Thus, universities play a fundamental role in agricultural research systems. Agricultural universities are home to some of the most highly skilled scientists, who have the essential task of training the researchers and technicians that staff research and development organizations in both the public and private sectors. In the 1960s many developing countries in Asia launched long-term initiatives to strengthen agricultural higher education; and India allocates more than a third of its total public agricultural R&D spending through universities (Lele and Goldsmith 1989). For Latin America, the share of agriculture R&D in universities is even higher, at around 40 percent (Stads et al. 2016). Countries in Sub-Saharan Africa, however, typically route less than 10 percent of public agricultural R&D funding through universities (Bientema and Stads 2017). Eicher (2004) and Osiru, Nampala, and Ekwamu (2016) document a serious decline in the quality of graduate training programs at African agricultural universities and argue that this is crippling the capacity of these institutions to train African scientists and to create effective agricultural research systems in this region.

Incentivizing Private-Sector Innovation and Technology Transfer

Private, for-profit agribusiness companies that sell inputs to and buy commodities from farmers are becoming an increasingly important source of innovation and technology transfer in agriculture. In many cases, however, these investments are constrained by market failures and government policies. These market failures can be due to high transaction costs, such as the costs associated with negotiating and enforcing contracts with a large number of producers, as well as information asymmetries regarding the quality of goods offered for sale. Government policies may explicitly limit agribusiness participation in agricultural input and output markets. State-owned enterprises or commodity boards, for example, may have monopolies over certain inputs like seed or fertilizer, or over the marketing of agricultural commodities.

In some cases, participation in agricultural markets is restricted to domestic companies. Market reforms that have opened up these sectors to private companies have stimulated significant private investment in agricultural research and technology transfer. Multinational companies have shown greater willingness to transfer their most advanced technologies if they are allowed to hold full or majority ownership in a local subsidiary.

Government regulations exert a large influence on the types of goods offered in agricultural markets. Regulations designed to ensure product safety and quality can help reduce information asymmetries when these attributes are not readily observable, but regulations can also hinder the introduction of new product innovations if approval procedures are onerous and time-consuming. Regulations for obtaining approval for marketing a new crop variety are often particularly costly, requiring multiple years of field testing in each country where a company wants to market the seed variety. While some progress has been made whereby countries would accept regulatory approvals from other countries, implementation of these agreements has been slow and has constrained technology transfer across national borders. Laws and regulations that protect patents and trademarks can provide a positive stimulus to private investment in innovation, but only if they are effectively enforced. Stronger intellectual property protection over new crop varieties has been an important factor stimulating private research into crops grown with the use of nonhybrid seed.

Many countries have been slow to establish biosafety protocols for genetically modified (GM) seed, despite abundant evidence of their economic value and safety. Investment in public goods like research, extension, and education help stimulate private investments in agricultural innovation and markets. Research that addresses key technical constraints to farm production can expand the supply and quality of commodities available for value-added processing and marketing. Expanding the university training of scientists, technicians, and engineers expands the pool of qualified personnel for private agribusiness. Some countries have used R&D tax incentives to encourage private investment in research. Tax credits for private R&D spending help compensate a company for economic "spillovers" that its R&D may create. These spillovers are economic benefits from the new technology that are not captured by the firm that developed it, but go to farmers, consumers, or other firms who may develop spinoff applications using the technology. An obvious role for government is to improve rural transportation infrastructure, electricity, and other infrastructure. Governments can target limited resources for infrastructure investment through consultation with private agribusiness, financial service providers, and producer groups, in order to identify where returns to infrastructure improvement may have the greatest impact on stimulating private investment in market value chains (Schlenker 2019).

To meet the growing demand for diverse and quality food products and to achieve scale, food companies will often establish contracts with farmers that specify prices to be paid and quality standards to be met for the farm products. Because negotiating and enforcing contracts with many small producers may involve high transaction costs, food companies will often prefer to contract with fewer, larger producers. Governments can assist small holder participation in market value chains through a number of approaches. One way is to use extension services to help organize and train producers in negotiating and meeting contract terms with food companies, both to ensure that producers' interests are respected and to reduce company transaction costs. Governments could also require companies to include small holders in their marketing chains as a condition of receiving business licenses or access to concessional loans or other public services.

Agriculture Labor and Rural Incomes

Macro statistics typically associate workers with the sector of their reported "main" occupation with the assumption that the workers pursue that activity full-time. Yet, agricultural workers often do not work full-time in agriculture. As such, even after the refinements in accounting for the sector of work, potential biases might remain, owing to mismeasurement of the actual time that individuals spend on specific activities (farming, nonfarm work, domestic work, and so on) (McCullough 2017). Rural workers typically work in multiple activities/sectors. Ignoring this leads to an overestimation of labor use in agriculture, as in the case of national accounts.

For instance, data from India provide detailed insights into rural labor markets. The comprehensive Village Dynamics in South Asia[7] surveys collect information on the myriad economic activities of households

---

7   A project launched in 2009 by ICRISAT, the International Crops Research Institute for the Semi-Arid Tropics.

and their individual members. These surveys allow researchers to estimate measures of labor supplied to various (agricultural and nonagricultural) activities. These surveys allow for estimation of three alternative measures of labor supplied to individual activities. One measure is
based on the self-declared "main occupation," which is the approach in
macro statistics—referred to as the *per-person* estimate. The second is
based on the number of labor days spent on specific activities—or a *per-
day* estimate. The third is based on the number of hours of labor spent
on each activity—the *per-hour*—estimate. Among these three measures,
the data on the hours of labor used for various activities throughout
the growing season, when combined with the detailed input and output
production accounts collected for each parcel the household cultivates,
provide the most accurate account of labor use on and off the farm
(Fuglie et al. 2019).[8]

The data clearly demonstrate that rural households follow multiple
strategies to secure livelihoods; households in the sample are engaged
in as many as six different activities, with the majority engaged in three
or four activities. A more nuanced picture emerges by age group and
gender. Focusing on working adults, and distinguishing between male
workers (who report 23 days of work) and female workers (who report
15 days of work), two main points are relevant to the measurement of
labor productivity. One is that the labor force engagement is significantly different for male and female workers. With the exception of salaried female workers, all others appear to be significantly less engaged
in economic activities. Male salaried and business workers also report
working more than full time (reflecting some participation in other activities), while farm-based workers (agricultural and livestock workers)
appear to be occupied slightly less (at about 92 percent of their labor
endowment). Importantly, however, the amount of time spent farming,
even by farmers, is significantly less, with a substantial part of their
time engaged in nonfarming activities. Farm laborers, on average, are
the least engaged, at about 82 percent of the time.

The second important point is the seasonality of labor use in agriculture. The observed slack in average worked time for farmers and
farm labor hides the seasonal nature of their work. This point is clearer

---

8 One piece of missing data is the hourly labor input for livestock, for which only
reported days are available. To derive labor productivity per hour, that data from
the cost of labor is used, divided by the village wage rates for livestock activities, as
available from a separate "village level" survey module.

FIGURE 7.3 The distribution of workdays each month for an average adult rural worker in South Asia, farm work versus nonfarm work, 2010–15

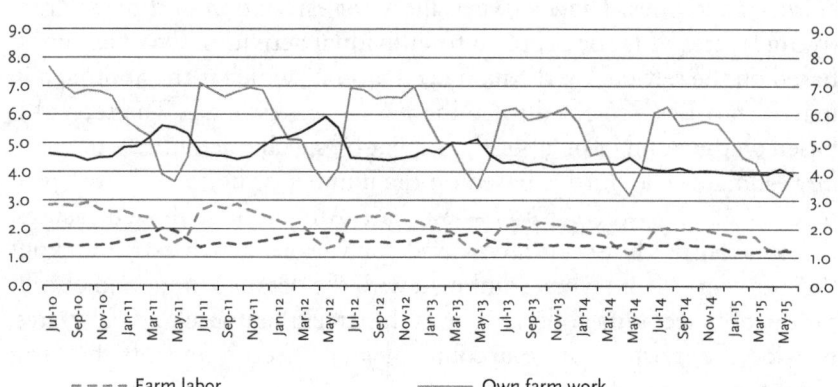

SOURCE: Village Dynamics in South Asia surveys, ICRISAT (International Crops Research Institute for the Semi-Arid Tropics).

in figure 7.3. While salaried workers are engaged at a constant level through the year, agricultural work, especially work related to crop production, has a distinct seasonal pattern. Farm labor supplied outside of the household farm shows an identical pattern to labor use on the household farm. Interestingly, nonfarm labor and business work show counter-cyclical patterns with supply of labor to those activities rising when agricultural activities are less. In other words, enterprises appear to be an important source of alternative employment in the "lean" agricultural periods.

The main conclusion emerging is that nonagricultural work is perhaps a "filler" for farmers' downtime. The implication for policy and strategy is to reduce the seasonality in agriculture through increased irrigation or temporal diversification, or through diversification into higher-valued crops and farm activities. Attractive, gainful employment for agricultural workers would better meet the needs of seasonally under- or unemployed agricultural workers. There is evidence of the counter-cyclical nature of rural nonfarm jobs, a trend that could be significantly scaled up through investments in nonfarm enterprises (Fuglie et al. 2019).

Finally, both agricultural productivity and gainful employment outside agriculture could be enhanced if there were better information about job opportunities outside agriculture, perhaps especially for young women (Jensen 2012) and if the workforce at all ages were healthier. Investments in human capital in terms of better education and better nutrition (reducing anemia, childhood stunting, etc.) can reinforce each other, enabling children to concentrate more in school; and such investments can be productive for households and the economy more broadly as the demographic transition proceeds, fertility declines, and working outside the home and outside of agriculture become more accepted options for many women. Women and older household members tend to have low rates of labor force participation, although evidence suggests they contribute to agricultural production and household labor in multifarious ways (Arokiasamy et al. 2012). Promoting health across the life course can facilitate healthy aging and increase the contributions of older individuals to the household and/or reduce caregiver burden by increasing the functional independence among older individuals and "compressing morbidity" into later years. This is especially important for rural India, because older individuals generally are more engaged with household activities than in high-income countries—working to support farm tasks, care for children, and doing other housework. As a consequence, time use among older adults in high-income countries may not provide the best counterfactual; and promoting healthy aging with specific interventions may have a higher value than what the high-income context would indicate (Sudharsanan and Bloom 2018). Improving their health would lead to potentially large gains from longer productive working lives and lower household burden from caregiving and medical expenses (currently borne mostly by households out-of-pocket).

The Power of Digital Technology for Productivity Growth

Mobile phones and the internet have significantly affected practically all sectors of the economy, and agriculture is no exception. Ever since people have grown crops, raised livestock, and caught fish, they have sought information from one another. What is the most effective planting strategy on steep slopes? Where can I buy improved seeds? Who is paying the highest price at the market? Over time, weather patterns and soil conditions change. Epidemics of pests and diseases come and go. Updated information allows farmers to cope with and benefit from these changes.

Providing such knowledge can be challenging. Agriculture is location-specific, and farmers need accurate local weather forecasts, advice on agricultural practices and input use, and real-time price information and market logistics. Harnessing the rapid growth of the internet and associated digital technologies such as mobile phones is critical to helping farmers obtain the information they need and to transforming agricultural development. Of specific interest has been access to extension services, marketing of output, and arrangement of logistics. There is a steady growth in rigorous, quantitative evidence on the ways in which digital innovations help improve the lives of rural people (Deichmann, Goyal, and Mishra 2016).

Agricultural productivity varies dramatically around the world. While credit constraints, missing insurance markets, and poor infrastructure account for some of this disparity, suboptimal agricultural practices and poor management are also to blame. New production technologies, such as improved seed varieties, nutrient management, and pest control methods, are not necessarily reaching farmers. Public extension agents can overcome information barriers on new agricultural practices and technologies, but such programs have been burdened by limited scale, sustainability, and impact.

Digital technologies help overcome these constraints and have revived agricultural extension and advisory services. In cooperation with agricultural research and extension services, organizations such as Digital Green, the Grameen Foundation, and Technoserve deliver timely, relevant, and actionable information and advice to farmers in South Asia, Latin America, and sub-Saharan Africa at a dramatically lower cost than traditional services can. Rather than always traveling to visit a farmer, extension agents use a combination of voice, text, videos, and the internet to reduce transaction costs and increase the frequency of interaction with farmers. Governments, in partnership with mobile operators, use phones to coordinate the distribution of seeds and subsidized fertilizers in remote areas through e-vouchers. Technology firms such as Climate Corp, based in Silicon Valley, are pioneering the provision of agrometeorological services for early warning of weather and climate risks. A number of innovations aim for real-time and accurate weather monitoring using remote sensing and geographic information system (GIS)– enabled technologies for climate-resilient agriculture.

Agricultural product markets in many developing countries are poorly integrated. High search costs have tended to lower competition and create an inefficient allocation of goods across markets. When the internet took off in the mid-1990s, it was often claimed that it would improve price transparency, cut out middlemen, and make markets more efficient. Indeed, rapid adoption of digital technologies has dramatically reduced the search costs incurred by farmers and traders, and hence has overcome an important constraint in the context of limited infrastructure. In Robert Jensen's classic 2007 study of Kerala sardine fishermen and wholesalers, new mobile phone service dramatically reduced price dispersion and waste, increasing welfare for producers and consumers. Similar effects have been shown for other communication platforms, such as e-Choupals in India, telecenters in Peru, and studies on Niger grain traders or Philippine farmers.

Digital technologies also improve agricultural supply chain management. With globalized food systems, ensuring food safety has become more complex. These trends have catalyzed innovations to trace the food supply from the producer to the consumer, which is important for developing countries that want to reach new export markets. Smallholder farms turn to cooperatives and aggregators who use digital tools to improve collection, transportation, and quality control. By opening up new specialized market opportunities, the internet improved consumer protection and farmers' livelihoods (Goyal 2010).

Why, however, do some of these innovations fail to scale up and achieve wider acceptance? One reason could be market fragmentation, even though market consolidation, over time, will enhance growth prospects. Another reason could be the lack of financially sustainable business models that will attract private-sector investments in innovative solutions for small-scale agriculture. There is great potential for the internet and related technologies to improve rural economies, but several lessons are important to keep in mind.

First, agriculture is becoming increasingly knowledge-intensive and high-tech. Some of the world's newest industries have started to put money and tech talent into farming—the world's oldest industry. Digital soil maps, remote sensing, and GPS guidance are critical tools for modern farmers. Big data for precision agriculture increases yields and efficiency. These high-tech tools mostly benefit big farms that can make large investments in technology. But there are also many innovative ways in which illiterate and otherwise disadvantaged people use digital technologies, such as basic mobile phones. Greater efforts to close the digital divide in rural areas can have great payoffs.

Second, basic price and market information systems can improve efficiency and welfare. The evidence, though strong, is still limited to certain countries and in certain contexts. A number of recent studies have cast doubt on the overall novelty of information provided to the farmer and the degree of competition in many markets. One explanation of weak effects is low take-up of fee-based price information services. But even when farmers are seemingly better informed, they may not necessarily be able to act on that information, because of inaccessibility alternative markets and the complex interlinked relationships between buyers and sellers in poor developing economies. Rather than assuming that a digital approach will always be cost-effective and yield a better outcome, a more nuanced understanding of the underlying institutional environment and constraints is warranted.

Third, technology-enabled interventions are no panacea in themselves, and must be backed by complementary investments in physical infrastructure, electricity, literacy, and so on. The versatility and near-constant innovation that characterize digital technologies can sometimes be a distraction that can cause interventions to focus more on the technology than on the demands and priorities of the intended beneficiaries and the tradeoffs imposed by resource-constrained environments.

Finally, IT policy and the broader regulatory environment in a country have to be discussed jointly. Whereas the expansion of mobile phone access has been rapid and commercially self-sustaining even among many people who are poor, the same is not true of the internet. In the long run, the internet can have an even greater impact on rural growth, and much depends on finding sustainable business models to encourage its spread in the poorest parts of the world.

Conclusion

Demographic transition can give society a "demographic gift" of higher per capita incomes (Bloom and Williamson 1998), especially if institutions adapt to longer lives by, for example, improving human capital, encouraging saving, and promoting healthy aging (Eggleston and Fuchs 2012). China's demographic dividend contributed a small but significant fraction of its unprecedented economic growth over the past several decades—no less than 15 percent of economic growth between 1982 and 2000.[9] India is poised to enjoy a demographic dividend in

---

9 See the discussion in Feng Wang and Andrew Mason, "The Demographic Factor in China's Transition," in *China's Great Economic Transformation*, ed. Loren

the coming decade or two, perhaps of similar magnitude, if its workforce is productively employed and innovation spurs a virtuous cycle of growth-enhancing productivity. Even as China and other economies of East Asia struggle with demographic "headwinds" and innovation for aging societies, India will face its own struggles with harnessing its younger population's potential for productivity growth. India's future prosperity will depend to a large extent on how well it innovates to reap the demographic dividend available from a large working-age population in an economy still overwhelmingly rural, by raising agricultural productivity.

Brandt and Thomas G. Rawski (Cambridge: Cambridge University Press, 2008), 136–66; and David E. Bloom, David Canning, Linlin Hu, Yuanli Liu, Ajay Mahal, and Winnie Yip, "The Contribution of Population Health and Demographic Change to Economic Growth in China and India," *Journal of Comparative Economics* 38, no. 1 (2010): 17–33; and Eggleston 2020.

References

Adamopoulos, Tasso, and Diego Restuccia. 2014. "The Size Distribution of Farms and International Productivity Differences." *American Economic Review* 104 (6): 1667–97.

Arokiasamy, P., David Bloom, Jinkook Lee, Kevin Feeney, and Marija Ozolins. 2012. "Longitudinal Aging Study in India: Vision, Design, Implementation, and Preliminary Findings." In *Aging in Asia: Findings from New and Emerging Data Initiatives*, edited by James P. Smith and Malay Majmundar. National Research Council (US) Panel on Policy Research and Data Needs to Meet the Challenge of Aging in Asia. Washington DC: National Academies Press (US).

Beintema, Nienke M., and Gert-Jan Stads. 2017. *A Comprehensive Overview of Investments and Human Resource Capacity in African Agricultural Research*. Agricultural Science and Technology Indicators. Washington DC: International Food Policy Research Institute.

Bloom, David E., David Canning, and Günther Fink. 2010. "Implications of Population Ageing for Economic Growth." *Oxford Review of Economic Policy* 26, no. 4: 583–612.

Bloom, David E., Mathew McKenna, and Klaus Prettner. 2018. *Demography, Unemployment, Automation, and Digitalization: Implications for the Creation of (Decent) Jobs, 2010–2030*. Working paper 24835. National Bureau of Economic Research.

Bloom, David E., and Jeffrey G. Williamson. 1998. "Demographic Transitions and Economic Miracles in Emerging Asia." *World Bank Economic Review* 12, no. 3: 419–455.

Caselli, Francesco, and Wilbur J. Coleman. 2001. "The U.S. Structural Transformation and Regional Convergence: A Reinterpretation." *Journal of Political Economy* 109, no. 3: 584–616.

Chenery, Hollis, and Moises Syrquin. 1975. *Patterns of Development: 1950–1970*. London: Oxford University Press.

Christiaensen, Luc, Lionel Demery, and Jesper Kuhl. 2011. "The (Evolving) Role of Agriculture in Poverty Reduction—An Empirical Perspective." *Journal of Development Economics* 96, no. 2: 239–54.

Clark, Colin. 1951. *The Conditions of Economic Progress*. London: Macmillan & Co. LTD.

Day-Rubenstein, Kelly, and Keith Fuglie. 2000. "The CRADA Model for Public–Private Collaboration in Agricultural Research." In *Public-Private Collaboration in Agricultural Research*, edited by

Keith Fuglie and David Schimmelpfennig, 155–174. Ames: Iowa State University Press.

Deichmann, Uwe, Aparajita Goyal, and Deepak Mishra. 2016. "Will Digital Technologies Transform Agriculture in Developing Countries?" Policy Research Working Paper Series 7669. World Bank.

Eggleston, Karen N. 2020. "Demographic Challenges: Healthcare and Elder Care." In *Fateful Decisions: Choices that Will Shape China's Future*, edited by Thomas Fingar and Jean Oi. Stanford, CA: Stanford University Press.

Eggleston, Karen N., and Victor R. Fuchs. 2012. "The New Demographic Transition: Most Gains in Life Expectancy Now Realized Late in Life." *Journal of Economic Perspectives* 26, no. 3: 137–56.

Eicher, Carl K. 2004. *Rebuilding Africa's Scientific Capacity in Food and Agriculture*. Background Paper No. 4, commissioned by the InterAcademy Council Study Panel on Science and Technology Strategies for Improving Agricultural Productivity and Food Security in Africa.

Fan, Shenggen, Ashok Gulati, and Sukhadeo Thorat. 2009. "Investment, Subsidies, and Pro-poor Growth in Rural India," *Agricultural Economics* 39, no. 2: 163–170.

FAO IFAD, UNICEF, WFP, and WHO. (2018). The State of Food Security and Nutrition in the World 2018. *Building Climate Resilience for Food Security and Nutrition*. Technical report, FAO, Rome.

Fuglie, Keith, Madhur Gautam, Aparajita Goyal, and William F. Maloney. 2019. *Harvesting Prosperity: Technology and Productivity Growth in Agriculture*. Washington, DC: World Bank.

Gollin, Douglas 2010. "Agricultural Productivity and Economic Growth." In *Handbook of Agricultural Economics 4*, edited by Robert Evenson and Prabhu Pingali, 3825–66. Amsterdam: Elsevier.

Gollin, Douglas, Stephen Parente, and Richard Rogerson. 2002. "The Role of Agriculture in Development." *American Economic Review* 92, no. 2: 160–64.

Goyal, Aparajita. 2010. "Information, Direct Access to Farmers, and Rural Market Performance in Central India." *American Economic Journal: Applied Economics*, 2, no. 3: 22–45.

Goyal, Aparajita, and John Nash. 2017. *Reaping Richer Returns: Public Spending Priorities for African Agriculture Productivity Growth*. Washington DC: World Bank.

IPCC (Intergovernmental Panel on Climate Change). 2018. "Global Warming of 1.5°C. An IPCC Special Report on the Impacts of Global Warming of 1.5°C Above Pre-industrial Levels and Related Global Greenhouse Gas Emission Pathways, in the Context of Strengthening the Global Response to the Threat of Climate Change, Sustainable Development, and Efforts to Eradicate Poverty." Geneva: IPCC. Accessed November 2018. http://www.ipcc .ch/report/sr15/.

Ivanic, Maros, and Will Martin. 2018. "Sectoral Productivity Growth and Poverty Reduction: National and Global Impacts." *World Development* 109 (September): 429–39.

de Janvry, Alain, and Elisabeth Sadoulet. 2020. "Using Agriculture for Development: Supply- and Demand-side Approaches." *World Development* 133.

Jensen, Robert. 2007. "The Digital Provide: Information (Technology), Market Performance, and Welfare in the South Indian Fisheries Sector." *Quarterly Journal of Economics* 122, no. 3: 879–924.

———. 2012. "Do Labor Market Opportunities Affect Young Women's Work and Family Decisions? Experimental Evidence from India." *Quarterly Journal of Economics* 127, no. 2: 753–792.

Kuznets, Simon. 1955. "Economic Growth and Income Inequality." *American Economic Review* 45 (March): 1–28.

Lee, Ronald D. 2003. "The Demographic Transition: Three Centuries of Fundamental Change." *Journal of Economic Perspectives* 17, no. 4: 167–190.

Lele, Uma, and Arthur A. Goldsmith. 1989. "Development of National Agricultural Research Capability: India's Experience with the Rockefeller Foundation and Its Significance for Africa." *Economic Development and Cultural Change* 37: 305–344.

Lewis, W. Arthur. 1954. "Economic Development with Unlimited Supplies of Labour." *The Manchester School* 22, no. 2: 139–91.

Ligon, Ethan, and Elisabeth Sadoulet. 2018. "Estimating the Relative Benefits of Agricultural Growth on the Distribution of Expenditures." *World Development* 109 (September): 417–28.

López, Ramón, and Gregmar Galinato. 2007. "Should Governments Stop Subsidies to Private Goods? Evidence from Rural Latin America." *Journal of Public Economics* 91, nos. 5–6: 1071–94.

Martha, Geraldo B., Jr., Elisio Contini, and Eliseu Alves. 2012. "Embrapa: Its Origins and Changes." In *The Regional Impact of*

National Policies, edited by W. Baer. Northampton, MA: Edward Elgar Publishing.

McCullough, Ellen B. 2017. "Labor Productivity and Employment Gaps in Sub-Saharan Africa." *Food Policy* 67, 133–52.

McMillan, Margaret S., and Kenneth Harttgen. 2014. "What Is Driving the 'African Growth Miracle'?" NBER Working Paper 20077, National Bureau of Economic Research, Cambridge, MA. doi: 10.3386 /w20077.

Osiru, Moses, Paul Nampala, and Adipala Ekwamu. 2016. "African Faculties of Agriculture Within an Expanding University Sector." In *Agricultural Research in Africa: Investment in Future Harvests*, edited by John Lynam, Nienke Beintema, Johannes Roseboom, and Ousmane Badiane, 229–52. Washington DC: International Food Policy Research Institute.

Schlenker, Woflram, ed. 2019. *Agricultural Productivity and Producer Behavior*. Chicago: University of Chicago Press.

Schultz, Theodore W. 1975. "The Value of the Ability to Deal with Disequilibria." *Journal of Economic Literature* 31, no. 3: 837–46.

Singh, Kavita, and Dorairaj Prabhakaran. 2019. "Healthy Aging Policies in India." In *Healthy Aging in Asia*, edited by Karen Eggleston. Stanford, CA: Shorenstein Asia-Pacific Research Center.

Stads, Gert-Jan, Nienke M. Beintema, Sandra Perez, K. Flaherty, and César A. Falconi. 2016. *Agricultural Research in Latin American and the Caribbean: A Cross-Country Analysis of Institutions, Investment and Capabilities. Agricultural Science and Technology Indicators*. Washington DC: International Food Policy Research Institute and the Inter-American Development Bank.

Sudharsanan, Nikkil, and David E. Bloom. 2018. "The Demography of Aging in Low-and Middle-Income Countries: Chronological Versus Functional Perspectives." In *Future Directions for the Demography of Aging: Proceedings of a Workshop*, edited by Mark D. Hayward and Malay K. Majmundar, 309–38. Washington, DC: National Academies Press.

Timmer, C. Peter. 2002. "Agriculture and Economic Development." In *Handbook of Agricultural Economics*, vol. 2A, edited by Bruce L. Gardner and Gordon C. Rausser, 1487–546. Amsterdam: North-Holland.

United Nations. 2018. "World Urbanization Prospects: The 2018 Revision. Key Facts." https://population.un.org/wup/Publications/.

Appendix B

FIGURE B.1   India's total population, 1950–2100

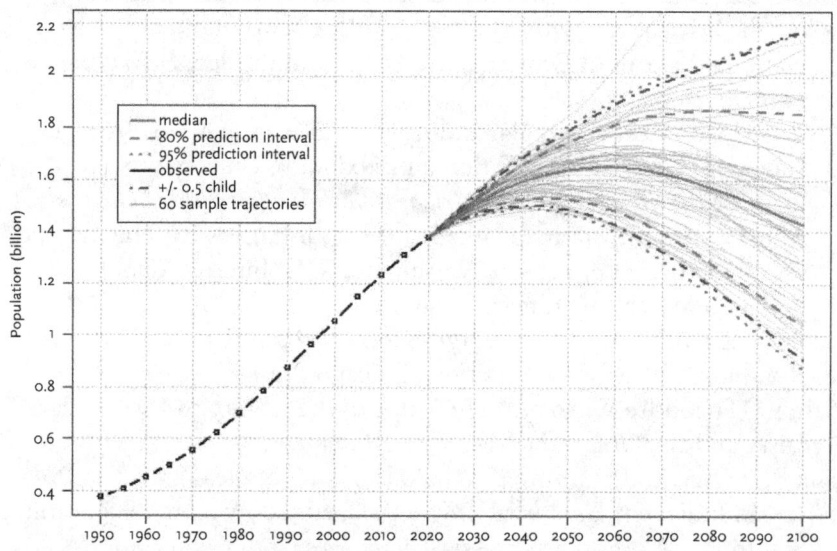

SOURCE: United Nations, *World Population Prospects 2019*, https://population.un.org/wpp/
Graphs/Probabilistic/POP/TOT/356.

FIGURE B.2 India's population, age 60 and over, 1950–2100

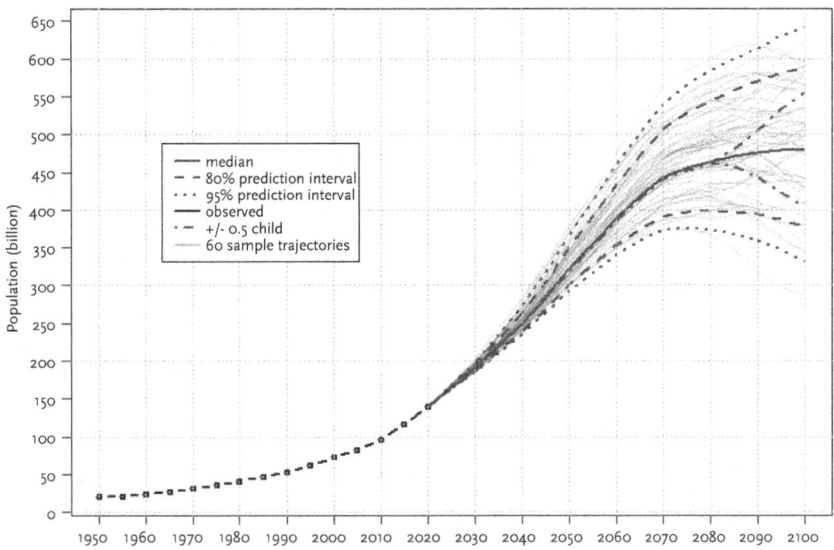

SOURCE: United Nations, *World Population Prospects 2019*, https://population.un.org/wpp/Graphs/Probabilistic/POP/TOT/356.

FIGURE B.3 India's old-age dependency ratio, 1950–2011

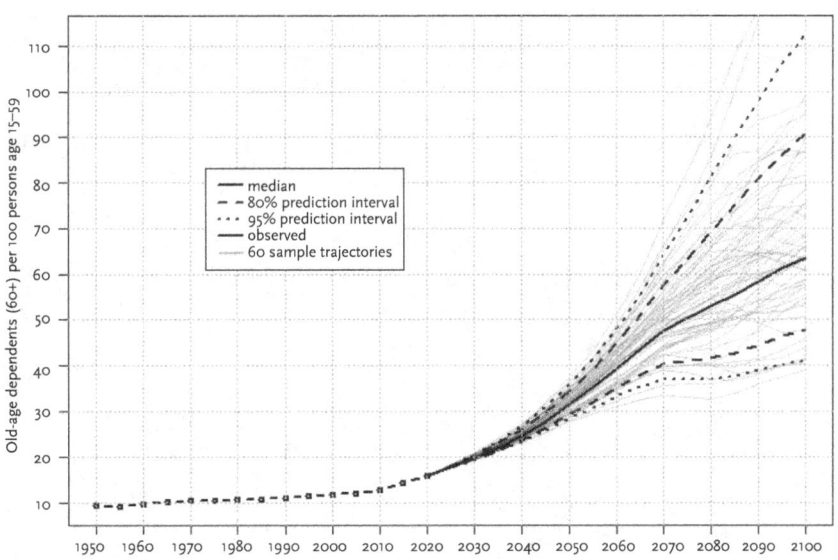

NOTE: Old-age dependency ratio = (number of those ages 60 and over) / (number of those ages 15–59).
SOURCE: United Nations, *World Population Prospects 2019*, https://population.un.org/wpp/Graphs/Probabilistic/POP/TOT/356.

8 Aging, ICT Innovation, and Media Literacy in South Korea

ICT Access Among the Elderly and the Remaining Divides

Sun Ho Jeong and Kyung Hee Kim

Makrye Park, a YouTuber in South Korea, started vlogging at the age of 71. She described her life before YouTube as "dead like rotten bean sprouts" (Lee 2017). According to an interview with the Associated Press, she said that her father did not send her to school because she was a girl. In her 20s, she was left with debts and three children as a single mother. For the next 40 years, she ran a restaurant to make a living. Her three children finished high school, and her granddaughter—the one who helped Park become a YouTuber—is a college graduate.

Even to this day, Park's writing is illegible due to spelling errors. However, she found a way to speak of her life through online videos. As of September 2019, her channel has more than one million subscribers. One of the reasons for her popularity may be that her story is familiar to many other South Koreans. For some people, it is their own story, and to others, it may be their mother's or grandmother's stories.

For Park, uploading online videos began as a way to prevent dementia. A doctor told the family that Park might soon suffer from Alzheimer's disease. With three sisters who had dementia, Park was more likely to develop it. At first, Park's granddaughter, Yoora Kim, tried to teach her to play games on a smartphone. While she did not enjoy the games, she tried to force herself to keep on playing, perhaps due to fear of the disease (Chang 2018). After searching the internet, Kim discovered that laughter and happy feelings aid dementia prevention. When Kim and her grandmother went on a trip to Australia, Kim uploaded a video of the trip to YouTube so that Park could watch it. The video was a big hit, and after more videos, Park became a celebrity in South Korea and internationally. Her videos are popular among both young and old. "We used to think, 'Since I'm over 70, my life is over.' But as I started doing this, I realized life starts at 71 years old," Park said (Lee 2017).

This story of Makrye Park received much attention from the South Korean media in light of the country's aging population. South Korea became an "aging society (with people aged 65 and over representing at least 7% of the population as defined by the United Nations)" in 2000, and an "aged society (with at least 14%)" in 2017, and is expected to become a "super-aged society (with 20% or more)" as early as 2026 (Kim 2020). According to this estimation, one out of five people in South Korea will be over 65 years old in less than a decade.

Theories on aging (e.g., activity theory) suggest that the life satisfaction of senior citizens increases when they remain active and involved in social interactions (Havighurst, Neugarten, and Albrecht 1964). While quality of life is often explained to have three dimensions (Lawton 1969)—physical health, psychological well-being, and social relationships/networks—prior research focused much more on information and communication technology's (ICT's) potential contributions to physical health rather than to psychological well-being or social relationships/networks. However, successful aging requires a low probability of disease and disability, high cognitive and physical function, and active engagement with life (Rowe and Kahn 1987).

This study began with an assumption that South Korea's digital transformation may have excluded its elderly. The Korean news media has referred to seniors as "the new middle age, 60–75," who have strength and intellectual ability, are able to work, and are wealthy (Chosun Ilbo n.d.). However, economic indicators show that nearly half (43.8%) of South Korean seniors (over 66 years old) live in relative poverty—the highest among OECD countries (OECD 2019b). Although South Korea is reported to have the smallest digital divide, with 96% of adults connected to the internet, 94% owning a smartphone, and 69% using social media (Choi 2016; Poushter, Bishop, and Chwe 2018), a digital divide persists in the everyday life of South Korean senior citizens. For example, as more train tickets are allocated to the online booking system, an increasing number of seniors fail to reserve seats and end up traveling on standing-room tickets during peak times (Go 2019). While offline bank services decline in South Korea, many seniors are still unaware of internet or mobile payment systems (Lee 2019). The self-ordering electronic kiosks at many fast-food restaurants are also challenging for aging adults (Park 2019).

In this regard, this chapter attempts to answer three questions: First, at the societal level, what kinds of efforts have been observed to provide aging adults with ICT access? Next, to what extent do seniors over the age of 65 years have ICT access? Finally, what factors influence seniors' ICT access?

Aging and Media Literacy[1]

Concepts related to aging are commonly divided into two distinct perspectives, from the fields of biology and developmental psychology. Biologists define aging as a process in which cells, tissues, or organs of an organic body start to decline and inevitably end with death. This concept contrasts with growth, which is a physical process from fertilization to maturity (Sigelman and Shaffer 1995). However, developmental psychologists describe life and death as a systematic process of changes and explain aging as part of human development (Sigelman and Shaffer 1995).

Whether it is a process of decline or development, aging falls in a later stage of the human lifecycle. Aging of human beings may be understood as biological aging, psychological aging, and social aging (Lim 2010). Biological aging is a normal change that can be observed from a person's appearance and organs. Psychological aging occurs frequently and can be explained as changes in how people sense, perceive, and respond to their environment, as well as changes in memory and personality. Social aging refers to changes in an individual's social relations and social roles that are found in the social environment where one belongs.

According to activity theory, seniors may gain positive perspectives and successfully adapt to the later stage of their lives by engaging in various activities (Havighurst, Neugarten, and Albrecht 1964). The theory suggests that when seniors stay active and maintain social interactions, they may have lower probabilities for disease and disability and maintain a high level of cognitive and physical functions.

Other scholars have also suggested the importance of social interactions in the lives of seniors. Lawton and Brody (1969) state that the quality of human life can be evaluated at three levels: physical health,

---

1   Part of this literature review section previously appeared in the *Journal of Cyber-communication Academic Society* 37, no. 3 (2020): 95–138.

mental well-being, and social relations/networks. Their study indicates that the formation of social relationships helps one to age successfully. But how can aging adults enhance their social interactions? The utilization of media is becoming absolutely critical for social interactions, because many activities are now facilitated through the internet.

Prior studies have shown that media use helps seniors to feel connected with society and to age successfully by enhancing their quality of life. According to these studies, the use of the internet mitigates depression (Cotten et al. 2014) and enhances a sense of self-efficacy (Erickson and Johnson 2011). Also, the use of social network sites helps aging adults to generate a higher sense of self-efficacy, better control, and more extensive social relations (Leist, Reljic, and Ferring 2012). Mobile and computer device usage among seniors has been found to be inversely correlated to feelings of loneliness (Öngun, Güder, and Demirağ 2016). The use of media plays a positive role in making the senior life satisfactory (Sun, Zhang, and Fan 2016), and it can also help to connect them with local communities and even volunteer opportunities (Kang 2013). Studies have shown that the use of the internet mitigates loneliness and improves social interactions, so that seniors may feel more satisfied with their lives and may participate more in society.

However, the problem is that the aging process undermines media literacy among aging adults and serves as a stumbling block in their media use. As people age, their sensory abilities (e.g., vision, hearing) decline, which then naturally lowers their ability to use media. The decline of capabilities to process information makes it especially difficult for aging adults to use media such as the internet, because it is a process that requires cognitive effort. Seniors are more easily tired and have less competence than younger generations for tasks like listening to lectures attentively for a long time or playing computer games (Kim 2007). However, the ability to be attentive and alert is necessary for understanding media content or communicating with others through messaging platforms. When the ability to stay alert declines, it becomes more difficult to notice a new message; when the ability to be attentive declines, it becomes more difficult to follow the message narratives.

Also, the amount of visual or audio information that can reach the perceptual span decreases among aging adults (Kim 2002). Since seniors are limited in the amount of information they can process at once, it is more difficult for them to understand media content conveyed in multiple instruments such as images, text, and audio. For example, it becomes difficult to understand television news when the anchor speaks rapidly, when there is video playing behind the speaker, and when a chyron appears at the bottom of the screen. It is also much more difficult to see content at a glance on small smartphone screens where texts, photos, and images are presented together.

Furthermore, selective attention, which allows a person to pay attention selectively to one target in the presence of complex interfering stimuli, declines as one ages (Kim 2002). This means that it becomes more difficult to select and read a pertinent message amid multiple messages or to select and read an article that one wants to read out of many different news articles available in a news app.

The aging process is a natural phenomenon and process that most people will experience. With ICT media literacy rapidly becoming a requisite for social interactions, society needs to address ways to enhance media literacy among seniors. This research looks into types of efforts that have been made to improve the media literacy of Korean seniors as South Korea transforms from an aging society into a super-aging society.

The Importance of Accessing Media in Old Age

Media literacy is the ability to read and use media. In the past, it was described as an ability to critically understand media messages and utilize the media, but as the internet and mobile technologies have advanced, communications and participation through media are defined as important parts of media literacy. Lee (2008) sees the concept of media literacy as

> an ability to access desired content through diverse media, critically understand media content based on one's understanding of the media, creatively produce media content to express one's thoughts, take responsibilities for the influence of the content, [and] take part in communications in society, using the media (47, authors' translation).

Diverse discussions are underway regarding the elements that comprise media literacy. Rheingold (2012) cites attention as the gate to necessary information, crap detection as a method to decipher truth from lies, participation as creating, diffusing, and enjoying together, collaboration as making the collective intelligence greater than the sum of its parts, and network smarts as the power of broad and loose ties among those elements. The European Association for Viewers Interests (EAVI

2011) includes environmental elements, apart from individual competencies, when explaining media literacy. For example, media context is cited as an environmental element that contributes to the improvement of media availability, i.e., individuals' physical access and media literacy. The EAVI emphasizes the importance of a social foundation to improve media literacy and social efforts to create such an environment.

In South Korea, a model consisting of media literacy elements was first designed using a Delphi study of experts, and the model was then tested using survey research. The media literacy elements verified in this study included access, critical understanding, creative utilization, and responsibility/rights (Kim, Kim, and Lee 2017). According to this study, access (i.e., technological usage) refers to basic operation skills that are required to select from diverse media, access necessary content, or prevent exposure to content that one does not want in line with the purpose of the use. The capacity for critical understanding refers to an ability to analyze and evaluate media content, while the capacity for creative utilization refers to an ability to express or share one's interest or knowledge and participate in and cooperate with each other using the media. Responsibility and rights mean that people act to protect their rights without violating others' rights when using media.

Seniors also need these four media literacy skills. Of these skills, access (i.e., technological usage) is most necessary for them, because their span of perception is shrinking and selective attention is weakening compared with that of younger generations. In modern societies where the internet is advanced to such an extent that most content is delivered through smartphones or computers, the capacity for access is most important for aging adults. A video clip of YouTuber Makrye Park's inability to use a self-service kiosk in a fast-food chain became a sensation in Korea because it demonstrates the experience of most of the older generation. Indeed, considering that disaster information is delivered through smartphone messages, the ability to access media is a survival-related issue.

Among the four main media literacy skills, the ability to access media must be first obtained not only for seniors to use the media as a tool for basic life but also to communicate and participate in society. In Finland, CareTV and its interactive services help isolated elderly people communicate with each other. This is one example of how the advancement of technologies, such as augmented reality and virtual reality, can bring about the emergence of diverse media that can increase seniors' social communications. Such media can give aging adults who live alone or in remote areas opportunities to form social relations, lessen loneliness, and feel happier.

The emergence of socially beneficial media will not benefit seniors if they cannot access it. Of course, the ability to access media cannot be obtained overnight. One must have the technological ability to use existing media so as to access a new medium in the future, yet aging makes it difficult to try new things. Many elderly people are not motivated to make attempts, and thus the number of elderly people who use new media is smaller than that of younger generations. Therefore, it is important to understand the current status of seniors' media access and to identify ways to enhance their ability to access media.

According to a study about new media adopters, social and economic status, such as income, education, and occupation, are important variables determining new media use (Rogers 1986). The study found that white-collar employees with higher incomes and more education adopt new media earlier and use them more effectively than others. Another study on the younger generation's use of personal media focused on young foreign students in South Korea who are expected to have a relatively high level of access to the media. This work found that an individual's socioeconomic status—especially one's economic status—has a large impact on their use of personal communication devices (Kim and Yun 2008). Mobile phone users were charged by the hour, and students' economic status influenced their patterns of use.

As observed from previous studies, seniors' socioeconomic status will also have an impact on their level of media access. Therefore, this study also aims to examine how the elderly's level of media access differs depending on their socioeconomic status.

National News Coverage and Survey Data

This study first examined South Korean news coverage of the elderly and ICTs to identify the topics discussed at the societal level. Headlines of news stories published between January 1, 2000, and March 31, 2019—from the time when the country became an "aging society" until the time this study was conducted—were collected using the country's most popular portal site, Naver's news service. Numerous search terms (i.e., elderly, senior, aged, ICT, IT, computer, PC, internet, phone, mobile, robot, AI, and IoT) were used to collect a comprehensive list of news stories related to seniors and ICTs (n = 2,177).

Next, an analysis of national survey data provided by the Korean Press Foundation was conducted to examine levels of ICT access among seniors (n = 729) in South Korea.

Analysis of National News Coverage Between 2000 and 2019

The analysis of news headlines from 2000 to 2019 indicated that there was an increasing number of news reports related to the issue of aging and ICTs over time (figure 8.1).

Table 8.1 lists the top 40 most frequently found words and phrases in these news reports. Excluding the original search terms, the most frequently found words and phrases (shown in bold) were "living alone," "care/help/support," "education," "dementia," "Japan," "disabled," "worry-free," "KT," "welfare center," "inexpensive," "safety," "victimization," "health," and "SK Hynix." News reports most frequently focused on the problem of seniors living alone and with risks of dementia. These reports saw such people as in need of support, which was expected to be provided through advanced technologies. When these news reports discussed new approaches to the aging population, Japan was the country most mentioned.

ICT education for the elderly was another important topic reflected in the news coverage. KT Corporation, South Korea's largest telephone company, was most frequently observed to offer ICT-related programs, hosting events, and signing MOUs. In addition, local welfare centers were also active in opening classes and competitions for seniors.

FIGURE 8.1 News coverage related to the issue of aging and ICTs, 2000–19

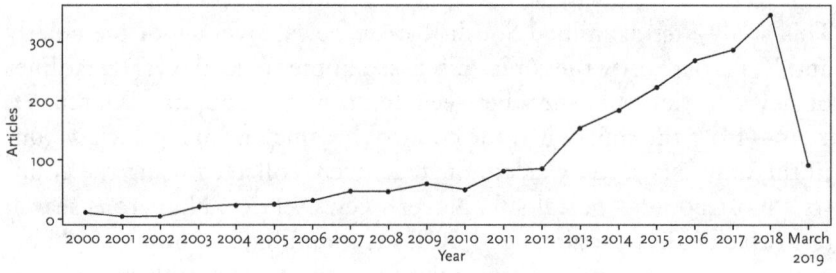

SOURCE: Author's survey of Naver portal news stories.

TABLE 8.1 Term frequency of words: news headlines

	Word	TF		Word	TF		Word	TF		Word	TF
1	elderly/aged/senior	2,106	11	phone	171	21	welfare center	82	31	information and communication	60
2	technology	453	12	dementia	149	22	inexpensive	82	32	business	55
3	robot	375	13	Internet	134	23	diffusion	79	33	safety	64
4	living alone	367	14	IoT	120	24	society	78	34	implement	53
5	information	351	15	use	120	25	silver	75	35	victimization	52
6	smart	270	16	Japan	104	26	develop	64	36	mobile	50
7	care/help/support	241	17	disabled	104	27	portable	63	37	share	50
8	AI	228	18	service	98	28	welfare	62	38	media	48
9	education	198	19	worry-free	96	29	industry	60	39	health	47
10	computer	172	20	KT	85	30	era	60	40	SK Hynix	47

SOURCE: Author's survey of Naver portal news stories.

Among private corporations, SK Hynix was the company that offered the most services for seniors, using their AI speakers. So-called worry-free phones with GPS tracking functions were also distributed and successfully used to locate lost elderly persons. As a result of these ICT services, senior citizens were expected to be able to live safe and healthy lives. However, in reality, they were also sometimes victims of cell phone fraud.

ICT Access Among South Korean Seniors

This study examined the level of ICT access among elderly South Koreans. According to the analysis of the survey results, most South Korean seniors had access to at least one ICT device (table 8.2). Television was the mostly widely ICT device available, and tablet PCs were the least. Respondents stated that they owned the following devices: television (99.5%), set-top box (56.8%), radio (26.4%), desktop computer (26.3%), laptop/netbook (10.3%), and tablet PC (4.1%).

While the survey did not specifically address whether the respondents had access to the internet, it did ask how many days in the past week they had used the internet with a smartphone or computer (table 8.3). Apparently, smartphones were more commonly used among South Korean seniors relative to computers. About 35% and 10% of the respondents said that they had used the internet at least once in the previous week with a smartphone and a computer, respectively. Although

TABLE 8.2 Senior citizens' access to ICT devices in South Korea, 2018

Number of devices in household	How many of the devices do you have access to?	
	N	%
0	1	0.1
1	211	28.1
2	299	40
3	138	18.4
4	58	7.8
5	38	5.1
6	5	0.6
Total	729	100

SOURCE: Korea Press Foundation Media Audience Survey, 2018.

TABLE 8.3 Senior citizens' frequency and method of internet access in South Korea, 2018

Frequency	Smartphone		Computer	
	N	%	N	%
No use	480	64.1	677	90.4
1 day	23	3.1	10	1.3
2 days	16	2.1	8	1.1
3 days	14	1.9	10	1.3
4 days	23	3	8	1.1
5 days	21	2.8	14	1.9
6 days	18	2.4	8	1
7 days	155	20.7	15	1.9

SOURCE: Korea Press Foundation Media Audience Survey, 2018.

TABLE 8.4 Senior citizens' frequency of use of traditional media in South Korea, 2018

	Television		Printed newspaper	
	N	%	N	%
No use	30	4	574	76.6
1 day	2	0.2	17	2.3
2 days	2	0.3	14	1.8
3 days	3	0.4	12	1.6
4 days	3	0.4	8	1.1
5 days	8	1.1	50	6.6
6 days	16	2.2	39	5.2
7 days	685	91.4	35	4.7

SOURCE: Korea Press Foundation Media Audience Survey, 2018.

20.7% and 1.9% of the elderly population surveyed used the internet every day with a smartphone or a computer, respectively, a majority of South Korean seniors responded that they had not used the internet in the past week, possibly due to lack of skills or interest.

These results contrast sharply compared to seniors' use of traditional media. Over 90% of the respondents said that they watch television every day, although the proportion that read the newspaper was relatively low (table 8.4).

Among our studied sample, only a limited number of seniors used (listed in order of their familiarity) messaging applications, portal news, social network sites, and online videos on a regular basis (table 8.5). However, a minority engaged in daily internet access: 18% used messaging apps every day, 10% accessed portal news, 6% viewed online videos, and 3% went to social network sites.

TABLE 8.5 Senior citizens' frequency of use and choice of platforms in South Korea, 2018

	Messaging		News portals		Social networking		Online video	
	N	%	N	%	N	%	N	%
No use	525	70.1	579	33.2	682	91	702	93.8
1 day	2	0.3	17	2.3	6	0.8	5	0.6
2 days	6	0.9	9	1.3	10	1.3	11	1.5
3 days	18	2.3	20	2.7	8	1	4	0.5
4 days	27	3.5	21	2.8	9	1.1	10	1.4
5 days	26	3.5	18	2.4	9	1.1	8	1
6 days	9	1.2	10	1.4	1	0.2	9	1.3
7 days	136	18.1	74	9.9	25	3.4	47	6.2

SOURCE: Korea Press Foundation Media Audience Survey, 2018.

With regard to the mean differences in access to ICT devices, there were significant differences by gender, age, monthly income, place of residence, level of education, and type of household (table 8.6). Significantly higher access to ICT devices was found in men, and those who are younger, as well as those with higher incomes and with more education, those living in an urban area, and those living with another generation or in a nonfamily household. The frequency of internet access through smartphones did not differ as much depending on those individual factors. The place of residence (urban or rural) was the only variable that generated a significant difference.

Conclusion

This study examined 20 years of news coverage of seniors and ICTs in South Korea to identify some of the related issues in Korean society, and then analyzed national survey data. The results show what level of access South Korean seniors have to ICT devices and the internet, as well as the extent to which their access differs based on their individual socioeconomic resources.

In light of its aging population, there have been continuous efforts to provide ICT devices and related education to senior citizens in South Korea. News coverage typically focuses on aging adults living alone and at risk of dementia, and how technology companies and local welfare centers can support these individuals by offering "worry-free" and

TABLE 8.6 Mean differences in internet access by gender, age, income, residence, education, and type of household

	n	Number of ICT devices in household				Number of days using internet in past week (via smartphone)			
		M	SD	t-test	ANOVA	M	SD	t-test	ANOVA
Gender									
Male	357 (47.6)	2.42	1.12	4.40***		5.69	1.98	1.682	
Female	393 (52.4)	2.06	1.12			5.26	2.18		
Age									
65–70	350 (46.7)	2.46	1.09		23.90***	3.92	1.94		0.44
71–75	166 (22.2)	2.44	1.35			5.24	2.21		
76–80	152 (20.3)	1.84	0.87			4.16	2.38		
Over 81	81 (10.8)	1.58	0.76			4.03	1.94		
Monthly income†									
Below 1,000,000	178 (23.7)	1.5	0.62		133.56***	4.87	2.43		0.45
1,000,000-1,999,999	212 (28.2)	1.87	0.84			5.49	2.09		
2,000,000-2,999,999	154 (20.6)	2.31	0.89			2.1	2.1		
Above 3,000,000	191 (25.5)	3.29	1.21			2.09	2.04		
Residence									
Urban	531 (70.9)	2.39	1.16	5.83***				3.80***	
Rural	218 (29.1)	1.87	0.98						
Education									
Elementary school and under	270 (36.0)	1.73	1		44.36***	5.21	2.29		2.14
Middle school	223 (29.7)	2.24	1.01			5.16	2.27		
High school	220 (29.4)	2.71	1.05			5.65	1.9		
Some college and above	36 (4.8)	3.09	1.5			6.16	1.92		
Type of household									
Two or more–generation and non-family household	174 (23.3)	3.24	1.34	15.33***		5.81	1.89	1.39	
One-generation household	575 (76.7)	1.93	0.86			5.41	2.13		

NOTE: ANOVA = analysis of variance; †In Korean won; ***P≤0.001.
SOURCE: Korea Press Foundation Media Audience Survey, 2018.

inexpensive cell phones, as well as ICT-related education. The result of these outreach efforts are covered by news reports both in a positive way (e.g., being able to locate lost senior citizens using these devices) and a negative way (e.g., seniors becoming victims of cell phone fraud). However, the news coverage rarely if ever describes examples of positive changes in the lives of the elderly in relation to healthy aging.

Although South Korea is often described as a country with the smallest overall digital divide, the gap between the haves and have-nots regarding ICT access persists among South Korean senior citizens. These differences were observed depending on one's gender, age, monthly household income, place of residence, education, and type of household. As such, socioeconomic resources were important in acquiring and learning to use ICT devices. When the frequency of internet use was analyzed, however, these differences were not significant except between people who live in urban versus rural areas.

These findings suggest the conclusion that aging adults in rural areas of South Korea are experiencing social isolation. Due to a shortage of infrastructure and related education—especially within a small community of people who are capable of adopting new technology and introducing it to others—the digital divide in these areas may be widening further. Additional attention is necessary to promote inclusion in these areas. For most seniors living in rural South Korea, there are basic barriers that hinder more advanced plans, such as implementation of eHealth services and remote care systems through ICTs.

In discussing differences in ICT access at the individual level—between generation or gender, for example—it is also worth noting that the level of education of South Koreans has changed dramatically over the last few decades. Differences in ICT access explained by demographic variables such as gender, age, and income are mostly related to the level of education. Among OECD countries, South Korea has the largest education gap between the younger and older generations (OECD 2019a). Only 23.1% of those ages 55 to 64 have attained tertiary education, while 69.6% of those ages 25 to 34 have the same level of education. For women, this difference between generations is even larger. While 15.5% of women between 55 and 64 have attained tertiary education, 75.7% of women between ages 25 and 34 have the same education level.

In the long term, such generational or gender differences in education are expected to decrease, and this might contribute significantly to closing the gap in utilizing new technologies by seniors. However, we also note that other socioeconomic resources, such as social networks and learning abilities, decrease drastically at later stages of life. Although these bring additional challenges in integrating ICTs into the lives of the elderly for healthy aging and generational solidarity, it is important that we continue our explorations of the reasons underlying such a divide so we can further support the aging population.

References

Chang, Eunkyo. 2018. "'K'oria kŭraenma' Pangmangnye 'insaengŭn mangnyech'ŏrŏm ojige reshitko'" ["Korean grandma" Makrye Park, "Live your life just like Makrye"]. *Kyŏnghyangshinmun*, December 22, 2018. http://news.khan.co.kr/kh_news/khan_art_view .html?art_id=201812220600045.

Choi, Sung-jin. 2016. "Korea Has 'Smallest Digital Divide' Among Major Nations." *Korea Times*, February 29, 2016. http://www .koreatimes.co.kr/www/news/biz/2016/10/123_199287.html.

Chosun Ilbo. n.d. "6075 shinjungnyŏn" [60–75 the new middle age]. http://issue.chosun.com/issue/issue_list.html?issu_id=10134.

Cotten, Shelia R., George Ford, Sherry Ford, and Timothy M. Hale. 2014. "Internet Use and Depression Among Retired Older Adults in the United States: A Longitudinal Analysis." *Journals of Gerontology* 69, no. 5: 763–71.

EAVI (European Association for Viewers' Interests). 2011. *Testing and Refining Criteria to Assess Media Literacy Levels in Europe.* Brussels: European Association for Viewers' Interests.

Erickson, Julie, and Genevieve M. Johnson. 2011. "Internet Use and Psychological Wellness During Late Adulthood." *Canadian Journal on Aging* 30: 197–209.

Go, Heejin. 2019. "Sŏl kich'a t'aboni ipsŏgen noindŭl" [In trains on New Year's Day, senior train passengers with standing tickets]. *Kyŏnghyangshinmun*, February 4, 2019. http://news.khan .co.kr/kh_news/khan_art_view.html?art_id=201902040900011.

Havighurst, Robert J., Bernice L. Neugarten, and Sheldon S. Tobin. 1964. "Disengagement, Personality, and Life Satisfaction in the Later Years." In *Age with a Future,* edited by P. From Hansen, 419–25. Copenhagen: Munksgoaard.

Kang, Seok. 2013. "The Elderly Population and Community Engagement in the Republic of Korea: The Role of Community Storytelling Network." *Asian Journal of Communication* 23, no. 3: 302–21.

Kim, Ae Soon. 2002. *Sŏngin paltalgwa saengae sŏlgye* [Development of adults and life design]. Seoul: Sigma Press.

Kim, Kyung-Hee, Gwang-jae Kim, and Sook-Jung Lee. 2017. *Midiŏ rit'ŏrŏshi chisu kaebal mit chiyŏkpyŏl kyŏkch'a ch'ŭkchŏng chosa* [Developing media literacy index and measuring the difference in media literacy levels between regions in South Korea]. Seoul: Pan'songt'ongshinwiwŏnhoe [Korea Communications Commission].

Kim, Kyung-Hee, and Haejin Yun. 2008. "Chaehan Ashiayuhaksaengŭi sahoejŏk maengnakkwa m'bailp'on iyonge ta'han t'amsaekch'k yŏn'gu" [The sociocultural context of Asian students in Korea and their uses of mobile phones]. *Han'gukpangsonghakpo* [Korean Journal of Broadcasting and Telecommunication Studies] 22, no. 2: 47–81.

Kim, Tae-Hyun. 2007. *Nonyŏnhak* [Gerontology]. Paju: Gyomoonsa.

Kim, Yon-se. 2020. "Korea Set to Be Superaged Society Within 4 Years." *Korea Herald,* April 22, 2020. http://www.koreaherald.com/view.php?ud=20200419000051.

Lawton, M. Powell, and Elaine M. Brody. 1969. "Assessment of Older People: Self-Maintaining and Instrumental Activities of Daily Living." *The Gerontologist* 9, no. 3: 179–86.

Lee, Ho-Jeong. 2019. "Mobile Finance Booms, But Seniors Are Unaware." *Korean JoongAng Daily,* May 11, 2019. http://koreajoongangdaily.joins.com/news/article/article.aspx?aid=3062919.

Lee, Sook-Jung. 2008. "Midiŏ rit'ŏrŏshinŭn muŏshin'ga" [What Is Media Literacy]. In *Tijit'ŏl midiŏ rit'ŏrŏshi* [Digital media literacy], edited by Han'gukpangsonghak'oe Midiŏgyoyukt'ŭkpyŏrwiwŏnhoe [Korean Association for Broadcasting and Telecommunication Studies Media Education Special Committee, 47–86. Paju: Hanwool.

Lee, Youkyung. 2017. "70-Year-Old YouTube Hit Redefining Beauty in South Korea." Associated Press, July 14, 2017. https://www.apnews.com/72aca250d7464424ad48c0f2dc5e44e9.

Leist, Anja K., Gabrijela Reljic, and Dieter Ferring. 2012. "Social Media Use in Old Age: User Profiles, Effects, Best Practices." *The Gerontologist* 52, S1: 563–564.

Lim, Yeon Ok. 2010. "Nohwae taehan ihae" [Understanding of aging]. In *Koryŏngsahoeŭi ihae: Nonyŏn'gwa sahoe* [Understanding of aging society: Old age and society], edited by Hallimdaehakkyo Koryŏngsahoeyŏn'guso [Hallym University Institute of Aging]. Seoul: Sowha.

OECD. 2019a. "Population with Tertiary Education." https://data.oecd.org/chart/5H6n.

OECD. 2019b. "Poverty rate" (indicator). https://doi.org/10.1787/0fe1315d-en.

Öngun, Erdem, Feride Zeynep Güder, and Aşkın Demirağ. 2016. "Elderly People's Choice of Media and their Perceived State of Loneliness." *Online Journal of Communication and Media Technologies* 6, no. 1: 35–47.

Park, Ju-young. 2019. "'Smart' Restaurants Challenge for Elderly." *Korea Herald*, February 15, 2019. http://www.koreaherald.com/view.php?ud=20190213000567.

Poushter, Jacob, Caldwell Bishop, and Hanyu Chwe. 2018. *Social Media Use Continues to Rise in Developing Countries But Plateaus Across Developed Ones*. Washington DC: Pew Research Center. https://www.pewresearch.org/global/wp-content/uploads/sites/2/2018/06/Pew-Research-Center-Global-Tech-Social-Media-Use-2018.06.19.pdf

Rheingold, Howard. 2012. *Net Smart: How to Thrive Online*. Cambridge: MIT Press.

Rogers, Everett M. 1986. *Communication Technology: The New Media in Society*. New York: The Free Press.

Rowe, John W., and Robert L. Kahn. 1987. "Human Aging: Usual and Successful." *Science* 237: 143–149.

Sigelman, Carol K., and David R. Shaffer. 1995. *Life-Span Human Development*. Pacific Grove CA: Brooks/Cole Publishing Co.

Sun, Shaojing, Shuangyue Zhang, and Xitao Fan. 2016. "Media Use, Cognitive Performance, and Life Satisfaction of the Chinese Elderly." *Health Communication* 31, no. 10: 1223–1234.

9 Population Cliffs, Crisis of Local Society, and the Politics of Innovation in South Korea

Young Bum Kim, Joon-Shik Park, and Dong-Il Jung

It is well-known that population aging is progressing rapidly in South Korean society. With respect to rapid population aging, there have been many debates regarding how changes to the population and its structure impact society (Ahn, Kim, and Ryuk 2017; Kim 2013; Choi and Yoon 2012). Statistics Korea reports that the size and ratio of Korea's senior population are currently increasing rapidly, and the overall population is projected to decline sharply in the long term due to a low birth rate. According to long-term medium estimates,[1] the 2017 population of 51.36 million is predicted to peak in 2028 at 51.94 million, and then decrease to 39.29 million—the size of the 1992 population—by 2067. Age distribution will also change drastically, as children aged 14 years and younger, constituting 13.1% of the population in 2017, will drop to 8.1% by 2067; furthermore, the ratio of those aged 65 years and older will increase from 13.8% in 2017 to up to 46.5% in 2067. Moreover, it is noteworthy that population and age distribution differ across regions. While the population tends to increase and the relatively high young population ratio is maintained in the capital region due to population influx, the population tends to decrease and the aging population is accelerating in medium-sized and small cities across the noncapital region.

The changes in the number and structure of population are predicted to have a negative effect on the development of Korean society in the

---

[1] Population estimates provided are classified into high, medium, and low estimates, depending on whether high or low levels of fertility, mortality, and international migration are used for the estimate (Statistics Korea 2019).

long run. In other words, population decline and aging are expected to lower the South Korean society's prospects for economic growth, and increase social welfare costs (Ahn, Kim, and Ryuk 2017; Woo, Shin, Park, and Kim 2014). The purpose of this study is to examine changes in the population and age structure in South Korean regions and to explore their implications for regional development. First, we describe how South Korea's demographic structure by age has changed over the last 20 years according to administrative area, and we investigate how changes to the population structure alter human-made amenities in the region. Second, we explain how the quality and quantity of human-made amenities can contribute to fostering regional innovations, and we suggest strategies for closing the gap between capital and noncapital areas, thereby achieving regionally balanced socioeconomic development in Korea.

To accommodate regional characteristics, data are analyzed in categories of counties, cities, and districts in metropolitan cities with a population of over 1 million. Using data from 2006 to 2017, this study examines the changes in the number and age distribution of the population by region, analyzes changes to elementary schools, medical facilities, and cultural facilities for each region, and determines whether there is a statistically significant relationship between the number of regional amenities and the population and its structure. Based on the results of the study, policy implications for regional innovation are provided.

Literature Review and Research Methods

Changes to population structure and their effects

Future changes in population can be summarized as a decrease in the number and an increase in the ratio of seniors in South Korea. According to the Special Estimate of Future Population (Statistics Korea 2019) reported in 2019, based on the medium-level estimation, the population of Korea is forecasted to peak at 51.94 million in 2028, and then continually decrease, reaching 47.74 million by 2050. Age distribution has also been predicted to change drastically. While the percentage of those aged 65 and older is estimated to increase from 13.8% in 2017 to 39.8% in 2050, the working population of 15 to 64 years of age will decrease from 73.2% to 51.3% in 2050. The population of children aged 14 and younger is predicted to decrease from 13.1% in 2017 to a mere 8.8% in 2050 (Statistics Korea 2019).

Population and age structure vary across regions. Changes in population, specifically population decline, vary by region in terms of when they begin. While the population began declining only recently or is still increasing in metropolitan cities of South Korea,[2] signs of population decline have already been witnessed in counties since the 1990s.[3] The early emergence of population decline in counties can be attributed to the younger generation's movement to metropolitan cities in pursuit of careers or education.

The population aging trends also demonstrate regional differences. According to a study (Kim 2013) on the level and rate of aging for cities, counties, and districts in metropolitan cities, although population aging began in counties earlier than in metropolitan cities, its rate was found to be extremely rapid in both divisions. The cause of population decline is reported to be low total fertility rate in metropolitan cities, whereas for counties, the reduced number of women of childbearing age due to population outflux is reported as the main cause. Therefore, in counties, population decline and aging are understood as being the consequences of the younger generation moving to metropolitan cities or other neighboring regions (Choi and Yoon 2012). Furthermore, population aging or decline in counties has not been caused by low birth rate, as no significant relationship has been found between regional birth rate and population aging.

Recently, a regional dissolution index has been used to gauge the possibility of population decline. Developed by Sang-Ho Lee (2016) and based on a study of regional dissolution by Hiroya Masuda (2014), this index is calculated by dividing the number of women aged 20 to 39 by the number of seniors aged 65 and over. If the index score is less than or equal to .5, there is a high possibility of regional dissolution. In other words, if the number of women of childbearing age is less than or equal to half of the number of seniors, it indicates that a region is predicted to be at high dissolution risk as it undergoes long-term

---

2   Statistics Korea provides the population by administrative divisions starting from 1992. For Busan, the population in 1993 was already lower than that in 1992. Metropolitan cities excluding Busan are mostly seeing a population increase or a recent decline.

3   For most counties outside of Gyeonggi Province (South Korea's most populous province), the population was not only lower in 1993 compared to that in 1992 but has been showing a continual decline.

population decline. According to this index, some counties in South Jeolla, North Jeolla, and North Gyeongsang provinces are at high risk of regional dissolution with an index value of less than or equal to .5.

The distribution of human-made amenities within a region influences population fluctuation, especially population movement. The life course–oriented approach claims that desirable amenities are perceived differently according to age (Whisler et al. 2008). That is, there is a difference in the quality of life perceived by each age group, depending on the facilities and services provided in the region. A particular region hosting the facilities and services that support an individual's desired way of life may be more attractive to the individual than other regions. Relating this to population movement, the difficulty of reproducing amenities preferred by a smaller age group may lead to their reduction or elimination and may cause that age group to move to other regions in a vicious cycle. While there are no established standards on distinguishing between amenities, they can generally be categorized into public goods and services such as medicine and education, private consumer goods such as restaurants and shopping malls, transportation and communication such as buses and town halls, and cultural facilities such as museums and movie theaters.

Population change, economic growth, and innovation

Population pressure has been at the heart of biological, cultural, and civilizational evolution, serving as a primal catalyst for industrialization and economic growth (e.g., Becker, Glaeser, and Murphy 1999; Kuznets 1967). Malthusian population theory (Malthus 1798) predicted the destructive consequences of population explosion, implying that population control should be implemented to enhance the efficiency of land use. Maintaining population size below the level of ecological carrying capacity would be required to keep economic growth. To the contrary, Marx (1867) claimed that population increases and the subsequent influx of the population into cities enable the primitive accumulation of capital, suggesting that population growth is one of the preconditions for the rise of capitalism and economic growth. He based this assertion on the fact that industrial reserve armies formed around cities, leading to a decrease in wages of urban labor and, by extension, increases in the value of capital. This process of population influx into cities was one that surfaced in the early years of industrialization in South Korea (Koo 2001).

One branch of modernization theory, demographic transition theory, has also highlighted the close relationship between population change and economic development (Notestein 1944). While the nature of the causal relationship is somewhat ambiguous, the decrease in birth rates after the takeoff of industrialization is regarded to have a positive effect on economic development, since the demand for skilled labor generally increases with the progress of industrialization such that the quality, rather than quantity, of human capital becomes increasingly important over time. The fewer the children per family, the greater the educational investment per child, and thereby the higher the quality of human capital. Korea's family planning policies, which were centered on the provision of birth control in the 1960s and 1970s, were alleged to be conducive to increasing the quality of human capital, thus promoting economic development.

Some studies claimed that population aging would negatively affect economic growth. According to a study (Maestas, Mullen, and Powell 2016) conducted in the United States, population aging was found to decrease per capita gross domestic product by 5.5 percent due to the reduced productivity of aging adults and the decrease in labor force. Conversely, some predicted that the negative effects of population aging on economic growth would be minor (Bloom, Canning, and Fink 2008). This study claimed that it was too simple to analyze the effects of population aging by solely examining the changes in the population of each age group; how people's behaviors change according to population aging must also be considered. The authors predicted that the negative effect of population aging on economic growth may not be strong, due to factors such as reduced youth dependency ratio caused by lower birth rate, increased participation of women in economic activity, and immigration. It was also emphasized that policies such as raising the retirement age or increased participation in economic activity could be implemented to ameliorate the effects of population aging. However, a study conducted in South Korea revealed that the economic growth rate was dropping as the population aging progressed (Ahn, Kim, and Ryuk 2017).

There were also two opposite claims on the effects of imbalances of population on regions. Based on Hirschman's (1958) theory of economic development, some claim that the concentration of population in capital areas is not only inevitable but also desirable, because it enables the so-called economies of scale, increases the efficiency of resource allocation, and eventually promotes a trickle-down effect in underdeveloped regions. However, others claim that the same demographic phenomenon, overpopulation in metropolitan areas and underpopulation in nonmetropolitan areas, is the root cause of various socioeconomic problems that obstruct the efficient and resilient use of spatial resources (Lewis 1954).

Research method

Data for this study were collected using official statistics released by the South Korean government. First, panel data were constructed after identifying the population, age distribution, number of cultural facilities, number of elementary schools, and number of clinics in 230 cities, counties, and districts in South Korea from 2006 to 2017. Next, the change over time in the number of each facility was examined, and finally, multivariate analyses were conducted using population, age distribution, and financial independence ratio as independent variables. Because cities, counties, and districts differ from one another in many aspects such as population and financial budget, it is crucial that such differences are controlled for analyzing the relationship between age distribution and amenities. A fixed-effect model was used in this study to analyze the panel data. By removing unexamined group characteristics, the fixed effect model could control the group characteristics in the analysis.

The major variables in the data are described in table 9.1.

Based on a life course perspective of population movement, this study presents the following hypotheses:

1. An increase in senior population may increase the number of facilities that are preferred by seniors.
2. A decrease in the number of children may decrease the number of elementary schools.
3. The number of cultural facilities may increase as the population increases.

Analysis of Population Structure and Human-Made Amenities

Changes in population structure

First, we examine how population and age distribution have changed over time (refer to figures 9.1 through 9.3). Figure 9.1 represents

TABLE 9.1 Data used in the analysis

Item	Detail	Years
Population	Total population	2006–17
Age Distribution*	• Ratio of population aged 5 years or younger (A) • Ratio of population aged 6–9 years (B) • Ratio of population aged 10–14 years (C) • Ratio of population aged 65 years or older • Ratio of population aged 0–14 years (A+B+C)	2008–17
Number of Cultural Facilities†	Total number of libraries, museums, art galleries, culture and art centers, regional cultural centers, and houses of culture	2007–09 2011–18
Number of Elementary Schools*	Number of elementary schools in the region	2006–17
Number of Clinics*	Number of clinics in the region	2009–18
Financial Independence Ratio*	Financial independence ratio of cities, counties, and districts	2006–18
Region‡	Cities, counties, and districts in metropolitan cities§	2006–17

NOTE: *Source for data is Statistics Korea; †Source for data is National Survey of Culture-Based Infrastructure by each year, Ministry of Culture, Sports, and Tourism; ‡regions are classified into districts in metropolitan cities (75), cities (76), or counties (79); §metropolitan cities: Seoul, Busan, Daegu, Daejeon, Incheon, and Ulsan.
Source: Authors.

FIGURE 9.1 Total population and age distribution of districts in metropolitan cities, 2008–17

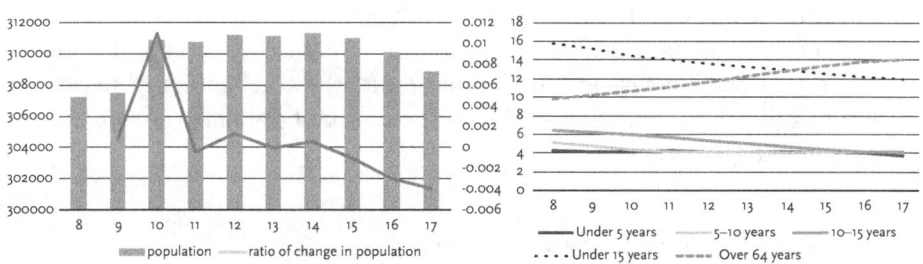

SOURCE: See table 9.1.

changes in the number and age structure of the population in districts within metropolitan cities with a population over 1 million. The change in population from 2008 to 2017 indicates that, on average, the population has increased during most periods. In terms of the rate of population change, it mostly remains above 0 until 2016—the year when the population began to decrease. While population decline began earlier in South Korea, especially for Busan, it is understood to be a recent phenomenon for most metropolitan cities such as Incheon, Daejeon, and Kwangju.

Age distribution in the districts of metropolitan cities shows that the ratio of population below 15 years of age is decreasing, while that of the population 65 or older is increasing. In these regions, the ratio of population 15 years old or younger was higher, at 16%, compared to the ratio of those 65 years old or older, at 10%, in 2008; however, continued change in these ratios led to their inversion in 2014. As of 2017, the ratio of population aged 15 and under is 11.9%, and the ratio of those 65 and over is 14.0%. These results suggest that the increased ratio of elderly population is a relatively recent phenomenon in metropolitan cities. Population decline is occurring mainly in the districts of Seoul and Busan, and this can be attributed to the younger generations moving to neighboring cities due to high living costs (Seoul) or lack of jobs in the region (Busan).

Population is continually rising in regular cities, unlike in metropolitan cities, as shown in figure 9.2. The average population has increased from 295,000 in 2008 to over 325,000 in 2017. A population change ratio of over 0 for all intervals also demonstrates that the population has been increasing. For age distribution, the ratio of population younger than 15 years old was higher than that of population aged 65 years or older, but this reversed in 2015 as the former decreased and the latter increased. In 2017, the ratio of population aged 15 and under was 13.6%, not far off from the ratio of population aged 65 and over, at 15.5%. The increase in population despite the acceleration of population aging is presumed to be due to the influx of population from the surrounding regions.

FIGURE 9.2 Total population and age distribution of cities, 2008–17

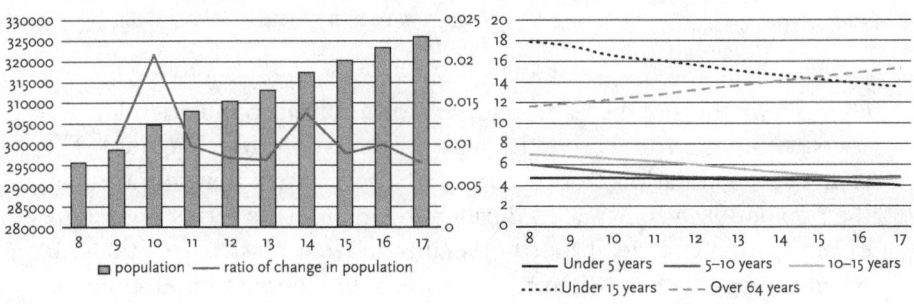

SOURCE: See table 9.1.

FIGURE 9.3 Total population and age distribution of counties, 2008–17

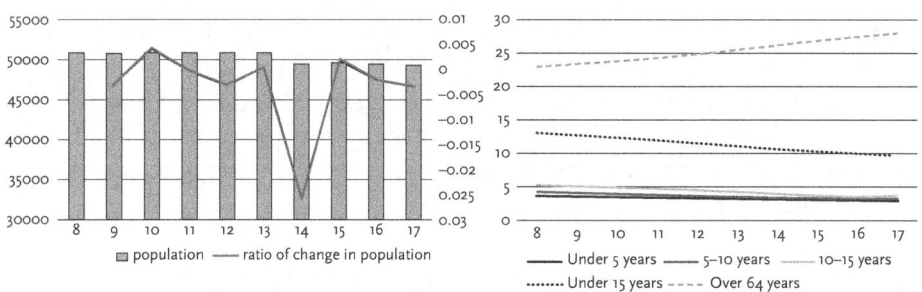

SOURCE: See table 9.1.

Figure 9.3 shows the time series analysis of the average population and age distribution of counties. The population is much smaller than those of regular cities or districts in metropolitan cities. The average population is shown to be around 50,000. Change in population reveals that population has been decreasing for most intervals. Only 2010 shows a change in population of over 0, and all other years show a decreased population compared to their prior years.

In terms of age distribution, the ratio of population aged 15 and under had already been considerably lower than the ratio of population aged 65 and older since 2008. The gap between the two age groups has expanded since then and reached an approximately threefold difference in 2017. It is clear that the population will continue to decline even more rapidly in counties over the long term.

The data on population and age distribution can be summarized as follows.

First, there is a large difference in the degree and rate of population aging among districts in metropolitan cities, other cities, and counties. In particular, both population decline and population aging began earlier in counties compared to other regions.

Second, population is still increasing in cities despite showing signs of population aging. While there are differences depending on the region, population aging, as well as decline, can be seen in metropolitan cities. The population decline in metropolitan cities can be attributed to people relocating to other neighboring cities, either metropolitan or regular. With population decline becoming a real issue in some metropolitan cities, it is necessary to devise measures to counteract this phenomenon.

Third, the ratio of seniors is extremely high in counties, whereas the ratio of adolescents is extremely low. There is also a high probability that increasingly more from the adolescent age group may move to a metropolitan city or a neighboring city in the future. Consequently, it is possible that population decline for counties will accelerate in the future. If a suitable policy for counties that suppresses adolescent movement is not proposed, the rhetorical expression of "regional dissolution" may become a reality.

Change in human-made amenities

This section explores how the number of elementary schools and clinics, which belong to public goods and services, and the number of cultural facilities have changed over time, and whether there are differences among regions.

Figure 9.4 examines how the number of elementary schools have changed over time by region. This figure shows that, on average, the number of elementary schools has slightly increased in cities and metropolitan areas, whereas it has decreased in counties. This is an unexpected phenomenon considering that the population under 15 years old has been consistently decreasing. A few measures can be taken in the case of decreased student enrollment: reduce the number of students per class, reduce the number of classes, and reduce the number of schools. In metropolitan and regular cities, as new schools were constructed from new housing developments, the average number of

FIGURE 9.4 Number of elementary schools by regional average, 2006–17

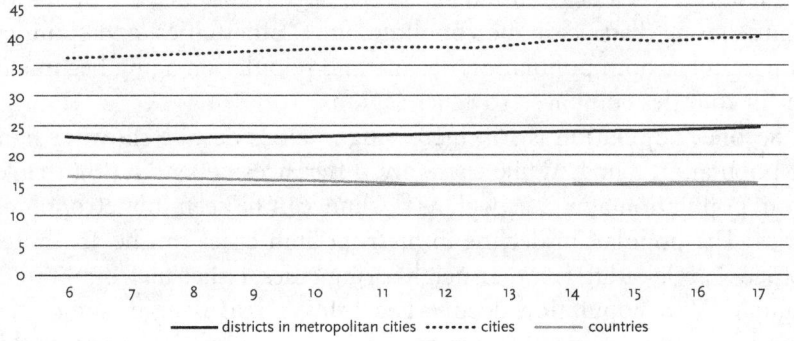

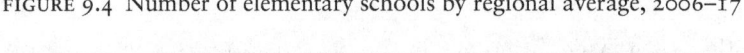

SOURCE: See table 9.1.

FIGURE 9.5 Number of clinics by regional average, 2009–18

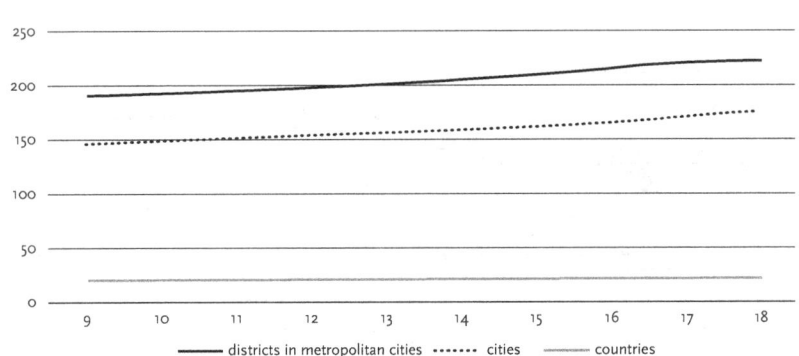

SOURCE: See table 9.1.

classes per school and the number of students per class is reduced. For counties, the options of reducing the number of classes or the number of students per class may have been exhausted due to the continued reduction of elementary grade population dating back many years, and thus the counties are ultimately responding by reducing the number of schools. If a decrease in the elementary-grade population continues, the number of elementary schools in metropolitan and regular cities may also be reduced.

Figure 9.5 illustrates the number of clinics. There is a considerable difference in the number of clinics per region. While an average of 150 to 200 clinics are located in metropolitan and regular cities, an average of 20 clinics are dispersed throughout a county. This can be understood as a natural effect of the major difference in population among the regions. Another difference is that while the number of clinics steadily increases in metropolitan and regular cities, no significant changes were observed for counties. The degree to which the number of clinics increased is also the greatest for regular cities. General clinics are primary care facilities that mainly treat children and seniors. From a population perspective, while the number of children is decreasing, the number of seniors is increasing; combining the population aged 15 and under and 65 and over, the population is shown to be slightly increasing. The population aged 15 and under and 65 and over, which constitute the main age groups using medical services, has increased by over 7,000 in cities, by approximately 1,500 in metropolitan cities, and by around 100 in counties. The fastest increase in the number of clinics

FIGURE 9.6 Number of nursing homes by regional average, 2009–18

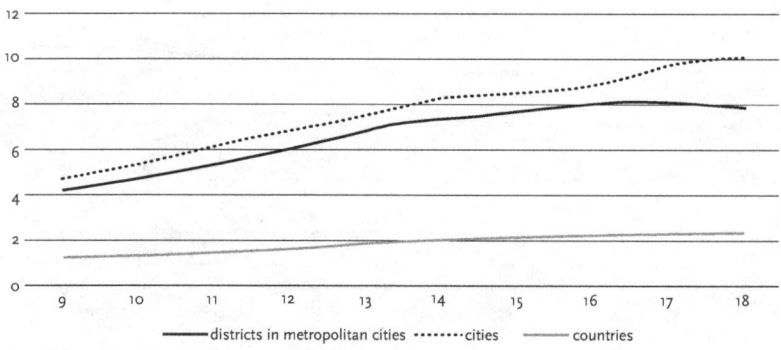

SOURCE: See table 9.1.

FIGURE 9.7 Number of cultural facilities by regional average, 2007–18

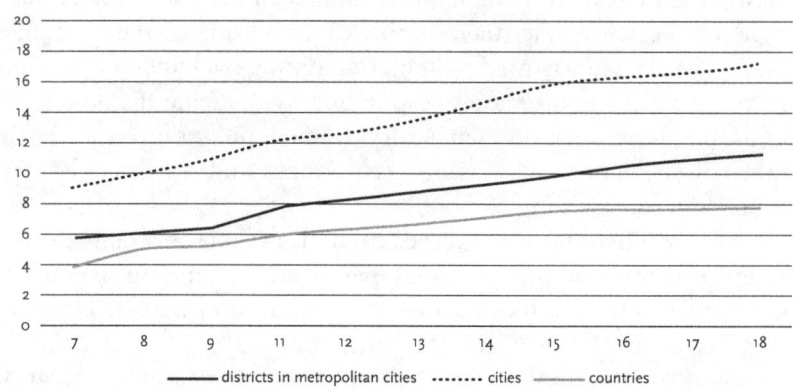

SOURCE: See table 9.1.

observed in cities and the stagnation in their numbers in counties seem to be related to the preceding population structure.

An interesting point is that while there is a difference in the number of nursing homes among metropolitan cities, cities, and counties, the number of nursing homes is steadily increasing over time, as shown in figure 9.6. This is probably related to an increase in the number of seniors in those regions, especially an increase in the number of older seniors.

Figure 9.7 depicts how the number of cultural facilities by region has been changing over time. Despite regional differences, the number of cultural facilities has been increasing overall across all regions. Cultural facilities are necessary for leisure time for all age groups. An increase in the number of cultural facilities across all three region groups could be related to an increase in the number of seniors.

Multivariate analysis: Relationship between age structure and man-made amenities

A multivariate analysis was conducted to examine the difference in the number of amenities according to the population structure by age. The number of each amenity was used as the dependent variable in the analysis, and population, ratio of population aged 15 or under, and financial independence ratio were included as independent variables.

Table 9.2 shows the results of the multivariate analysis on the number of elementary schools. A significant relationship was observed between the population and the number of elementary schools for all regions, including metropolitan cities, regular cities, and counties. In other words, the number of elementary schools increases as the population increases. For the major variable—the ratio of population aged 15 and under—a positive relationship was observed in metropolitan cities and a negative relationship in counties. The negative relationship between the number of elementary schools and the ratio of population aged 15 and under in metropolitan cities can be attributed to the strategy of shrinking the size or number of classes instead of reducing the number of schools. In counties, where the response is to reduce the number of schools due to a long history of decline in elementary

TABLE 9.2 Multivariate analysis: number of elementary schools

	Metropolitan Cities		Cities		Counties	
	b(se)		b(se)		b(se)	
Population	.00006	***	.00008	***	.00004 ***	
	(.2.04e-06)		(2.60e-06)		(.00001)	
Ratio of population aged 15 or under	−.31(.02)	***	.009(.04)		.20(.02)***	
Financial Independence Ratio	−.01(.006)		−.02(.02)		.01(.01)	
Constant	10.79(.63)	***	12.95(1.27)		11.18(.59)***	
	F=332.29	***	F=400.48	***	F=53.11 ***	
	roh=.99		roh=.98		roh=.98	

NOTE: *p < 0.05, **p < 0.01, ***p < 0.001

TABLE 9.3 Multivariate analysis: number of clinics

	Metropolitan Cities		Cities		Counties	
	b(se)		b(se)		b(se)	
Population	.0005	***	.0005	***	.0004	***
	(.00006)		(.00002)		(.00003)	
Ratio of population aged 15 and under	.06(1.01)		−2.21(.55)	***	.0004	**
					(.0003)	
Ratio of population aged 65 and older	3.76(.78)	***	.75(.55)		.41(.09)	***
Financial Independence Ratio	−1.09(.17)	***	.002(.11)		.08(.03)	***
Constant	21.97(30.53)		34.82(16.94)	*	−18.15(4.33)	***
	F=53.11	***	F=347.77	***	F=47.4	***
	roh=.99		roh=.96		roh=.92	

NOTE: **p ≤ 0.01; ***p ≤ 0.001.

students, a positive relationship is shown between the ratio of population aged 15 and under and the number of elementary schools.

Table 9.3 shows the results of analyzing the number of clinics as a dependent variable. A larger population leading to more clinics was found to be statistically significant in all three regions. A large population means a high demand in medical services. For metropolitan cities and counties, the population aged 65 and over also has a significant relationship with the number of clinics. In other words, the number of clinics increases as the number of people who use medical services increases. Although the ratio of population aged 15 and under is not significant for metropolitan cities, regular cities and counties show significant as well as conflicting results. In the case of regular cities, a higher ratio of population aged 15 and under led to fewer clinics, while in counties, a higher ratio of population aged 15 and under led to a higher number of clinics. Additional research is required for determining whether regular cities yield negative results.

The analysis performed using the number of cultural facilities as a dependent variable is shown in table 9.4. A significant relationship was observed between population and the number of cultural facilities in all three regions. Increased population leads to more cultural facilities. While the ratio of population aged 15 and under also shows a statistically significant relationship in all three regions, it shows a negative relationship contrary to population. That is, a greater ratio of such population leads to fewer cultural facilities. This could be due to the

TABLE 9.4 Multivariate analysis: number of cultural facilities

	Metropolitan Cities		Cities		Counties	
	b(se)		b(se)		b(se)	
Population	.00004	***	.00007	***	.0003	***
	(4.56e-06)		(4.42e-06)		(.00003)	
Ratio of population aged 15 and under	−51(.07)	***	−1.13(.14)	***	−.60 (.10)	***
Ratio of population aged 65 and older	.36(.06)	***	.02(.15)		.16(.07)	*
Financial Independence Ratio	−.09(.15)	***	.14(.03)	***	.08(.02)	**
Constant	2.33(2.41)		6.51(4.55)		−6.99(3.57)	
	F=200.07	***	F=199.16	***	F=130.44	***
	roh=.97		roh=.97		roh=.96	

NOTE: *p ≤ 0.05; **p ≤ 0.01; ***p ≤ 0.001.

fact that cultural facilities include only those that are not readily used by children and adolescents, such as museums, art galleries, and culture and art centers. Conversely, they had a significant relationship with the ratio of population aged 65 and over in counties and metropolitan cities. In other words, a higher ratio of the senior population aged 65 and over leads to an increased number of cultural facilities in that region. This increase may be due to the age group having relatively more free time and a greater desire to use cultural facilities, which results in the expansion of such facilities.

The results can be summarized in relation to several hypotheses. First, hypothesis 1 predicted that an increase in senior population is related to the number of clinics. Results indicated that an increase in senior population is related to the expansion of cultural and medical facilities. An increase in the ratio of seniors increases the demand for the services they desire and brings about the expansion of the facilities that meet such needs. In the long term, there is a high chance that an increase in elderly population will restructure the distribution of amenities in a manner reflecting their desires.

Second, hypothesis 2 predicted that a reduction in the number of children will reduce the number of elementary schools. The results indicate a significant relationship between population aged 15 and under and the number of elementary schools only in counties. This can be attributed to the fact that metropolitan and regular cities respond to the decrease in the number of children by reducing the size or number of classes. However, continued reduction in the number of children will inevitably require reducing the number of schools.

Third, hypothesis 3 predicted that the number of cultural facilities will increase with an increase in population. Change in population was found to influence the changes to amenities in that region. In particular, cultural facilities and medical facilities such as clinics were found to increase when the population increased and decrease when the population decreased. Counties where the population has already declined considerably may face a situation where the population may not receive the necessary services. Some counties are even missing specific medical facilities, such as maternity clinics.

Fourth, if senior-centric amenities are constructed due to population aging, it will be difficult to attract the younger generation to the region or stop them from leaving. One young mother residing in a county expressed the following complaint in an interview held by one of the authors: "In this region, there are no places for kids to go over the weekend. There is at least the Kkumjaram playground in Chuncheon; here, there is nowhere to take the kids."

To solve the problem of regional population decline, meeting the conditions required for the younger generation to remain or to come into the region from elsewhere is a crucial goal. Such conditions include not only the availability of jobs but also of amenities that meet the demands of the younger generation. This is a politically challenging task in counties, because it is difficult to place the interests of the relatively fewer in the young generation above those of the senior majority.[4] Unless they actively prepare for population aging, metropolitan and regular cities will also face the unwanted situation of population aging and population decline.

The role of human-made amenities in regional innovation

The results presented earlier suggest that South Korea is falling, or may have already fallen, into a "vicious cycle" triggered by dramatic demographic transformation since the 1960s. The demographic crisis

---

4   For reference, the following objection was raised in an interview hosted by the researchers regarding the need for day-care centers. "Although it's good to newly construct a regional day-care center for children who cannot reach one due to distance, I'm not sure how many children will attend. There are not many children in this region. You can build senior centers anywhere because there are a lot of seniors."

is worsening, with the fertility rate falling to a record low of 0.98 in 2018. However, this is only a part of the bigger picture. The interregional population imbalance has already reached a serious level: About half the total population resides in the capital and its surrounding areas that occupy just a tenth of the total land area. To make matters worse, the age structures of populations remarkably differ across regions, which is accelerating the spatial and social segregation based on age, segregation characterized by relatively young metropolitan areas and extremely aged nonmetropolitan areas. The interregional disparity in terms of demographic composition as well as population size has arguably been attributable to the uneven distribution of economic resources and job opportunities, especially for young people.

However, interregional imbalances in human-made amenities also play a significant role in worsening the vicious cycle. First, regions with more human-made amenities attract people who seek more and better life opportunities, and overpopulated regions, often with greater financial power, tend to enjoy a greater chance of having more amenities for their residents. Supply creates its own demand, and demand creates its own supply. Second, such a Matthew effect of accumulated advantage also operates in spatial differentiation of human-made amenities leading to intensified spatial segregation along the age line. Facilities that cater to seniors tend to be located in areas where there are many seniors, and facilities that cater to the young are relatively abundant in areas where there are higher numbers of young people. This serves as a negative feedback mechanism that further reinforces the spatial segregation of age groups. For instance, parents tend to avoid living in places where school facilities are lacking, thus they migrate to cities with rich educational opportunities for their children. While the Korean government has attempted to alleviate interregional imbalances by relocating public institutions to non-capital areas and making disproportionate social overheard capital investments in less-advantaged communities, it seems that the interregional gap has not yet been closed and will continue to widen in the future.

Based on these observations, we now turn to explaining how the quality and quantity of human-made amenities can contribute to fostering regional innovations, thereby bridging the gap between capital and non-capital areas, and achieving regionally balanced socioeconomic development in Korea. To this end, let us begin with the commonly accepted argument that population changes may have a profound impact on economic outcomes.

From this perspective, population change in South Korea has a dual character. On the one hand, rapid population changes and increased concentration in metropolitan cities, especially in the capital area, have contributed, in part, to South Korea's astonishing economic development. On the other hand, the vicious cycle of regional imbalances established through this process, in addition to the rapidly changing population structure due to low birth rates and increased population aging, has left a substantial burden not only on the current generation but also on those to come.

There are conflicting viewpoints about addressing this vicious cycle; it is a topic that has been the subject of heated political and academic debate in recent decades.

It must be recognized that population aging and population imbalances are the conjoined twins born from the industrialization model; thus, the two problems are inseparable. One cannot be justified while the other is neglected, and addressing one issue while maintaining the status quo on the other is impossible. For example, many young people in Korea are reluctant to get married and to bear children because of high living costs, including those of housing, due to the concentration of residents in the capital area. Employment is another factor that discourages childbirth. Although cities are a repository of jobs, rising populations that exceed the number of jobs available leads to increased unemployment rates. In 2018, the region with the highest unemployment rate was Seoul, at 4.8 percent, with cities around Seoul in Gyeonggi Province, such as Anyang, also recording high unemployment rates (5.8 percent). In contrast, most provinces, including Jeju, Jeonbuk, Chungbuk, and Chungnam, recorded unemployment rates of approximately 2 percent. Detailed analysis is required on job quality and stability, but it is likely that jobs will provide diminishing returns when the population of a city exceeds a certain level. Compared to the unipolar system of a highly concentrated capital area, a multipolar system of quite even distribution of appropriately sized cities will arguably heighten overall life opportunities such as jobs, housing, and education, and this can ultimately raise fertility.

Imbalance between regions can also increase social risks due to population aging. As discussed earlier, the severe lack of human-made amenities in aged regions deprives the inhabitants of the opportunities to adequately care for the various risks (diseases, social isolation, etc.) associated with aging. As such, the two demographic issues—population aging and regional imbalances—are closely related to each other, and thus require a comprehensive approach rather than two separate approaches.

The industrial age, which brought forth the two related problems, is waning. A new trend described by some as the fourth industrial revolution, and by others as the digital transformation, is replacing the industrial age. It is commonly accepted that while productivity was crucial in the industrial age, various forms of innovation are at the core of the digital age. In the industrial age, cities required a massive population influx to achieve economies of scale and improve productivity. Can the same city model be applied in the digital age? Will the concentration of half the population in the polarized capital be beneficial for widespread entrepreneurial activities in the digital age? Is population aging or low fertility rates a scourge or a boon in the digital age? To review such issues, one must consider how innovation is related to the nature of and changes in population structures.

While remarkably detailed studies have been conducted on the relationship between demographic changes and economic development, little has been investigated concerning the relationship between population structure and economic innovation in the context of regional development. As such, we first explore the impact of demographic changes caused by low fertility and aging on innovation outcomes in the digital age, and then proceed to examine how the theoretical angle from spatial issues can enhance our understanding of the relationship between demography and innovation.

Low fertility and aging are products of the demographic transition accompanied by rapid industrialization. As of 2018, the total fertility rate of South Korea stands at 0.98, which is less than half of the replacement level. Meanwhile, life expectancy is 80 years or longer and is expected to steadily rise in the future. South Korea can be regarded as one of the most aged societies with the greatest imbalance in age structure. With a drop in birth rates and increased life expectancy, the population structure is predicted to be closer to an inverted pyramid shape by 2050. Even if the shape can be somewhat altered by various factors such as policy interventions, technological development, and immigration, it must be an inevitable reality that South Korea suffers from one of the world's lowest fertility rates and will be unable to escape the tragic trap of low fertility in the near future.

As Malthus (1798) states, population is a primal and original condition that exerts enormous influence on all facets of state functions, including politics, economy, society, and national defense. The sharp decline in labor force and steady increase in support costs are expected to become massive social burdens. Characteristics of the workforce are also expected to change. As the workforce ages, businesses will have to work with seniors, and it will become relatively difficult to find younger talent. While the unbalanced population structure of South Korea is a product of a rapid industrialization process, it cannot be overcome through the industrialization paradigm.

Despite the preceding risks, the potential impact of low fertility and aging on innovation is not totally negative. First, if the quantity of human resources was important in the industrial age, their quality is important in the digital era. The reduction in school-aged population will provide an opportunity to improve the quality of education. The standardized, assembly-line approach to education can be replaced with one that focuses on creativity and entrepreneurship, which will boost the innovative capabilities of human resources. Secondly, population pressure caused by a reduced labor force and increased support costs can promote a range of technological innovations. The various social problems brought about by aging provides the opportunity to boost innovative activities. For instance, Japan's Society 5.0 is a roadmap for transnational growth, which aims to solve social problems, such as labor shortages due to population aging, by applying the technology of the fourth industrial revolution, such as artificial intelligence, robots, and the internet of things. The Society 5.0 initiative largely consists of the extension of healthy life, realization of the mobility revolution, establishment of a next-generation supply chain, creation of comfortable infrastructure and regions, and fintech, all of which are strategies to tackle such social problems as aging and reduced labor force. Much progress can be made in technological, cultural, and social sectors related to the health, culture, leisure, and livelihood of seniors. Such innovation can also contribute to reducing the social burden resulting from a reduced labor force as well as enhancing social vitality by expanding the opportunities for seniors to participate in the labor market and society.

In summary, as low fertility and aging progresses, the industrialization model is expected to rapidly decline, and innovation is gradually moving toward the central stage of the economy. In terms of the labor force, as its quantity decreases, it will be possible to supply high-quality human capital adept in digital technology, creative thinking, problem solving, and cultural sensibility. To achieve this, the current education paradigm, which is focused on supplying "industrial armies," must be fundamentally reformed. It will also be necessary to expeditiously

establish a lifetime education system for seniors to be able to participate in the labor market. On the demand side, social problems associated with population aging will provide opportunities for qualified and
creative young talents to make a wide variety of innovations.

Now, the question is how to detect and utilize such opportunities.
Regions are at the heart of a strategy to generate innovative break-
throughs. Is the concentration of residents in capital regions and the
resulting age segregation across regions beneficial to the nationwide
innovative capabilities? To address this question, several issues must
be addressed.

First, we need to consider what would be the optimal population
size appropriate for a region to be innovation-friendly. It is certainly
true that innovative capabilities of a region increase with its population size. Geoffrey West (2017), a physicist studying complex systems,
demonstrated the increasing returns of population size of a city on the
number of patents generated. He showed that the number of patents
increases at an approximate rate of 1.15 per capita when the population doubles. This is because of the so-called network effect—the more
people there are in a city, the easier it is to exchange and integrate ideas
through the dense social network within the city. It is certainly difficult to achieve innovation in a small and isolated region. With a large
population, however, a region can accommodate numerous inventors
and technological pioneers with diverse ideas and skills, which makes
it easy for new ideas and inventions to circulate through dense social
networks.

Although West's analysis yields a law-like regularity of increasing
returns, the maximum population size of the cities analyzed by West
was around 3 million. The population size of San Jose, California,
located in the Silicon Valley, is only 1 million, and that of Boston is
around 0.6 million. In comparison, Seoul has a population of 10 million, and the population of the Seoul metropolitan area combining the
city of Seoul and Gyeonggi Province is approximately 22 million. This
means that around half of the South Korean population resides in the
capital area. Could the law of increasing returns still be applied to
a city this large? This may not necessarily be possible. The number
of applications for international patents in Seoul from 2012 to 2016
was approximately 37,000, which was roughly similar to that of San
Jose, a city with a much smaller population. While Seoul's population
is 15 times that of Boston, it only has three times as many international
patent applications.

The applications for international patents per capita in Seoul are low even when compared to other major cities in Asia. The number of patents by Seoul is only two-thirds of that by Hong Kong, which has a population of 7 million; moreover, it is marginally higher than Osaka, which has a population of 2.5 million. While various factors may be involved in building innovative capabilities of a city, there may be a fixed ceiling to the maximizing effect of population growth on innovation in cities. Further detailed analysis on the relationship between innovation and the population size of a city must be conducted after controlling for several confounding factors, including the city's industrial composition and research and development infrastructure. If a ceiling does exist, however, the unipolar system, in which a super-big city absorbs all human, financial, and technological resources, may not be an effective way of augmenting nationwide innovation outcomes. From a national standpoint, for instance, two cities with a population of 5 million each may be more conducive for innovation than one city with a population of 10 million.

Second, the relationship between population structure and innovation must be examined. While it is difficult to find reliable literature on this topic, according to one study (Richter 2014), regions with greater percentages of the population aged 50 to 60 showed the highest level of innovation, as measured by the number of patents. In contrast, regions with more young people around 20 to 30 years of age, or those with more seniors aged 60 and over, did not show consistent results. This may result from the fact that the age group in the 50s, which is young enough to remain in the labor market and old enough to accumulate experience, leads to entrepreneurial activities. Another interpretation is possible. The children of people aged 50 to 60 fall within the 20 to 30 age group. Therefore, there is a high chance that the population aged 20 to 30 is relatively greater where there is a large population of seniors aged 50 to 60. Furthermore, regions where many people aged 50 to 60 reside will have relatively more human-made amenities that they or their children can use, and such facilities can also be used by seniors aged 60 or older. In other words, cities with a large population aged 50 to 60 may be regions where age distribution is relatively even and varied. From this perspective, if a multipolar system is to be seen as more innovation-friendly than a unipolar system, a balanced age distribution must also be considered as potentially more innovation-friendly.

Clusters are regarded as the core in the system of regional innovation. In South Korea, comparatively successful clusters are concentrated in the capital area. While there can be many reasons for this, probably the most important one is that it is relatively easy to find individuals with various talents and experiences there. The accessibility to those various talents is extremely limited in non-capital regions. Even if there are universities in non-capital regions, many university students decide to abandon such regions after graduation for capital areas. Furthermore, those areas lack clusters that link local businesses and industries with educational institutions and regional communities. Despite various benefits, such as corporate tax exemptions incentivizing the establishment of new businesses or the relocation of existing ones, the chances of a successful cluster emerging are meager if the talent pool of the surrounding area is limited. Without qualified human capital, not only is it difficult to expect competitive businesses to relocate into those areas, but there is also a high chance that their survival is short-lived even if they are drawn in. Various policy approaches should be implemented, such as attracting businesses, establishing business-friendly legal and policy institutions, and creating a system of university-research-industry collaboration; yet, from a demographic viewpoint, these must be coupled with the provision of an appealing labor pool with diverse backgrounds.

Can demographic changes bring forth a new type of innovation? The rapid increase in the number of seniors, acceleration of aging in rural areas, and the concentration of population in cities are certainly inevitable. Social problems that did not receive much recognition in the past may resurface due to such demographic changes. Increased life expectancy will boost the demand for various social services related to eldercare and healthy living. Demand for leisure, cultural, and educational services will continue to rise. The importance of social innovation will subsequently be heightened, and new markets are likely to be established based on these needs. Such markets are dispersive and locally based by nature, because the spatial distance between the supplier and the consumer must be close. Therefore, regionally led grassroot innovations are necessary, and such grassroot innovations will serve as a platform for various social economic actors in the region, including social enterprises and cooperatives. Especially in light of the growth in the use of general-purpose digital technology such as information and communications technology, opportunities to create value through grassroot innovations will likely increase. This type of innovation not only will resolve social problems but also will contribute to the socioeconomic development of regional communities by creating jobs and increasing social capital.

Conclusion

In sum, demographic problems such as population imbalance due to low fertility and aging, and spatial segregation resulting from the concentration of residents in capital areas, have considerable implications for boosting socioeconomic innovations. Population change may provide opportunities for innovation, which has the potential to resolve the various problems caused by demographic changes. The two gigantic demographic problems faced by South Korea—population aging and regional imbalance—are not separate issues, and thus a comprehensive approach is necessary to adequately address them.

The key to a comprehensive approach lies ultimately in the regions. Multipolarization of areas, each supporting regional innovation, must be achieved through the dispersion of the population, and various forms of innovation using social, economic, spatial, and cultural resources are necessary for all regions. Such innovation initiatives will in turn lead to balanced development through population dispersion, increased fertility rates, and effective responses to population aging. A mutual feedback process between population changes and innovation must be established for the vicious cycle to be transformed into a benign one.

Public investment in regional amenities may be a starting point for fostering this transformation. Regional amenities are both an appealing asset to attract populations and infrastructures for innovation. Schools and lifetime education facilities are spaces that foster and attract the creative talents necessary for innovation. Hospitals and health facilities can promote various types of physical and mental activities by expanding life opportunities. Libraries and meeting places provide the opportunity to trade and merge information, knowledge, and ideas.

It is well known that the coffee houses that spread in London in the eighteenth century contributed to the scientific, technological, and ideological innovation of modern times. Bold public investments in regional amenities may be the small flutter that will result in the massive typhoon in the form of balanced development across all regions.

References

Ahn, Byung Kwun, Ki-Ho Kim, and Seung Whan Ryuk. 2017. *Inku goryungwhaga kyungje sueungjangae michieun younghyang* [The effects of population aging on growth]. *Economic Growth* 23, no. 4: 1–33.

Becker, Gary S., Edward L. Glaeser, and Kevin M. Murphy. 1999. "Population and Economic Growth." *American Economic Review* 89, no. 2: 145–49.

Bloom, David E., David Canning, and Günther Fink. 2008. "Population Aging and Economic Growth." Program on the Global Demography of Aging at Harvard University, working paper no. 31.

Choi, Jae-Heon, and Hyun Wi Yoon. 2012. "Hankook inku koryungwhayee jiyukjuk junkie yangsang" [The changing spatial patterns of aging population in Korea]. *Journal of Korean Geographical Society* 47, no. 3: 359–74.

Hirschman, Albert O. 1958. *The Strategy of Economic Development.* New Haven: Yale University Press.

Kim, Hyun Sik. 2013. "Inku goryungwhagauey geoyukguek chaiy" [Regional differences in population aging]. In *Inguwa boguenye sahoehak* [Sociology of population and health], edited by Bongoh Kye et al. Seoul: Dasan Publishing.

Koo, Hagen. 2001. *Korean Workers: The Culture and Politics of Class Formation.* New York: Cornell University Press.

Kuznets, Simon. 1967. "Population and Economic Growth." *Proceedings of the American Philosophical Society* 111: 170–193.

Lee, Sang Ho. 2016. *Jiyuk goyongdonghyang simcheung bunseuk* [Analysis of regional labor market trends]. *Regional Labor Market Brief* 16 (Spring).

Lewis, W. Arthur. 1954. "Economic Development with Unlimited Supplies of Labour." *The Manchester School* 22, no. 2: 139–91.

Maestas, Nicole, Kathleen Mullen, and David Powell. 2016. "The Effect of Population Aging on Economic Growth, the Labor Force and Productivity." NBER Working Paper no. 22452.

Malthus, Thomas R. (1798) 1986. *An Essay on the Principle of Population.* London: W. Pickering.

Marx, Karl. (1867) 1976. *Capital,* vol. 1. New York: Penguin.

Masuda, Hiroya. 2014. *Chihō shōmetsu tōkyōikkyokushūchū ga maneku jinkō kyūgen* [Local extinction: Rapid population decline caused by overconcentration in Tokyo]. Tokyo: Chūōkōren shinsha.

Notestein, Frank W. 1944. *The Future Population of Europe and the Soviet Union: Population Projections, 1940–1970*, vol. 2. Geneva: League of Nations.

Richter, Doreen. 2014. "Demographic Change and Innovation: The Ongoing Challenge from the Diversity of the Labor Force." *Management Revue* 25, no. 3: 166–184.

Ryu, Bang Lan, Kyung Ae Kim, Keun Tae Kim, Du Whan Kim, and Ki Gon Nam. 2018. *Ingu jukbyuk sidae kyoyookjungchakyei banghyang tamsa* [Exploring the direction of education policy in the age of the demographic cliff]. Korean Educational Development Institute.

Statistics Korea. 2019. *Jangrey ingu tookbul chugae: 2017–2067* [Special estimation on population change: 2017–2067]. http:// kostat.go.kr/portal/korea/kor_nw/1/2/6/index.board?bmode =read&aSeq=373873.

West, Geoffrey. 2017. *Scale: The Universal Laws of Life, Growth, and Death in Organisms, Cities, and Companies*. New York: Penguin Books.

Whisler, Ronald L., Brigitte S. Waldorf, Gordon F. Mulligan, and David A. Plane. 2008. "Quality of Life and the Migration of the College-Educated: A Life-Course Approach." *Growth and Change* 39, no. 1.

Woo, Hae bong, Hwa-yeon Shin, In-wha Park, and Sunhee Kim. 2014. *Ingu kyurngwha wa bokji jichun* [Population aging and public expenditure in South Korea]. Sejong: Korean Institute for Health and Social Affairs.

Index

Locators in **bold** refer to tables; those in *italics* refer to figures.